MEDIA, SURVEILLANCE
AND IDENTITY

Steve Jones
General Editor

Vol. 84

The Digital Formations series is part of the Peter Lang Media and Communication list.
Every volume is peer reviewed and meets
the highest quality standards for content and production.

PETER LANG
New York • Washington, D.C./Baltimore • Bern
Frankfurt • Berlin • Brussels • Vienna • Oxford

MEDIA, SURVEILLANCE AND IDENTITY

SOCIAL PERSPECTIVES

EDITED BY ANDRÉ JANSSON AND MIYASE CHRISTENSEN

PETER LANG
New York • Washington, D.C./Baltimore • Bern
Frankfurt • Berlin • Brussels • Vienna • Oxford

Library of Congress Cataloging-in-Publication Data

Media, surveillance and identity: social perspectives /
edited by André Jansson, Miyase Christensen.
pages cm. — (Digital formations; vol. 84)
Includes bibliographical references and index.
1. Social media. 2. Electronic surveillance. 3. Group identity.
I. Jansson, André, editor of compilation.
II. Christensen, Miyase, editor of compilation.
HM742.M4194   302.23'1—dc23   2013018181
ISBN 978-1-4331-1880-7 (hardcover)
ISBN 978-1-4331-1879-1 (paperback)
ISBN 978-1-4539-1166-2 (e-book)
ISSN 1526-3169

Bibliographic information published by **Die Deutsche Nationalbibliothek.**
Die Deutsche Nationalbibliothek lists this publication in the "Deutsche
Nationalbibliografie"; detailed bibliographic data is available
on the Internet at http://dnb.d-nb.de/.

The paper in this book meets the guidelines for permanence and durability
of the Committee on Production Guidelines for Book Longevity
of the Council of Library Resources.

© 2014 Peter Lang Publishing, Inc., New York
29 Broadway, 18th floor, New York, NY 10006
www.peterlang.com

Printed in the United States of America

To Lara Charlotta

Contents

PART II: PRACTICES

PART III: POLITICS

Acknowledgments

This volume is the outcome of a number of different research endeavors, the combination of which yielded a rich body of data and a framework to work with. The primary resource that we benefited from was a three-year research grant that we were awarded by the Swedish research foundation Riksbankens Jubileumsfond for our project "Secure Spaces: Media, Consumption and Social Surveillance" (project number P2008–0667:1-E). The grant enabled us to work in a more focused manner with issues related to surveillance. We were also able to gather field data in a systematic manner and in several contexts, giving us a deeper understanding of the social nature of surveillance today. We are most grateful to Riksbankens Jubileumsfond for their support.

We are also grateful to our partners within the EU-funded COST Action network Living in Surveillance Societies, who have been great supporters and discussants of our work. We also would like to thank our colleagues who have contributed intellectually and by way of providing assistance: David Kvicklund, James Pamment and Ilkin Mehrabov. Finally, we would like to extend our thanks to the professional team at Peter Lang for their collaboration and support throughout the process of putting together this volume.

April 2013
André Jansson, Karlstad
Miyase Christensen, Stockholm

Introduction

André Jansson & Miyase Christensen

Some of the most significant outcomes of the mediatization meta-process in our age are the immensely complex forms and conflicting meanings surveillance takes: from domesticated techno-pet for security, to entertaining voyeurism to counter-power tool for civic activism. Technological transformations of private means of communication, such as interactivity, convergence and mobility, paired with an increasingly pervasive social and cultural saturation of these media, inevitably complicate deep-seated notions of surveillance pertaining to the modern era—notably the view of surveillance as a top-down administrative process (Giddens, 1985) and/or as self-discipline (Foucault, 1979). Social theory perspectives, such as that of Giddens (1985), that construed surveillance as the key element in the structure and organization of power in modernity provided insights and analytical frameworks that were instrumental in the way we approached questions of power and monitoring. If, as Giddens has it, the rise of modernity and the nation-state system ran parallel to the inception of surveillance practices (or bureaucratic surveillance) as part of administrative power, what are we to make of current surveillance practices and their relationship to late-modernity?

Writings on the dynamics generated by the more recent phase of surveillance include suggestive concepts focusing on destabilized relations of monitoring, such as "synopticon" (Mathiesen, 1997), "surveillant assemblage" (Haggerty & Ericson, 2000) and "cryptopticon" (Vaidhyanathan, 2011), as well as on the complicated positioning of social agency, such as "lateral surveillance" (Andrejevic, 2005) and "participatory surveillance" (Albrechtslund, 2008). In spite of their (sometimes radically) diverging theoretical and ideological points of departure, these notions are all based on an interest in the contested relationships between expressivity and control; privacy and publicness; structure and agency. At the most fundamental level, these are questions about the relationship between self and society—a relationship in which technologized (and culturally mediated) surveillance has become an integral part. An increasing variety of interconnected and personalized media for "seeing and being seen" are successively drawing social actors more fully into the very structures and logics of surveillance in exploitative yet seemingly playful ways.

Despite the growing interest in mediated surveillance, empirical knowledge and theoretical progress regarding individual perceptions and practices of surveillance (understood here in a more constructivist sense) are still lagging behind. Most work so far—notably within disciplines such as political science, science and technology studies, geography and philosophy (or, what has been broadly termed as "surveillance studies")—has focused on mapping out and theorizing the new systemic and technological dynamics of these developments, and their implications in terms of reproduced/remodeled power structures in society (e.g., Graham, 2006; Haggerty & Ericson, 2007; Gates, 2011). Such theoretical and conceptual discussions also informed some empirical work in the field.

Earlier work, which focused heavily on vertical dimensions of monitoring, cameras and "dataveillance" (Clarke, 1994), also commonly paid tribute to the Foucauldian notions of discipline and panopticism (e.g., Gandy, 1993). Theoretically, a significant volume of research invoked surveillance in relation to issues of crime/security and loss of privacy. As Haggerty and Ericson (2007:3) discerned, the conceptualization of surveillance as the collection and sorting of information about groups and communities with the purpose of governing their activities opened up further analytical possibilities, beyond camera and secret monitoring, to uncover the increasingly complex dimensions of surveillance.

The multiplication of technological artifacts and associated practices is one such dimension. New media forms afford faster, more powerful and cheaper surveillance capabilities both for the industry and state-military. Such capabilities go beyond mere monitoring and data storage as (1) the scale has grown considerably; and (2) monitoring has changed form and content, now including radically new practices with complex implications for who we are (made to be) and where we are positioned socially. Digitization of health records and sequencing of human genomes, if they become routine, might have grave consequences for large segments of the society who will be denied health insurance in a highly commercialized environment. Converging various gadgets, such as heart monitors or cameras, to immediately share input on social media sites and targeted advertising are some of the many practices that add to the ubiquitous character of the technology and taps into identity.

Considering we live in social environments where such tools and capacities are multiplying exponentially, it is not surprising that at its recent phase much of what has been written on surveillance focuses on digital technologies.

One problem with such heavy emphasis on the medium, however, has been an analytical approach that lacks not only contextuality but also historicity. As Lauer (2011) notes, the linkages between old and new forms of surveillance, whenever noted, were glossed over. While the architecture and widespread forms of digital media put so much at stake, as Lauer rightly notes (2011:567), "privacy has died many deaths." Throughout modern history, every new technology from the telegraph to telephone and television had strong implications for identity and how subjectivities were formed and situated socially. What is important, then, is to understand technology use and surveillance in relation to the political, cultural and social environments within which they are shaped. To go back to the patient information example, sequencing of genomes, where healthcare is a universal service, can save lives rather than destroy them.

While there have been studies addressing such crucial dimensions, more comprehensive volumes that bring together research on social and identitarian aspects are limited in number. A number of recent articles have explored emergent social dynamics in relation to technological questions (e.g., Ball, 2009; Best, 2010; Christensen, 2012; Jansson, 2012; Marwick, 2012). And, to some extent, subjective and everyday dimensions of social monitoring and voyeurism have been taken up in cultural studies, for example in relation to reality shows, social networking and identity politics (e.g., Koskela, 2004; McGrath, 2004; Jacobs, 2011). In our previous work, we have addressed the ways in which the handling of mediated surveillance, seen also as part of symbolic strategies, interweaves with everyday communicative routines and rituals pertaining to particular social fields, communities and/or lifestyle sectors (Christensen, 2011; Jansson, 2012; Christensen & Jansson, 2012). In general, however, we can discern a common pattern in the way surveillance is inquired today, which places a rather heavy emphasis on artifacts and digitality.

The objective of the current volume is to provide social perspectives on contemporary surveillance at the juncture of macro-social elements and individualized processes that currently shape and define the overarching manifestations and structural absorption of surveillance. The realm of everyday mediations challenges and, in certain sociopolitical settings, potentially subverts surveillant practice through locational, identitarian, mundane as well as strategized practices. Of course, this does not necessarily translate into the toppling down of surveillance regimes and agents, or achieving social change. Yet, attending to both structural and everyday subjective dimensions yields a more rounded approach. The chapters that follow account for dominant power structures (such as state surveillance and commercial surveillance) and social reproduction as well as political economic considerations, counter-privacy discourses, and class and gender hegemonies. Potential ruptures in such processes of domination, identity politics and everyday practices of expressivity and control are also discussed. Through empirically grounded inquiries of these aspects, the volume seeks to advance a complex framework of research for future scrutiny. In order to achieve this goal, the authors take on board a comprehensive view of current debates in the field.

Three key concepts—media, surveillance and identity—and the linkages amongst them, are problematized throughout the book. The accents are diverse. For instance, while some chapters go deeper into analyses of particular media types, formats or platforms (such as loyalty cards or location-based services), others account for the composite dynamics of media ensembles within particular spaces of surveillance or identity creation (such as consumerism or the domestic sphere). The volume also aims to inspire a rethinking of the very concept of surveillance, bringing it into dialogue with associated social phenomena, such as economic debt, gifts and game/play, and discusses complementary terms for grasping the socially integrated nature of surveillance in a mediatized society. Amongst these concepts are "complicit surveillance," "collaborative surveillance" and "interveillance."

On the whole, mediatized conditions of surveillance affect a wide range of social dynamics related to identity processes. The volume adopts a number of different conceptual and analytical axes to address these dynamics: individual privacy versus social integration; reflexivity versus trust; expressivity versus recognition; complicity and resistance. With the aim of generating a holistic and up-to-date view of contemporary social conditions, the analyses presented in the book build bridges between various theories of modern and late-modern society, socialization and identity construction, ethical and normative considerations, and point to the importance of both "big-picture" diagnoses and contextual sensitivity within surveillance studies. Integrating outlooks and insights from different social realms and different parts of the world, the volume highlights the socially negotiated, diversified and ambiguous cultural forms of mediated surveillance (cf. Williams, 1974).

The structure of the book represents three analytical realms, which bind together the individual chapters: *Perceptions*, *Practices* and *Politics*. As we discuss further on, each part attends to a certain set of research questions arising at the intersections of media, surveillance and identity processes. Before turning to these aspects, and the structure of the book, in what follows we offer further reflections on the rationale behind this volume and try to unpack what "social perspectives" entail.

Social Perspectives

At a fundamental level, surveillance can be understood as a social conduct and phenomenon signifying a particular type of relationship amongst human beings and institutions. Surveillance refers to the systematic gathering and organizing of information about individuals and their activities, opinions and values in order to exercise various types of control (e.g., political, economic or social) over the subjects and/or a certain social territory (e.g., the nation-state, commercial spaces or the private home). Surveillance is thus not a condition that emerges at random, or without any underlying social logic or force. Yet, many such processes today take on more liquid appearances (Bauman & Lyon, 2012). Surveillance is an integral part of the reproduction and negotiation of power structures in society, whether we speak of direct forms of control exercised by authoritarian states or more reciprocal processes of "soft" surveillance based on, for example, commercial exchange. In order to understand how such processes are legitimized and put into practice, we need perspectives that can help us unpack various social dynamics and imperatives that sustain human relations at large, often in culturally taken-for-granted ways.

Furthermore, under mediatized social conditions, new technological affordances make it easier for "ordinary people" to gather information about their peers (and others), and private information (generated through communicative and spatial online-offline practices) circulates in an increasingly open-ended manner. This, in turn, increases the need for conducting contextualized in-depth studies exploring social life and everyday dimensions. This is not to suggest that interpersonal relations in general are becoming "panoptic," even though such tendencies can be discerned, too (Andrejevic, 2005). Above all, social perspectives are needed to account for why and under what conditions social actors comply with (or resist) various forms of surveillance, such as the digital disclosure of personal information, and the ways in which everyday social practices and mediations become part of and de facto legitimize overarching structures of surveillance (Christensen & Jansson, forthcoming).

Of course, "social perspectives" may be seen as an overly simplistic label meant to capture too much, yet saying too little. Social perspectives may indeed range from phenomenological and interactionist outlooks concerned with the maintenance of (inter)subjective lifeworlds to more macro-level considerations of ideology, power and social reproduction. This volume does not intend to provide symmetry amongst the social perspectives its chapters put forth. Rather, it highlights precisely the importance of avoiding what it eludes: uniformity of analytical perspectives. We contend that a multitude of approaches that rest upon varied sets of theories and methodologies would help vitalize the field of surveillance studies today. This said, there are also certain common denominators, for the purposes of offering a meaningful framework, that underlie the studies presented in this book. Three broad features can be highlighted.

First, the studies adopt varying degrees of non-media centricism (Morley, 2009), where technological and textual affordances are not regarded in isolation or foregrounded over social and cultural processes. While some chapters address particular media phenomena, the analytical focus remains on the social and cultural registers through which these media are received and experienced. The same applies to the discussions of how processes of surveillance are perceived, negotiated and potentially subverted. In line with Raymond Williams' (1974) classical account of television, the media are regarded as cultural forms with inherent materialities. This means that the overt or dormant potential of various media as means of surveillance, as dual agents of liberation and control, is taken as culturally and ideologically embedded, and thus contested. This applies not only to the culturally diverse ways in which particular technologies are integrated in social life, but also to the shifting and converging manifestations of surveillance that they may bring along. As illustrated throughout this volume in various ways and through varying vocabularies, mediatization (here, broadly understood as the growing media saturation of social life and cultural lifeworlds on the whole) implies that logics and practices of surveillance seep into even the most fundamental and mundane areas of social life, and blend with a whole range of needs, desires and social rituals.

Second, what follows from this is that surveillance is interwoven with identity processes in an increasingly seamless manner as "projects of the self" incorporate various media. Identities are multilayered and in flux, as well as socially and culturally negotiated. As Giddens (1991) notes, a sense of ontological security, that is, basic trust in the sustainability of one's Self, depends on two complementary aspects: on the one hand, the maintenance of a personal, autonomous existence; and on the other hand, integration in social environments through which identity can achieve confirmation. In late-modern pluralistic societies, this oscillation between autonomy and social integration necessitates a certain degree of reflexivity on the part of social actors. This, in principle, also means that (mediated) practices of inclusion and exclusion, enclosure and disclosure of information (about oneself and others, institutionally or individually), and thus questions of surveillance, are integral to both transparent democracy and to identity processes. First, private media technologies, networking platforms and mobile applications, which are all embedded in institutional and personal life, allow for various forms of social monitoring and self-surveillance as part of social, professional and everyday practice. Second, a broad range of commercial industries and institutional entities are equipped with greater opportunities for data and information collation for more targeted purposes. Undoubtedly, this may lead to concerns regarding personal privacy, such as "the right to be left alone" and the ability to "control one's filters," evoking feelings of social anxiety and moral dissonance. On the flip side, such practices (which the users might or might not be aware of) could be "normalized" and perceived as commonsensical. As such, new media technologies and processes are enmeshed with the moral spectra of social exchange.

Third, the social perspectives adopted in this volume open the way to approach relations of media, surveillance and identity in a contextualized manner, taking social space and intersectional power structures as a broad starting point. The notion of power here points to various dimensions of structural domination, conditioning control over information and technological means of communication as well as citizens' rights to privacy, recognition and expression in society. The book puts forth critical views of the ways in which power is negotiated between public entities (such as corporations and state institutions) and citizens in different socio-cultural contexts. It also includes reflections on and empirical accounts of how diverse forms of surveillance and monitoring activities become part of social relations (in terms of how gender, class, sexuality and other positionalities are constructed) as well as the discursive construction of "surveillance."

Overall, social perspectives enable us to see how material, symbolic and discursive forces come together, often in contradictory ways, as part of identity processes and power struggles in the context of mediated surveillance. These insights, in turn, can help us unveil and problematize the fluctuating and often context-specific meanings attached to surveillance as a social and ideological phenomenon.

Structure of the Book

The chapters that constitute this volume unveil the social complexities and inherently ambivalent nature of most forms of mediated surveillance today. To bring out arguments and ideas for future research in a synthesized manner, the book is divided into three inter-related parts: Perceptions, Practices and Politics. The chapters in Part 1, Perceptions, address how social actors regard, cope and comply with surveillance, and what kinds of analytical issues and concerns emerge from a research perspective. Each new media technology constitutes a paradigmatic intervention shaping both the conduct and experience of surveillance. Yet, it is the characteristics of the overall social-cultural climate at a given time and place that provide the context within which such conduct and experience are made sense of. Current environments are increasingly marked by an intense level of mediatization, commercialization and spatialized relations. Added to these are cultural and political trends that foreground features such as network capital and self-branding, entertainment and fear. The chapters problematize, amongst other things, a high level of direct and indirect reliance on institutional, largely commercial, processes and procedures, and thus a cultural condition marked by complicity with surveillance.

The fact that perceptions and values are sometimes at odds with actual (mediated) social practices, such as in cases of information disclosure, is further elaborated in Part 2, Practices. These chapters also direct their attention to more horizontal processes of peer-to-peer monitoring and the structures of social norms, values and conventions through which such practices are sustained. Through case studies from diverse social contexts it is demonstrated how social desires for maintaining a sense of ontological security and interpersonal trust contribute to the moral legitimation of surveillance in everyday life, as well as to the making of digital media into indispensable properties.

In the final part of the book, Politics, we move from moral to more overt political agendas. The chapters present contextualized analyses of how monitoring practices sometimes resonate with dominant discourses of citizenship and civic responsibilities, while at the same time having the potential to feed into more expressive forms of (identity) politics. Furthermore, such basic values as protection of privacy and control of information are far from symmetrically distributed across social space. Rather, they are in themselves constitutive of political lines of division and positional struggles. As such, in this final part of the book, we are brought back, once again, to the social ambiguities that surround the media-surveillance-identity complex.

Perceptions

In "Complicit Surveillance and Mediatized Geographies of Visibility," Miyase Christensen discusses the contemporary forms and logics through which surveillance manifests itself. While surveillance is nothing new, the intense level of mediatization we find ourselves in renders current forms of surveillance significantly different in character. Drawing upon fieldwork and interviews with individuals from various segments of Swedish society, Christensen offers reflections on the complicit character of current practices of surveillance. As the author argues, factors such as increased dependence on the media, commodification of communication and a geopolitics of fear yield social practices and formations of space where we are no longer positioned vis-à-vis surveillance, but we are situated *in* it.

Nils Zurawski, in "Consuming Surveillance," takes, as a departure point, that surveillance of the consumer is the most prominent form of surveillance today and is virtually unavoidable due to ubiquitous computing. The author suggests that commonly used analytical models such as the panopticon and surveillant assemblage are not entirely useful to define what surveillance means in the context of consumption. On the basis of his empirical study on loyalty cards issued by commercial entities, Zurawski explores how interdependencies of consumption, control and social formation mediate surveillance without defining it as such.

In the next chapter, Allmer, Fuchs, Kreilinger and Sevignani provide an analysis of the political implications of targeted advertising on social networking sites. They use both survey and interview methodologies to explore the ways in which Facebook users are positioned vis-à-vis the notions and related practices of privacy and surveillance. This chapter advocates abandoning bourgeois notions of privacy and advancing a socialist understanding of privacy in order to strengthen the position that consumers and citizens need protection against corporate surveillance.

In the chapter "The Emerging Surveillance Culture," which closes this first part of the volume, David Lyon offers an engaging discussion of how surveillance is integrated into everyday life and how it becomes ordinary, natural and normal. In order for surveillance researchers to grasp what he labels "an emerging culture of surveillance," Lyon suggests the emphasis should be placed upon how surveillance has become an everyday social experience. He draws our attention to the importance of maintaining a historical perspective rather than overemphasizing the role of digital technologies. Lyon concludes that we should explore the growth of surveillance culture by way of studying the experiences of surveillance, the rise of surveillant imaginaries and the engagement of ordinary people in surveillance as compliant or complaining "data subjects."

Practices

The second part of the book opens with Mark Andrejevic's chapter "The Infinite Debt of Surveillance in the Digital Economy." The author draws on theories of "debt" to explore the nature of the obligation imposed on consumers of the online economy and their reactions to it. The online economy requires "free" services and content in exchange not simply for ad exposure, but also for willing submission to data collection processes used to profile, sort and target users. The original research data presented here illustrate that people have a high level of concern about the terms of exchange, even as they acquiesce. Andrejevic argues that we need to move beyond the fact that consumers "agree" to provide information about themselves in exchange for access to goods and services in order to interrogate the power relations that structure this agreement.

In the following chapter, "Mobile Social Networks and Surveillance: Users' Perspective," Lee Humphreys examines how people think about privacy and surveillance when using mobile social networks. In a field study of Dodgeball, the author found most informants were not concerned about privacy when using the mobile social network because they felt they were in control of their personal information. However, as Humphreys argues, the study also exposed three kinds of surveillance present in the everyday usage of Dodgeball: voluntary panopticon, lateral surveillance and self-surveillance.

In "Collaborative Surveillance and Technologies of Trust," Jennie Germann Molz provides an original analysis of online reputation systems in the "new" sharing economy. In this new economy, where individuals and small enterprises use the internet and online peer-to-peer networks to rent, swap, gift, barter and share material resources with strangers, trust is a fundamental element. However, since trust is fostered via new mechanisms, such as online reputation systems, it also necessitates surveillance. Studying the websites CouchSurfing.com and Airbnb.com, Molz suggests that the online reputation systems that operate on these sites constitute a form of interpersonal surveillance that disciplines members' behavior, securitizes the network and binds members together in a "like-minded" community. Ultimately, Molz argues, the interpersonal surveillance implied by these reputation systems is part of a larger trend towards the "surveillancization" of social relations.

The final chapter of Part II is André Jansson's "Textures of Interveillance: A Socio-Material Approach to the Appropriation of Transmedia Technologies in Domestic Life." Jansson's chapter extends the discussion on "horizontal" monitoring practices and introduces the concept of "interveillance" for capturing the normalization of such mediated practices as part of identity creation. Studying the appropriation of new (trans)media technologies in Swedish small-town households, Jansson contends that interveillance, despite its open-ended, transmediated character, abides and reproduces deep-seated moral values. The interview data unveil how the managing of private information and the judgment of other people's online behavior operate through taken-for-granted registers of "common sense." Jansson's chapter thus underscores the importance of approaching the spread of surveillance culture as a socio-materially embedded, negotiated process.

Politics

In "The Non-Consensual Hallucination: The Politics of Online Privacy," David Barnard-Wills starts his discussion with the assertion that online privacy is a political issue, and that a single social theory is unlikely to explain the extent of phenomena experienced online. This chapter links the politics of online privacy to surveillance through an engagement with the discourse theory of Chantal Mouffe, Ernesto Laclau, David Howarth and Jason Glynos. Barnard-Wills remains critical of reducing the highly complex character of social mediations through simplistic and deterministic terminology such as "online" or "digital." Bringing together political philosophy and social scientific analysis, the author examines the politics of online privacy from two related constructs—hegemony and identity.

Next, Mäkinen and Koskela examine cases where people themselves conduct surveillance in game-like settings. The authors pay attention to how uses of surveillance are constantly changing and being negotiated by different groups in different times. As discussed in the chapter, while people participate in surveillance in numerous ways, there are patterns of unconventional politics through which ordinary people express opposition to surveillance and dissent. Mäkinen and Koskela also discuss the aspect of playfulness and how the latter is related to both using the equipment in a playful manner and turning surveillance itself into a game.

Since its establishment, the People's Republic of China has imposed a nation-wide ban on pornography. The mechanisms of monitoring included top-down measures such as persecution and moral reinforcement through bulletins as well as policing of online and offline venues. In "Sexual Bodies and Surveillance Excess on the Chinese Internet," Katrien Jacobs discusses how Chinese netizens employ subversive discourses and open displays of sexuality in response to the ideology and morality imposed by the state. To illustrate her points, Jacobs offers examples from amateur or "DIY" pornography sites, internet activism sites and practices, and online vigilantes or the Human Flesh Search Engine (*Renrou Sousuo*). The chapter demonstrates how the internalization of surveillance as methods of gazing and identity management goes hand in hand with an online porn culture and sexual revolution.

In the final chapter, Patrick Burkart and Jonas Andersson Schwarz offer reflections on the counter-discourse of "post-privacy" that has become prevalent amongst some net activists. The post-privacy position advocates the abandonment of privacy activism and personal privacy hygiene based on the conviction that digital privacy is both untenable and socially unrewarded. This laissez-faire attitude towards surveillance reveals deep anxieties about the loss of control over domains previously associated with autonomy, self-presentation and personal visibility. In their effort to make sense of post-privacy advocacy, Burkart and Andersson Schwarz propose a framework within which post-privacy ideology is interpreted through the doxa and the praxis of maintaining personal online privacy under conditions of state and corporate surveillance.

References

Albrechtslund, A. (2008). Online social networking as participatory surveillance. *First Monday*, *13*(3). http://firstmonday.org/article/view/2142/1949/

Andrejevic, M. (2005). The work of watching one another: Lateral surveillance, risk and governance. *Surveillance & Society*, *2*(4), 479–497.

Ball, K. (2009). Exposure: Exploring the subject of surveillance information. *Information, Communication and Society*, *12*(5), 639–657.

Bauman, Z., & Lyon, D. (2012). *Liquid surveillance*. Cambridge: Polity.

Best, K. (2010). Living in the control society: Surveillance, users and digital screen technologies. *International Journal of Cultural Studies*, *13*(1), 5–24.

Christensen, M. (2012). Online mediations of sociality in transnational spaces: Cosmopolitan re/formations of belonging and identity in the Turkish diaspora. *Journal of Ethnic and Racial Studies*, *35*(5), 888–905.

Christensen, M. (2011). Online social media, communicative practice and complicit surveillance in transnational contexts. In M. Christensen, A. Jansson, & C. Christensen (Eds.), *Online territories: Globalization, mediated practice and social space* (pp. 222–238). New York: Peter Lang.

Christensen, M. & Jansson, A. (Forthcoming). *Cosmopolitanism and the media: Cartographies of change*. Basingstoke: Palgrave Macmillan.

Christensen, M., & Jansson, A. (2012). Fields, territories, and bridges: Networked communities and mediated surveillance in transnational social space. In C. Fuchs, K. Boersma, A. Albrechtslund, & M. Sandoval (Eds.), *Internet and surveillance: The challenges of Web 2.0 and social media*. London: Routledge.

Clarke, R. (1994). Dataveillance: Delivering 1984. In L. Green & R. Guinery (Eds.), *Framing technology: Society, choice and change* (pp. 117–130). Sydney: Allen & Unwin.

Foucault, M. (1979). *Discipline and punish: The birth of the prison*. Harmondsworth: Penguin.

Gandy, O. (1993). *The panoptic sort: A political economy of personal information*. Boulder, CO: Westview.

Gates, K. (2011). *Our biometric future: Facial recognition technology and the culture of surveillance*. New York: New York University Press.

Giddens, A. (1991). *Modernity and self-identity: Self and society in the late modern age*. Cambridge: Polity.

Giddens, A. (1985). *The nation-state and violence: Volume two of a contemporary critique of historical materialism*. Berkeley: University of California Press.

Graham, S. (2006). Surveillance, urbanization, and the U.S. "revolution in military affairs." In D. Lyon (Ed.), *Theorizing surveillance: The panopticon and beyond*. Cullompton: Willan.

Haggerty, K. D., & Ericson, R. V. (Eds.). (2007). The new politics of surveillance and visibility. In K. D. Haggerty & R. V. Ericson (Eds.), *The new politics of surveillance and visibility* (pp. 3–25). Toronto: University of Toronto Press.

Haggerty, K. D., & Ericson, R. V. (2000). The surveillant assemblage. *British Journal of Sociology, 51*, 605–622.

Jacobs, K. (2011). *People's pornography: Sex and surveillance on the Chinese internet*. Bristol: Intellect.

Jansson, A. (2012). Perceptions of surveillance: Reflexivity and trust in a mediatized world (the case of Sweden). *European Journal of Communication, 27*(4), 410–427.

Koskela, H. (2004). Webcams, TV shows and mobile phones: Empowering exhibitionism. *Surveillance & Society, 2*(2/3), 199–215.

Lauer J. (2011). Surveillance history and the history of new media: An evidential paradigm. *New Media and Society, 14*(4), 566–582.

Marwick, A. E. (2012). The public domain: Social surveillance in everyday life. *Surveillance & Society, 9*(4), 378–393.

Mathiesen, T. (1997). The viewer society: Michel Foucault's panopticon revisited. *Theoretical Criminology, 1*(2), 215–234.

McGrath, J. (2004). *Loving big brother: Performance, privacy and surveillance space*. London: Routledge.

Morley, D. (2009). For a materialist non-media-centric media studies. *Television and New Media, 10*(1), 114–116.

Vaidhyanathan, S. (2011). *The googlization of everything (and why we should worry)*. Berkeley: University of California Press.

Williams, R. (1974). *Television: Technology and cultural form*. London: Fontana.

PART I

Perceptions

1

Complicit Surveillance and Mediatized Geographies of Visibility

Miyase Christensen

Rethinking Surveillance Today

Over the past few decades, surveillance expanded in scale and diversified in form, prompting a remarkable increase in interest from both academia and popular culture. In terms of the latter, the 1980s were about towering bureaucracies such as those represented in *Brazil* and *1984*; the 1990s witnessed a fascination with reality shows and entertaining voyeurism in the likes of *EDtv*, *The Truman Show* and *Sliver*; and the first decade of 2000 was awash with intelligent and invasive everyday technologies as in *Eagle Eye*, *Echelon Conspiracy* and *Bourne Identity*. In relation to academia, the rapid spread of online and mobile social media platforms from the mid-2000s onwards, and the questions they raise in relation to loss of privacy and digitized tracking, have been the subject of a sizable volume of research in the area of "surveillance studies" (cf. Albrechtslund, 2008; Andrejevic, 2005; Ball, 2009; Best, 2010; Fuchs, 2010; Haggerty & Ericson, 2007, 2000; Lyon, 2007; Marwick, 2012; Christensen & Jansson, 2012), scrutinizing both economic and cultural aspects. In the other disciplines of humanities and social sciences, there are a rising number of studies linking mediated surveillance to various phenomena, such as urbanization, globalization, migration, wealth disparity and a steep jump in the number cases of paranoia in the U.K. (Durrant, cited in Christensen, 2009).

The current volume is dedicated to exploring, from a social perspective, various dimensions of surveillance, particularly in relation to media and identity. Given that information and communication flows accent who we are, and reshape, to a great degree, not only how we are socially positioned but how we are coded and traded, this interest is well-justified. On an everyday level, our lives and routines, professional and private environments are indeed densely infused with a plethora of technologies and applications that see and show. Yet, while more intense and complex than ever before, mediatization of society, contrary to the way it has often been portrayed in media studies, is not a haphazard occurrence of post-1990s globalization and digitalization, but part of an historical continuum and not exclusively a technological phenomenon.

As discussed elsewhere (Christensen, forthcoming; Christensen & Jansson, forthcoming), I take mediatization broadly to mean an ongoing sociocultural meta-process where the media ensemble (forms, texts, interfaces, technologies and institutions) permeate all spheres of life (cf. Krotz, 2008, 2007; Schulz, 2004), regardless of how one chooses to mediate through a particular form of media. It is more than the sum of its constituents, and although some of us do opt out—unless it is done on a massive scale—this does not reverse its macro influence. On an everyday level, with which this chapter concerns itself, we see the consequences of mediatization in terms of, for instance, the increased migration of both social and personal relations and political communication onto social media platforms such as Facebook. In conjunction with other meta-processes such as globalization, commercialization and individualization (Krotz, 2008), mediatization yields strong currents that shape and drive relations of production, and not least identity processes, which are part and parcel of social and economic formations.

Mediatization, then, is one of the key defining features of late-modernity and a force that sustains (and is sustained by) today's global consumer cultures, or what I label here "cultures of compliant exchange." So far, in addition to the discussions related to its theoretical scope, the more commonly addressed questions borne out of mediatization have been the implications of digitalization and individualization of media technologies for politics or religion, or the intertwining of technological connectivity and tradition (cf. Morley, 2007). I invoke it here as a general conceptual trope as it frames current practices of surveillance in fundamental ways. As Lauer (2011:567) notes, at the end of the 19th and beginning of the 20th centuries (touched by an early phase of mediatization), a number of then-new evidence-producing technologies (from the telegraph to photography) not only served as communication venues, but shaped the "information environment" significantly.

The late 20th and early 21st centuries have ushered similarly radical technological interventions, but at an unprecedented, exponential rate of multiplication and transmutation of artifacts and interfaces. Nearly all media devices and applications today come with tracking and storing functions and many of them cater specifically to surveillance needs. Thus, while surveillance as an apparatus of state and capitalism is nothing new, the intense level of mediatization along with a number of other key social factors that characterize our times renders current forms of surveillance significantly different in character.

As I discuss in this chapter, against the backdrop of global network capitalism (market) and the increased enmeshing of social life and information flows (media), the contemporary forms and logics through which surveillance seeps into the fabric of social life necessitate rethinking on the basis of an assemblage of further aspects: namely, technology (i.e., the medium itself), place (i.e., the lived space of social relations), and cultural absorption of politics (or, everyday geopolitics). Each dimension, and their various combinations at a given time, bring a paradigmatic intervention to surveillance. On the basis of the fieldwork that resulted from our research project "Secure Spaces: Media, Consumption and Social Surveillance" (2009–2012) funded by Riksbankens Jubileumsfond, and my analysis of more recent developments, I suggest that current forms of surveillance increasingly depend on the compliant exchange of information and services through various mediated practices, giving surveillance a complicit character.

Drawing partly upon qualitative interviews in Sweden and a discussion of current examples, I seek to grasp and exemplify in what ways and under what conditions we consent to and comply with surveillance and commercial-political control of personal information. As crucial as they are, narratives that focus solely on the implications of commodified communications, or on the painfully obvious systemic subordination of individuals and social life to the forces of capitalism, reveal but part of the picture of how such dynamics are absorbed.

Theoretically, the purpose here is not to produce an analysis and an accompanying instrumental concept, merely to illustrate the fact that consumers agree to provide personal information in "exchange for access to goods and services" (see Andrejevic, Chapter 5 in this volume, who also points to the importance of maintaining a political economic lens). On the contrary, complicit surveillance, which involves humans as well as machines, is suggested here as a critical and rounded framework within which to consider social practices, economic structures and accompanying power hierarchies that re-produce particular forms of relations. In the nebulous communication environment shaped by the coercive-forces of market and media, we are no longer positioned vis-à-vis surveillance, but we are situated *in* it. While loyalty cards and smart cards produce commercial attachments through the lure of "better deals" (see Zurawski, this volume), surveillance on the whole is generative of debt (Andrejevic, this volume) as well as a cultural condition, interveillance, where identity creation and mediated peer-to-peer monitoring merge (Jansson, this volume; Jansson, 2012; Christensen & Jansson, forthcoming).

In what follows, I offer a description of the fieldwork I draw upon, before I discuss everyday dimensions of surveillance and user attitudes as well as a selection of popular examples.

Description of the Study

This chapter and preceding publications that I cite here, on various dimensions of social surveillance and subjective responses to it, are based largely upon fieldwork (2009–2012) associated with the research project "Secure Spaces: Media, Consumption and Social Surveillance." One set of interviews with migrants of Turkish and Kurdish origin residing in the Stockholm area and one set of interviews conducted with Scandinavian expatriates who are employed as development workers in Nicaragua took place in 2008. As the project commenced in 2009, our first step was taking part in the Society Opinion Media survey conducted at Gothenburg University. The survey generated representative data about perceptions of and attitudes toward surveillance as well as the perceived social functions of various media in everyday life.

In terms of devising our qualitative research strategy, we sought to include samples from different segments of Swedish society and focused on three such sample groups: (a) transnational migrants (originating from Turkey and of Kurdish-Turkish ethnicities) living mostly in the suburban areas of Stockholm; (b) middle-class individuals from Swedish small towns (see Jansson, this volume); and (c) middle-class individuals with mixed Swedish and international backgrounds and high global mobility living in inner-city areas of Stockholm. Each study package involved both site visits and in-depth, semi-structured interviews. A gender balance was observed in the selection of informants, and, during the data collection and analysis phases, both thematic similarities and different patterns were accounted for.

The first sample group was selected because Turkish migrants (of Turkish and Kurdish ethnicities) constitute one of the major migrant populations in Sweden. The informants in this group varied in terms of their class and educational backgrounds, but most lived in the suburban areas of Stockholm where the old and the new, or modern life and traditionalism abide side by side. Individuals in the second and third groups were of middle-class origins, well- to fairly well educated, and with varied political, cultural and religious orientations. The second group of individuals living in small-town settings were more locally rooted with episodic experiences of stays abroad and global mobility. The third group, which is more central to my discussion here, was constituted of ten informants between the ages of 23 and 69. One was originally from Germany and another from the U.K. All were employed at the time of the fieldwork, except for one pensioner who still worked with development projects, and most were career professionals in areas such as biochemistry, journalism, political science and education.

All collected data were recorded, except in the cases of some Turkish migrants who preferred that we took notes rather than voice-recorded the interview. The timing of the study, primarily 2009 and 2012, is important as this was the period when there was a high degree of interest in social media platforms, and new online meeting points and networking sites were rapidly flourishing. There is clearly adequate scope to further consider follow-up studies to gather data on the continued uptake of technology and potentially changing understandings of privacy and surveillance.

Although I draw upon the results of the overall study in my discussion of mediatization and surveillance, of central significance here is the third group of individuals who live in urban, big-city settings and who have a high degree of mobility. In this brief essay, my analysis of the interviews is combined with a discussion of key phenomena and a number of recent examples in the context of surveillance practices.[1]

Cultures of Compliant Exchange

Understanding a phenomenon as complex as surveillance necessitates several lines of attack to pin down its key elements: the institutional and technological points of its origin and economic imperatives; the modalities through which it travels; how it is received, experienced and resisted by individuals and groups; and, the kinds of social and historical contingencies it produces. While the ideal of well-rounded results is always a research aspiration, due to disciplinary, material and spatiotemporal constraints, bringing together all lines of inquiry within a unified research agenda remains a great challenge.

As discussed earlier, against the backdrop of market and media, I concern myself here with "the interactional system in play in a particular context" (Morley, 2007:250), and more specifically, the subjective perception and absorption of particular technologies, and of surveillance, in particular places and geopolitical climates. Such a focus, in and of itself, poses an empirical challenge. As Best (2010:7) observes, "whereas quantitative surveys appear to indicate that people voice privacy concerns, qualitative research demonstrates a much more apathetic public sentiment."

Technology and Place

In the case of technology, each artifact that channels information—from identification cards that we are prompted to produce in order to legitimate our presence at certain locales, to digital TV recorders and face-recognition devices to social media—is imbued with different "molding powers" (Hepp, 2012) that structure social relations. In this study, Ihde's (1990) post-phenomenological conception of human-technology relationship where we are not merely positioned vis-à-vis technology but are reconstituted in it has been instrumental for grasping the mediatized everyday and controlled space (see Christensen, forthcoming; Christensen & Jansson, forthcoming). More specifically, concerning surveillance, the Deleuzian (1992) dissolving of panoptic disciplinary gaze (Foucault, 1979) into more diffuse forms of surveillance also has purchase, especially in explaining subjective attitudes toward online and mobile surveillance versus more traditional forms of monitoring. It is not only humans who are made complicit in surveillance. The architecture of media technologies, home and office spaces and commercial zones are all designed to comply with and facilitate the gathering of information.

When it comes to considerations of space and urban life in conjunction with technology, we rely heavily on abstract systems (Giddens, 1991, 1990) such as transport, banking and personal communication technologies for self-maintenance, security, speed and leisure. It is not uncommon to make payments and purchase bus tickets via mobile phones in metropolitan areas, but the place and context of such exchange is significant. As Giddens (1991:120) notes, "With the development of abstract systems, trust in impersonal principles, as well as in anonymous others, becomes indispensable to social existence." Such elements have a more pronounced character in big cities and urban environments where the level of dependence on abstract systems might be higher than other social contexts defined by closer relations and proximity.

Our qualitative interviews point to the significance and persistence of both locational elements and increasingly complex variations of technological features that condition everyday mediations (Christensen, forthcoming; Jansson, this volume). On the whole, how individuals and groups are positioned socially, pursuits of identity formation and acquisition of material and symbolic wealth are closely entangled with geographic markers and spatial elements in addition to a variety of other factors such as education, class, gender and familial characteristics. The real and the virtual were often dichotomized in media studies, producing a disconnect between technology and technology use and the "places" and material reality in which such use is situated. Each technology intervenes in space in specific ways, and the place of such intervention conditions the way it's experienced and adopted.

The use of Google Glass, for instance, is but one recent and highly illustrative example of the influence of space upon surveillance and where we draw up the lines of complying or complaining (see Lyon, Chapter 4 in this volume). It provides an illustration of the split between how people might view external and personal hardware. Google Glass, Google's "augmented-reality wearable computer," are light-weight eyeglasses—essentially a hands-free portable computer. It is intended as a ubiquitous computer with a head-mounted display and voice recognition. While many are excited at the prospect of such technology and the resultant affordances, concerns have been raised by, for example, online groups such as Stop the Cyborgs, who have started a campaign to have the glasses banned from public spaces (if and when that happens), so as to avoid surveillance and recording of unwilling citizens. The use of such technology within confined urban spaces, containing millions of people, leads to myriad questions and issues regarding how such spaces shape (or not) complicit surveillance and compliant exchange.

Another example is locational practicalities, which come in increasingly mediated forms. For instance, in early 2013 the city of Stockholm decreed that tickets purchased for city busses or underground metro via mobile phones would be required to use a new centralized purchasing system. Residents of Stockholm had been able to purchase tickets via their mobile phones for more than five years, but the recent decision was the end-point for a period of transformation within Stockholm's local transport system. In recent years, there has been a move toward "ticketless" travel within the city: either via travel cards or mobile phones. Coin-operated ticket machines at bus stops have been removed, and drivers are no longer able to accept cash payments for tickets on board. Thus, users of busses and the underground metro in the city are forced to have their travel movements monitored via smartcards or cellphones. Such an action was possible in Sweden due to a number of factors, including high mobile phone penetration, secure online payment systems and, importantly, a high degree of trust in both municipal and corporate entities in relation to both payment and the potential use and/or abuse of data gathered. In other words, what functions in Stockholm in terms of citizens' willingness to participate in a system that surveils their movements is economically, technologically and socio-culturally specific. Surveillance, therefore, must be seen within clear contextual boundaries.

Amongst the urban group of respondents whom I focus on here, attitudes toward more ambiguous forms of surveillance and spatial control, such as online tracking, were varied, and, at times, equally ambiguous. A 42-year-old Swedish male university lecturer noted, in response to questions about his social media use:

> I've used Facebook to attract people to courses, to training days, to discussion groups and comments, to link to articles, all to use it for building opinion, a little bit of marketing, a little bit like a telephone catalogue. But I don't use it for personal contact, no private photos. I don't have that kind of use for it. I have 460 friends and that's everything from colleagues to employers to old customers, students, contacts, relatives. I don't have a wall you can write on or anything like that. If they force me to have a timeline I'll leave.

Q: How do you feel about commercial tracking?

A: I'm not positive towards commercial use of tracking online but I'm less bothered, it's of very little consequence so long as it doesn't disturb or lead to a greater interaction with people who SMS you or phone and try to sell things. If it's the same amount of ads but they're aimed at me, it doesn't really disturb me as much. (Personal interview, 2012)

Another Swedish male, 37, commented:

Q: How do you feel about exposure in social media?

A: I don't have a problem with it because I'm quite careful about what I put out. Certain things I don't put out, you know, I wouldn't put anything personal on my own site. I wouldn't discuss family matters online. What I put out is pretty basic, football scores, expressing my hatred towards Manchester United [laughs]. I'm quite careful about what I put out, that's the main thing, so I can stand up for whatever's been put there, no problem. I might get annoyed about what other people put up about me, that has happened, I've asked other people to untag me before, I wouldn't think twice about it. I'd never post that picture up on Facebook, as far as I'm concerned, they shouldn't. It's actually only happened once.

Q: Why are you so careful?

A: Because of that reason. It's hard to control the information once it's out there. I'll not be able to know how it's used. I also know that basically everything I put out on Facebook is the property of Facebook, and I don't necessarily want to give them, well I'll give them trivial stuff, but it's not like it's a thing against Facebook, basically I don't want my private life posted online unless I choose to myself. And I've chosen not to. (Personal interview, 2012)

As in the case of the interviews with younger individuals from the Turkish–Kurdish migrant community, this set of interviews was also indicative of a different understanding of privacy, where vertical collection of personal data is not necessarily seen as invasion of privacy (exceptions notwithstanding), but horizontal exposure (to peers) of personal data in online space more likely is (Christensen, 2012).

In the interviews conducted, many respondents indicated a specific understanding of surveillance in relation to technology. This understanding was one in which the use of what we might term "external" hardware—such as Closed-Circuit Television (CCTV) cameras or other security cameras—was seen as prototypical surveillance in which the state utilized visual technologies to monitor public spaces. Respondents offered varying levels of support for such surveillance: from an acceptance that such activity might, for example, deter crime in dangerous urban areas, to more skeptical positions on the use of such technology and the implications for personal freedoms. The same university lecturer quoted above commented:

Q: How do you feel about surveillance in public places?

A: I'm torn. On the one side it's good for solving crimes, fights, gangs, that's more positive, but in principle I think it should be restricted. I don't buy the argument if you got nothing to hide it doesn't matter, I think it can be misused, and personal integrity is important. (Personal interview, 2012)

What is noteworthy in these discussions on surveillance, however, is the fact that respondents generally (although not exclusively) seemed to link external hardware and *otherness* with surveillance. A 32-year-old female biochemist commented:

Q: How do you feel about freedom and control in relation to online platforms?

A: It's enabling more control. But in terms of security that could be good because it enables control over criminals.

Q: Are you bothered by it?

A: I am slightly bothered by the invasion of our privacy and that's why I don't really like using social media, I have very limited online activity in that way. Of course I don't like it but there's very little you can do about it. In terms of police surveillance, I feel safer that they check people's emails for say terrorist plans than if they don't. (Personal interview, 2012)

Or, to put it another way, overt surveillance was something done by someone else, using technology belonging to someone else (with the camera being the most obvious symbol), in places where it is necessary and being done *to* someone else.

With technologies such as CCTV cameras, the "exchange" taking place between surveillor and surveilled is overt, and is one of security in exchange for privacy. What was less overt, however, and was somewhat more difficult for the respondents to articulate their feelings about, were surveillance forms that remain "hidden" within what we might describe as "personal" technologies such as cell phones. A 37-year-old male professional who works in the press sector responded:

Q: How do you feel about privacy risks in relation to mobile communication?

A: Not that I can be tracked by GPS, I couldn't care less. Personal integrity as far as someone being able to, if they wanted to, see what I'm doing or being able to download my passwords as such, yeah, that can worry me sometimes. (Personal interview, 2012)

As recent news reports have indicated, state and government officials in the U.S., as well as private corporations, are increasingly making use of the tracking possibilities found in phones to monitor users' online activities as well as physical movements. The use of personal phones for this purpose raises a number of interesting questions regarding the notion of "compliant exchange." In particular, it forces us to consider the extent to which the relative "externality" of a technology influences how individuals perceive it in relation to surveillance.

In this case, we can think of "external hardware" as equipment, which does not "belong" to us (such as CCTV cameras, scanners at stores or metal detectors). Expanding upon Ihde's (1990:3) "technologically textured ecosystem" or "technosystem," the culturally embedded nature of technology and how the terms of that embeddedness is contextualized on the basis of both material and ontological elements such as experiences of externality and internality are of importance here. In addition to being owned by someone else, the technologies in question here are also created for the specific purpose of monitoring or scanning. Sentiments toward camera surveillance differed. One Swedish resident, a 30-year-old British female who migrated from the U.K., noted:

> It's a double-sided question. For me personally I have absolutely no problem with being photographed or registered. I can see for some people that they would feel it was Big Brother checking up on them, but on the other side it's a safety measure, a way of protecting property such as schools. In an ideal world you wouldn't need it but we're not in an ideal world. (Personal interview, 2012)

While a Swedish male student, 23, responded:

> Q: How do you feel about surveillance in public spaces?

> A: I don't have anything against it so long as you can show it gives an effect or is used properly. If you can't show it's there for a reason or it doesn't give results…I don't really have more to say. (Personal interview, 2012)

Cell phones, on the other hand, are highly personal pieces of equipment, often held close to the body for large portions of the day, and used to make contact with family and friends. Thus, they are a far cry from the cold, impersonal "eye" of the in-store surveillance camera or airport full-body scanner. It would be fair to say that the respondents in our study did not see cell phones in the same surveillance league as cameras, despite the fact that both enable significant surveillance possibilities. The same student commented:

> Q: How do you feel about tracking through mobile phones?

A: I'm not really bothered by it. People can follow me if they want to. I suppose my personal integrity isn't majorly important to me. Even though it can be a pain, especially the way the laws are tightening up. I'm more worried about SOPA [Stop Online Piracy Act] and that kind of thing because I'm an active downloader. So at that level I am.

Q: What do you think about future trends, about freedom and control?

A: Well, *freedom under surveillance*, I guess [italics mine]. I don't know really, it feels very uncertain. It could go many different ways. I don't really have an opinion. (Personal interview, 2012)

How people might view external and personal hardware in relation to both space and the circumstances that surround their subjective existence remain significant.

Everyday Geopolitics

Finally, our experiences of and response to both mediation and social space are informed not only by the general climate of formal politics, but, relatedly, how we perceive the world through the prism of everyday sentiments. In *The Geopolitics of Emotion: How Cultures of Fear, Humiliation and Hope Are Reshaping the World*, Dominique Moisi (2009), in response to Huntington's (1996) *Clash of Civilizations*, argues that geopolitics today is characterized by a clash of emotions. The West is dominated by fear. Due to humiliation and condescension, the Arab and Islamic world is host to a fermenting culture of hatred; while Asia stands for hope for a better future. While the accuracy of such grand claims certainly remains questionable, Moisi's discussion of a culture of fear resonates with other studies of a popular immersion in fear, particularly in the U.S. (cf. Downing, 2013).

As we discuss elsewhere (Burkart & Christensen, 2013:4), critical geopolitics, developed in the aftermath of the Cold War, necessitates thinking of geopolitics not only in terms of international relations and foreign policy, but as current economic and political shifts in which media and cultural elements play a key role in shaping power dynamics. A popular understanding of geopolitics is particularly important to consider in the framework of mediatization where the role of everyday imaginaries, as they circulate through various communication channels, is of key importance in influencing perceptions and attitudes. In their piece on geopolitics, Dittmer and Gray (2010:1665) also call upon scholars to consider the ways in which geopolitics are more than simply functions of elite discourse, but can be understood through an examination of "diffuse and relational" forms of power to be found in the everyday (see also Dittmer & Dodds, 2013). In an article on the relationship between the geopolitical and the popular, Downing (2013) discusses the everyday in relation to the culture of fear that has been prevalent within the U.S. for centuries, and not simply in the current post–9/11 environment. This combination of popular geopolitics and a culture of fear has a clear and important impact upon studies of surveillance, and the extent to which individuals are willing to agree to potentially invasive uses of technology in exchange for, once again, a sense of security and well-being.

A prescient example of a surveillance technology used in the wake of widespread fear is the full-body scanner installed at airports throughout the U.S. in the aftermath of an attempt in 2010 by a Nigerian national to blow up a flight to Detroit by detonating an explosive device located in his undergarments. The scanners were installed shortly thereafter, with just over 150 in use throughout the country. The scanners were controversial because they produced an image of the passenger showing the full body without clothing. Public response to the scanners was mixed, with travelers expressing a belief that the scanners were necessary in order to combat terrorism, while at the same time indicating they felt the scanners constituted a violation of personal privacy. This included a lawsuit filed by the Electronic Privacy Information Center in 2010 to halt the introduction of the scanners on the grounds that the use of such technology by the U.S. Transportation Security Administration (TSA) was in violation of the U.S. Administrative Procedure Act, the U.S. Privacy Act, the U.S. Religious Freedom Restoration Act and the Fourth Amendment ("unreasonable search and seizure").

Despite these fears, the scanners have been in use for three years at U.S. airports, although the TSA has announced that they will be withdrawn by the end of June 2013. The reason for the withdrawal is that the images produced by the scanners were too accurate, thus giving investigators a *de facto* view of those being scanned in a state of virtual undress, and subsequent attempts to adjust the software so as to modify the images proved unsuccessful. What is noteworthy about the use of the scanners, in addition to the length of time they were used, is the fact that the notion of privacy, which proved key in the complaints against the technology, were corporeal in nature: travelers simply did not want their bodies to be seen by others. Thus, while all other forms of travel surveillance has been conceded to (if not approved of) by a majority of travelers—including other forms of body scanning, bag searches and biometric data in passports—a line was drawn at what could be considered a clear boundary: seeing one's body naked. Thus, morality played a clear part in determining how far individuals were willing to go in order to obtain security.

Due to a continuum of factors such as the Cold War followed by globalization and mobility, 9/11 and perceived terrorist threats, and migration and urban crime, an everyday geopolitics of sustained fear plays into how we comply with or confront invasive technologies. As a result, we enter into certain relations where the power dimension might be explicit or invisible and adopt attitudes and mediated practices of particular sorts. A 32-year-old female respondent noted:

Q: How do you feel about the impact of globalization on Sweden?

A: It's made me feel unsafe in certain suburbs because I don't really understand the people that live there. I don't really know what they do, that makes me feel unsafe. I'm also annoyed by some of the EU legislation that's been on, for instance food products. But there's a great deal of better restaurants than there were before, and there's also better shopping. (Personal interview, 2012)

A 69-year-old Swedish female noted:

Q: How do you feel about future trends and freedom and control?

A: In one way it's a reduction of freedom and it becomes more of a surveillance society. But at the same time it gives opportunities, I wouldn't say freedom, but opportunities to be used in positive ways. Unfortunately it's becoming more surveillance. Like when you fly, it's become so much, all the controls, it feels like you're being harassed. It used to be nice to travel, now you're like cattle. Some countries are worse for this of course, like the U.S. and U.K. (Personal interview, 2012)

In sum, the growing prominence of surveillance is closely linked to its commodity value, new technological possibilities, spatial and locational factors and the political-cultural context in which we find ourselves. It is not static, but continuously changing and morphing. At its current level, the relational forces of market and media yield a surveillance environment, which relies on positioning users, technologies and spaces in a manner of complicit partaking in it. The ways in which such technologies and practices are adopted at the everyday level and in specific sociocultural contexts remain less explored. While survey research reveals certain beliefs and attitudes toward technology, mediation of artifacts and communication routines is a complex phenomenon necessitating a sociological approach to pin down both the structural and contextual and moral dimensions, which, at times, might be at odds with each other (Christensen, 2013; Christensen & Jansson, forthcoming).

Freedom Under Surveillance?

It was a rather common tendency of earlier studies of the internet to frame digital communications, the "placeless" and "liberating" channels of new media, profile maintenance, avatars and "maintaining of the Self" in a celebratory manner. Precisely two decades after the web browser (first Mosaic, then Netscape) entered our lives, we know all too well that place matters; identity, in many ways, is constituted of both *actual* (Morley, 2011) embodied states and *virtual* (ibid) flows, and that there is no such thing as a free lunch. What we comply with or resist, in essence, are not the geographies of visibility per se that are produced by the data collecting and sorting capabilities of media technologies themselves, but the institutional and commercial centers of control into which those data flow and the implications such flows carry.

As things stand today, the two powerful forces that shape the world we live in, the market and the media, impose upon us a neoliberal sense of social presence and self-achievement. Terms of success, in personal, social and professional spheres, as well as senses of both security and enjoyment depend increasingly on how connected, technologically armed we are and to what extent we comply with "the system" and the ensuing cultures of exchange that bond as much as they bound and oblige. Added to these are the sentiments of a geopolitics of distrust that saturate everyday culture and anxiety-ridden urban routines. As Caldeira (1996) notes, modern cities today celebrate an "aesthetics of security." We can observe similar patterns of segregation in online environments. Vertically, mediated venues remain ultimately porous and open to intrusion. As such, the market-driven technological colonization of social and domestic life bestow upon commercial and state institutions unprecedented power through surveillance. Horizontally, a logic of boundary maintenance and exclusivity of access to each other's information (granted on the basis of various criteria) apply and give the users a sense of control (Christensen, 2011) as well as enjoyment through their self-created *data-doubles*.

Our national survey data indicated that politically left-leaning individuals (Jansson, 2012; see also Jansson, this volume) remain more concerned over privacy control and vertical intrusion. The overall interviews are indicative of a somewhat similar trend, although there are disjunctures between what people express in surveys and how they regard media, technology and security-related questions in private. While we observed varying degrees of awareness of and concern over invasion of privacy, commercial exploitation and state surveillance amongst the range of informants included in this study, on the whole mediated surveillance was regarded as the hidden injury of pervasive penetration of communication technologies.

Interestingly, many informants were indifferent to or less concerned over vertical collation and distribution of data, which was regarded as one of the terms of the culture of exchange, than they were about horizontal visibility, or interveillance (see Jansson, this volume). Oftentimes, the informants did not consider themselves to be the subject of commercial and state monitoring, or surveillance to be boundless and ubiquitous (beyond one's own networks). The external (e.g., CCTV cameras) versus the internal (e.g., mobile phones and online applications) nature of the surveillant artifact also emerged as a significant determinant in shaping attitudes and beliefs. The platforms and modalities through which we are subjected to and experience surveillance continue to multiply. Overt technologies such as airport body scanners receive more media and public attention than civic concerns over potentially even more intrusive new software, such as the face-recognition application of Facebook that identifies its users' faces in each photo uploaded.

Going back to where we started, if mediatization is a defining characteristic of our society, and if surveillance and its different modalities are integral to today's mediated cultures of compliant exchange, then critical social theory needs more honed and rounded approaches to these dynamics in explorations of social-economic relations in general and identity processes and power in particular. Where mediatization extends not only to particular social fields such as politics and health but to the entirety of social and individual conduct from professional networking to distant-mothering[2] and dating services, power inequalities and subordination through acquisition of personal information should flag even greater concern.

The particular interviews noted here are, of course, representative of a social segment whose members possess relatively high degrees of knowledge and cultural capital. Yet, on the whole, the fact that (1) many of us have little or no information on the actual terms and conditions of use, which change continuously, and (2) often concede to using these channels to avoid exclusion, indicate that practical considerations currently outweigh ethical concerns. The solutions can no longer be sought exclusively in the micro-spheres or problems attributed to individual (lack of) responsibility.

Notes

1. Both the conceptual-theoretical and analytical dimensions of the discussion here are put forth in the form of a brief essay. More in-depth analyses are provided in the cited and forthcoming publications related with the project.
2. Such as the Filipino nannies who work in the U.K. and keep in touch with their children via Skype and Facebook (Madianou & Miller, 2011).

References

Albrechtslund, A. (2008). Online social networking as participatory surveillance. *First Monday*, *13*(3). http://firstmonday.org/article/view/2142/1949/

Andrejevic, M. (2005). The work of watching one another: Lateral surveillance, risk, and governance. *Surveillance & Society*, *2*(4), 479–497.

Ball, K. (2009). Exposure: Exploring the subject of surveillance information. *Information, Communication and Society*, *12*(5), 639–657.

Best, K. (2010). Living in the control society: Surveillance, users and digital screen technologies. *International Journal of Cultural Studies*, *13*(1), 5–24.

Burkart, P., & Christensen, M. (2013). Geopolitics and the popular. *Popular Communication: The International Journal of Media and Culture, 11*(1), 3–6.

Caldeira, T. (1996). Fortified enclaves: The new urban segregation. *Public Culture, 8*(2), 303–328.

Christensen, M. (forthcoming). Technology, place and mediatized cosmopolitanism. In A. Hepp & F. Krotz (Eds.), *Mediatized worlds: Culture and society in a media age.* New York: Palgrave Macmillan.

Christensen, M. (2012). Online mediations of sociality in transnational spaces: Cosmopolitan re/formations of belonging and identity in the Turkish diaspora. *Journal of Ethnic and Racial Studies, 35*(5), 888–905.

Christensen, M. (2011). Online social media, communicative practice and complicit surveillance in transnational contexts. In M. Christensen, A. Jansson, & C. Christensen (Eds.), *Online territories: Globalization, mediated practice and social space* (pp. 222–238). New York: Peter Lang.

Christensen, M. (2009, October) Complicit surveillance and social networking: Watching me watching you. *Le Monde Diplomatique* (Eng. Edition).

Christensen, M., & Jansson, A. (Forthcoming). Complicit surveillance, interveillance and the question of cosmopolitanism: Towards a phenomenological understanding of mediatization. *New Media and Society.*

Christensen, M., & Jansson, A. (2012). Fields, territories, and bridges: Networked communities and mediated surveillance in transnational social space. In C. Fuchs, K. Boersma, A. Albrechtslund, & M. Sandoval (Eds.), *Internet and surveillance: The challenges of Web 2.0 and social media,* p. 15. London: Routledge.

Deleuze, G. (1992). Postscript on the societies of control. *October,* 59: 3–7.

Dittmer, J., & Dodds, K. (2013). The geopolitical audience: Watching Quantum of Solace (2008) in London. *Popular Communication: the International Journal of Media and Culture, 11*(1), 76–91.

Dittmer, J., & Gray, N. (2010). Popular geopolitics 2.0: Towards new methodologies of the everyday. *Geography Compass, 4*(11), 1664–1677.

Downing, J. D. (2013). "Geopolitics" and "the popular": An exploration. *Popular Communication, 11*(1), 7–16.

Foucault M. (1979). *Discipline and punish: The birth of the prison.* Harmondsworth: Penguin.

Fuchs, C. (2010). StudiVZ: Social networking in the surveillance society. *Ethics and Information Technology, 12*(2), 171–185.

Giddens, A. (1991). *Modernity and self-identity: Self and society in the late modern age.* Cambridge: Polity.

Giddens, A. (1990). *The consequences of modernity.* California: Stanford University Press.

Haggerty, K. D., & Ericson, R. V. (Eds.). (2007). The new politics of surveillance and visibility. In K. D. Haggerty & R. V. Ericson (Eds.), *The new politics of surveillance and visibility* (pp. 3–25). Toronto: University of Toronto Press.

Haggerty, K. D., & Ericson, R. V. (2000). The surveillant assemblage. *British Journal of Sociology, 51,* 605–622.

Hepp, A. (2012). Mediatization and the "molding force" of the media. *Communication, 37*(1), 1–28.

Huntington, S. (1996). *The clash of civilizations.* New York: Touchstone.

Ihde, D. (1990). *Technology and the lifeworld: From garden to earth.* Bloomington: Indiana University Press.

Jansson, A. (2012). Perceptions of surveillance: Reflexivity and trust in a mediatized world (the case of Sweden). *European Journal of Communication, 27*(4): 410–427.

Krotz, F. (2008). Media connectivity: Concepts, conditions, and consequences. In A. Hepp, F. Krotz & S. Moores (Eds.), *Network, Connectivity and Flow: Key concepts for Media and Cultural Studies.* New York: Hampton Press.

Krotz, F. (2007) The meta-process of 'mediatization' as a conceptual frame. *Global Media and Communication* 3(3), 256–260.

Lauer, J. (2011). Surveillance history and the history of new media: An evidential paradigm. *New Media and Society, 14*(4), 566–582.

Lyon, D. (2007). *Surveillance studies: An overview.* Cambridge: Polity.

Madianou, M., & Miller, D. (2011). *Migration and new media: Transnational families and polymedia.* London: Routledge.

Marwick, A. E. (2012). The public domain: Social surveillance in everyday life. *Surveillance & Society, 9*(4), 378–393.

Moisi, D. (2009). *The geopolitics of emotion: How cultures of fear, humiliation and hope are reshaping the world.* New York: Doubleday.

Morley, D. (2011). Afterword. Electronic landscapes: Between the actual and the virtual. In M. Christensen, A. Jansson, & C. Christensen (Eds.), *Online territories: Globalization, mediated practice and social space*, pp. 273–290. New York: Peter Lang.

Morley, D. (2007). *Media, modernity and technology: The geography of the new.* London: Routledge.

Schulz, W. (2004). Reconstructing mediatization as an analytical concept. *European Journal of Communication, 19*(1), 87–101.

2

Consuming Surveillance

Mediating Control Practices Through Consumer Culture and Everyday Life

Nils Zurawski

Introduction

In many societies exchanges and contracts take the form of presents, though in theory these are voluntary, in reality they are given and reciprocated obligatorily. (Mauss, 1989)

Surveillance of the consumer is the most prominent form of surveillance today (Samatas, 2004; Marx, 2006). The issue of consumer surveillance evokes images of massive data collections, built through the ambient data-gathering strategies that constantly check for new data and behaviour profiles. Ubiquitous computing and mobile technologies have transformed the internet into a constant companion for the average consumer so that surveillance has become almost unavoidable.

In trying to analyse the modes of surveillance to which the modern day consumer is unconditionally subjected, it is difficult to apply commonly used analytical models—e.g., panopticon, surveillant assemblage—in order to define what surveillance is in the context of consumption. Indeed, we may even question whether surveillance is still a good term to describe modes of monitoring customers. Basically, forms of an overarching power as central to Foucault-oriented approaches, (cf. Haggerty, 2006), are somewhat absent. Furthermore, to describe data gathering itself as surveillance implies that this is aimed at steering, managing and influencing people to a defined end. But what could this end eventually be in the context of consumption?

Data gathering is a major business in itself, and acquiring as much data as possible seems to be one end in all the control, monitoring and profiling practices employed today. However, it becomes increasingly difficult to describe all such practices as surveillance, as much of what happens is not as straightforward as an analytical use of the term surveillance suggests. To study issues of surveillance within the context of consumption also means to look at what is actually perceived as surveillance—and why some practices that look like surveillance may not be perceived as such. The key to such an approach lies in the understanding of surveillance as a social practice (cf. Monahan, 2011; Zurawski, 2011a, 2011b) that is hidden in a multiplicity of everyday activities and social relationships. Phenomena that are defined as surveillance from an analytical standpoint may be appropriated by users, citizens or consumers through different media in different contexts. Consumer surveillance can be viewed as a form of mediated surveillance. It is "hidden" in the sense that it surfaces in forms of control that are disguised as social relationships or everyday practices, and yet this does not necessarily make certain surveillance practices appear more attractive or less intrusive. Our perception of the phenomenon of surveillance needs to change from seeing it as direct control to seeing it as a part of a social relationship. Thus, in this article I will argue that surveillance itself transforms into an item of consumption, that will be consumed under the logic of the consumer culture's modes of social formation.

In this article, I will discuss some findings from a study[1] on loyalty cards as issued by shops or corporations. I will explore how these loyalty cards are situated within practices of consumption and how surveillance or monitoring strategies are embedded in their use. I will use theories of reciprocal gift exchange to highlight the interdependencies of consumption, control and social formation, in which the latter provides forms that mediate surveillance without defining it as such. Since loyalty cards are at the heart of shopping, which is itself an iconic activity of consumer culture, the study yielded rich material in support of my argument, not least because, as a marketing device, they are used to establish a relationship between customers and shops as the basis for all of the data gathering that follows. Although collecting data from customers is a primary aspect of loyalty cards, their function cannot be reduced to this feature alone.

Following this introduction, I will begin with a discussion of some features of "consumer society" or "consumerism," as the main mode of social formation today, and its interdependence with surveillance. Then I will show why shopping can be viewed as a social practice rather than a purely rational, economic act, and how relationships are constructed through loyalty cards in the act of shopping. I will place loyalty cards within theories of gift exchange and discuss how surveillance itself becomes part of the social relationships that are established through such exchanges.

I will use interview material from a study on shopping and loyalty cards to highlight and support my argument. In my conclusions, I will draw from the analysis to argue for an approach that understands surveillance as consumption established within social relationships by way of seemingly reciprocal exchanges of goods, information, trust and data.

Consumer Society, Surveillance and Shopping

From a sociological perspective, consumer culture can be viewed, as "the dominant mode of cultural reproduction developed in the West over the course of modernity" (Schrage, 2009). It is being formed by mass production and the all-encompassing commodification of goods, social relations and social life itself (cf. Slater, 1997:8; Bauman, 2009; Ullrich, 2006 on the history of consumer culture). This logic of consumerism features such aspects as constant choice, self-discipline, control for exclusion and the management of the self (cf. Hellmann, 2005:7ff; Bauman, 2009). In a consumer society, it is not only goods that are consumed, but also the meanings that are attributed to them.

Theoretical discussions about surveillance suggest that the disciplinary model will be replaced with a more control-oriented model, in which individuals becomes self-dependent and responsible for their actions. There is less direct coercion and more indirect control through self-management and the presentation of seemingly endless choices and desires (cf. Bogard, 2006). Consumer society controls by means of desire and seduction. Following from this, it seems easy to criticise consumers for walking into the obvious marketing traps and fallacies of industry and its agents. However, this criticism fails to recognise the possibilities that open up from a perspective that pays close attention to everyday practices. Such a perspective does not ignore the wider sociological framework but opens up to narratives of practices in which people also negotiate life and try to make sense of their surrounding world. Narratives about shopping are not only about shopping, but also about all other aspects of daily life, social relationships, society and the world. It is through consumption that social relations are expressed and negotiated (cf. Schrage, 2009:103–104).

According to Gudeman's (2007) concept of the economy as being split into the two realms of community and market, loyalty cards are part of both, which seems to be the key to their success in marketing and profiling. They are also directly linked to economic and cultural logics and are an expression of the political economy in a consumer society, as much as they constitute a cultural practice in themselves. The latter, however, is only possible because of the former. As much as the consumer wants and performs individuality through forms of consumption (e.g., shopping, cf.

Langman, 1992), the data collectors (e.g., corporations) want individual information in order to tailor their supplies, ranges of products and services. Although neither party gets exactly what they wish for, the consumerist logic makes them believe they do. The behaviour of both parties ignites further dynamics and leads to what is discussed widely as "the surveillance society," being the product of social dynamics.

Consumer culture and its modes of production and re-production have spread globally, bridging social diversities and incorporating local modes of consumption. Personal data that is used to monitor people's consumption behaviour, habits and patterns is a central aspect of the conditions under which social formation is possible today. The personal information used for the monitoring processes is generated locally as part of practices that, at first glance, connect neither to the global dynamics of an economy concerned with personal information nor to strategies of monitoring and surveillance that are dependent on such data. Consumer society and surveillance converge through the global data flows that are the backbone of most digital consumer-monitoring strategies today. The generation, processing and trade of data are essential to an advertisement-oriented, internet-based global economy of goods and ideas, which also thrives because of an economy that trades in personal information (Turow, 2006:292–293; Pridmore, 2008; Zureik & Mowshowitz, 2005; Zureik, Harling Stalker, Smith, Lyon, & Chan, 2010). Most data about consumers is generated by consumers themselves—mostly during an everyday practice such as shopping (Zurawski, 2011a). Contrary to primarily viewing loyalty cards as part of a strategic surveillance system, I want to propose a perspective that looks at surveillance through social and cultural practices. It is not the meticulous rituals of power (cf. Staples, 1997:3) that are important here, but the perceptions and narratives of the consumers and the interpretation of their actions within the wider framework of consumerism. My assumption is that surveillance, in an analytical sense, is part of commodified social relations that are enabled through acts of shopping within the logic of consumption. Therefore the focus of this study is on consumption, represented in shopping, and the social relationships that are established or maintained through it. This implies being concerned with the wider implications of the technological artefact, the materiality of the card and the social relations that may exist through this artefact (cf. Miller, 1998:32; Vannini, 2009:18). Loyalty cards are representations of a globally spread culture of consumption and its monitoring strategies, as well as material objects.

Shopping, Loyalty and Everyday Life

In *A Theory of Shopping*, Miller (1998) advances the argument that shopping is a form of lovemaking; that is, it's about social relations and not necessarily a self-centred activity of conspicuous consumption. Earlier, Ben-Porath (1980) had stressed the role of economic exchange for the quality of family connections and identity formation (and vice versa). In the analysis, this perspective helps to show how shopping is, on the one hand, a mundane everyday practice and, on the other hand, a vehicle to negotiate and reconstruct everyday life as a sphere of practice and agency (cf. Slater & Miller, 2007:8–9). Practices are routine types of behaviour. They are co-ordinated, but also require performance for their existence. Consumption is a process whereby agents engage in the appropriation and appreciation of goods, services or information; hence consumption is part of every practice, not a practice itself (cf. Warde, 2005:133ff).

As an everyday practice, shopping provides a setting in which human relationships with other members of society and with society itself are expressed and negotiated, and thus also a field of resistance and identity formation (cf. Hellmann, 2005; Scanlon, 2005). The following statements (from the research interviews) on shopping may highlight how social relations are narrated and produced as part of shopping. It is clear from the interviews that "shopping" often meant to shop with somebody and not necessarily alone. Three quotations from different interviews give examples of this narrative trope.

> I often accompany female friends when they go shopping, as a consultant. I love to spend other people's money [laughs]. (11-b-163)[2]

> If we go shopping for a lot of groceries, we mostly do it with our mother, because then we take her car. But if it is only for small stuff for now or just tomorrow, we walk or take the bus. (12-b-190)

> We go the weekly market together because it is such a nice thing to do. Once you stop working, you have more time and you arrange it differently too. And I love to go shopping at the market every week. (9-a-242)

In the first statement, the person not only refers to relationships with friends, but also voices attitudes towards shopping as a pastime or leisure activity. In the second statement, social relationships, in this case familial relationships, are described— underlined by the use of a familial "we." The reader also learns about the apparent lack of a means of mobility available to the interviewee. The third statement discloses the regularity of the interviewee's shopping practices. It also reveals something about the changes in his routines since retirement, including the changes in the relation to his spouse and their shopping practices. The everyday lives of people are expressed within their narrations about shopping practices. The quote "We're socialized to shop" (cf. Hellmann (2005: 9) has to be inverted to "We shop to socialize"—a more fitting description of what actually happens in and during shopping.

Although loyalty cards are part of shopping practices, because they are used during the actual act of paying for goods, they are incongruous to the idea of social relationships. The bargains and bonuses promised by loyalty card systems tend to invoke a more egoistical and calculable economic approach. However, the cards neither replace money nor are they really needed for shopping as such. In the act of shopping itself, they appear to be a technological artefact that represents a particular part of shopping practices.

Generally, there are two ways to understand the logic of loyalty cards. One way is in light of their role in data collection within the global economy of personal information. As consumer advocates would argue, these marketing devices provide a cheap deal in exchange for valuable data (cf. Maurer, 2012). The other perspective on loyalty cards emphasises their role as an interface between a customer and a shop, chain or brand. Although not all loyalty card schemes work in the same way—some even without collecting personal data—they all share the idea of loyalty. Loyalty is a part of social relationships and this is why I find it appropriate to connect loyalty card use to shopping as a social practice. While inquiring into the uses of loyalty cards in shopping practices, I was able to generate distinctive lines of reasoning from the narratives of the interviews. These rationalised the possession of the cards and enabled me to link them to shopping practices in particular and to a wider framework of consumerism in general. The most important *lines of* reasoning were the following:

- *Bonuses/points*—arguments explicitly broaching or relating to the offered benefits offered by loyalty cards, both negatively and positively
- *Trust*—arguments that articulate people's relationships with and feelings towards a particular business, mostly in a positive manner
- *Shopping habits*—explanations for shopping habits, including rationalisations for shopping: "I always buy there" (a precondition for trust)
- *Family*—narratives in which family and friends are mentioned, either as beneficiaries of points or bonuses or because they play a role when using the card, e.g., shopping together or for someone else

These above lines of reasoning root loyalty cards in narratives of shopping, as they refer to tropes identified in the more general narratives of shopping—family, social relationships or proximity to a particular shop. Shopping can be used as a means to uncover something about people's practices (cf. Miller, 1998).

People negotiate their everyday lives within shopping and thus establish or maintain social relations. These social relationships include those that are directed towards shops. The use of loyalty cards not only serves the purpose of securing bargains and discounts, but also manifests relationships beyond the customer–shop relationship. In order to explore this relationship, the role of loyalty cards and the consequences this has for the perception of surveillance and its analytical framing, I want to return to theories of gift exchange. The social nature of shopping practices and the lines of reasoning identified in the interviews give reason to believe that such theories could add to the theoretical understanding of surveillance within consumer culture.

Gifts, Loyalty and Social Relations

If shopping is socialising, it may be so only if it is not a purely economic activity, but something that reaches beyond a market logic. As the lines of reasoning indicate that social relations and trust are two important issues, it is relevant for this study to examine the nature of the exchanges that take place within shopping when loyalty cards are used. This also assumes that loyalty cards have features and facilities that are not obvious and that reach beyond their original purposes as a marketing instrument. One of the reasons for looking into gift exchange in regards to shopping and loyalty cards lies in the fact that "obligation" surfaced as a strong, explicit argument against their use.

> I do not want to be compelled to go shopping there, because of the card, even if I do not go there most of the time. (9-a-966)

> You feel obligated to buy there. (12-a-551)

> … then you must buy there, because of the bonus points. (12-b-552)

The concept of obligation is at the core of Marcel Mauss' (1989) seminal work on the gift and the reciprocity of exchanges. Much of my research indicates that loyalty cards are more a form of gift than of commodity exchange (i.e., a simple act of economic transaction). However, it also became clear that, within the context of consumption, other readings are possible and this is the reason why surveillance can attach to consumption practices and be transformed into a social relationship itself. This ultimately leads to a reading of surveillance as consumption.

Marcel Mauss published the original *Essai Sur le Don* (*An Essay on the Gift*) in 1923, and it has since become a classical masterpiece in sociology and anthropology. Obligation is one of its central concepts. Thus it seems consequent to explore the importance of the concept in terms of the role it plays in the use of loyalty cards and how this may structure and form modes of consumption and thus social relations. While I will not discuss the long history of academic debate of the work itself (cf. Berking, 1996; Gudeman, 2007; Osteen, 2002; Sykes, 2005; Hénaff, 2009;

Därmann, 2010), I will highlight some of its aspects and try to develop a reading of the use of loyalty cards that reflects features of gift exchanges.

While bearing in mind that interpretations of the original concept, as introduced by Mauss (1989), have been contradictory and controversial, I will use interview material collected in the mentioned study (cf. Zurawski, 2011a, 2011b) to discuss the ambiguity of gifts in their relation to commodities. Furthermore, I want to show how the gift as an object has an impact on concepts of the person, especially in relation to a personal information economy, and I will explore the role of reciprocity in respect to loyalty cards. Reciprocity could be a key aspect through which strategies of consumer profiling attach to practices such as shopping that appear rather disconnected from control or surveillance regimes. The above-quoted interview material also suggests other aspects beyond obligation or reciprocity. The card itself is not only addressed as a material thing (although this is not a strong aspect in the narratives), but also as an idea that comes to represent the relationship that it establishes.

Reciprocity

For Mauss, reciprocity and the obligation to respond to a gift are elementary in exchanges (1989: 20ff). Although those exchanges are often made by individuals, they pertain to the whole community, as the individuals represent groups (cf. Gudeman, 2007: 83). Fundamentally, gifts are exchanged between individuals who are bound together by social relationships (or they begin to be related through an initial gift exchange). Economic marketing is rooted in a world shaped by consumption and aims to sell an increasing number of products to customers. However, as shown by the following quote from an interview with a marketing executive, marketers may have understood that loyalty may serve as a form of reciprocity within a consumer society and even suspect that their customers know what stands behind a loyalty card scheme.

> Consumers are not stupid. They understand that they engage in an exchange in a way: I yield my data, but in return, I want to be addressed more personally. Everybody engaging in a loyalty cards scheme knows that. (Interview with marketing executive of Budnikowsky, a local drugstore chain in Hamburg)

This quote resonates well with existing academic, economic literature on loyalty marketing, which focuses also on its ambivalent implications. Although much of the literature does not show an interest in what the consumer as a customer actually does and how they themselves may interpret loyalty, some approaches indicate that marketers have understood aspects of everyday practices such as shopping. For instance,

Gómez, Arranz, and Cillán (2006) look at how loyalty programmes affect different kinds of loyalty, i.e., behavioural and affective (see also Lim & Razzaque, 1997). Rundle-Thiele (2006) conceives loyalty as a relational construct that helps to establish a reciprocal relationship that eventually sets a brand apart (see also Prus, 1987 in an ethnographic study concerned with the development of loyalty as a social relation; and Arvidsson, 2005, on brands). Others ask if loyalty programmes are actually increasing customer loyalty or not. Rosenbaum, Ostrom, and Kuntze (2005) integrate a notion of community into their research. Their notions go beyond the mere economical rationale of marketing and link to Gudeman's approach of economic practices as constituted in the realms of market and community—the latter being the realm where gift exchange in a Maussian sense becomes relevant (cf. Gudeman, 2007:5, 80–81). Beckett and Nayak (2008) also stress the fact that loyalty cards are not only concerned with knowledge about the consumer, but also with collaboration between the consumer and the retailer, which may lead to "new marketing opportunities and greater loyalty" (Beckett & Nayak, 2008: 306). Their argument is that loyalty cards can achieve what is not possible through traditional mass marketing. In many cases, the strategies behind loyalty marketing can be recapitulated as "rewarding repeat purchase behaviour and, through communication acts to stimulate loyalty trends for the further repeat purchase" (cf. Capizzi & Ferguson, 2005:80).

Ultimately, all loyalty programmes' purpose is to establish and foster a close connection between a business and its customers with the intended collection of data for further marketing use. However, as Beckett and Nayak (2008:300) argue, "the significance of CRM (customer relationship management) lies not only in its individualization of marketing and the objectivization of the consumer, but also in its attempt to subjectivize the consumer through the construction of forms of identity with which consumers are encouraged to identify. The emphasis here is not one of the individual being governed by producers, but individuals governing themselves through association with forms of identity promoted by producers."

According to the interview material, community is an important aspect of the practice of shopping. These relationships are based on reciprocity in the context of community and are concerned with the maintenance of social bonds. Gifts are never fixed entities, but contested constructions of social transactions (cf. Algazi, Jussen, & Groebner, 2003:10). Thus, giving and receiving gifts lie at the core of the constructions of meanings and hence the establishment of social bonds. "Loyalty" describes such a social bond, which is not primarily focused on an economic exchange (cf. Hénaff, 2009:175) but on the negotiation of a social order or a relationship between individuals. Giving enables individuals to reach out and establish social bonds, while receiving gifts produces the obligations with which those bonds are stabilised over time. However, loyalty cards do not establish bonds between individuals, but between individuals and larger commercial entities. This did not seem to concern one interviewee, who described "unfaithful" behaviour with regards to shopping practices and the possession of a loyalty card (in this case, for a car-washing chain):

> I can become unfaithful when going to Mr. Wash instead. (11-b-616)

This quote indicates that loyalty cards and the exchanges taking place form social bonds to which a person may become unfaithful—although such disloyalty actually does not have social ramifications. In consumerist economic terms, choice or calculation should determine where someone washes his or her car, without favour towards any particular company. However, the quote indicates that loyalty, in this case manifested by possession of a card, is also a factor in decisions (cf. Komter, 1996:8). The exchange manifested in a loyalty card generates an obligation.

There remains a question over what is actually exchanged and whether the card itself is the gift. Loyalty cards are part of shopping practices, as explained above, and these are clearly situated within part of a consumer culture, where everything has been turned into a commodity. Goods and services are bought and exchanged. Loyalty cannot be bought, but it appears to strengthen the ties between consumers and shops in a similar way to the obligations that are generated in gift exchange practices. However, the cards themselves do not seem to be the gift.

Gift or Commodity

The distinction between gift and commodity has been extensively debated. I do not want to pursue this debate about whether one is the replacement for the other, or whether they can only exist in mutual exclusion (cf. Callon, 1998; Gregory, 2004; Osteen, 2002). I will rather show the ambivalence of the concepts in respect to loyalty cards and their role in the asymmetric form of exchange that they facilitate.

Gift and commodity exchange are not the same. The gift does not represent a prior form of the commodity exchange and both may exist side by side (cf. Gregory, 2004, 1982; Hénaff, 2009). Hénaff (2009) also stresses that gifts are no alternative for commodity exchanges. However, with the expansion of consumption as the dominant model of social formation, less room exists for more public forms of gift exchange, which become an entirely private issue. Social bonds are not reproduced through these kinds of exchanges (cf. Hénaff, 2009:169). The use of loyalty cards can be seen as being situated at the interface of gift and commodity exchange. To regard loyalty cards as non-commercial would neglect their characteristics as marketing tools. However, as I have argued, the use of loyalty cards evokes certain features that can be analysed as gift exchanges—processes in which social relations are negotiated and maintained. The following three quotes may exemplify the two-sided nature of loyalty cards in regards to gift and commodity exchange.

> I threw mine away—because I wasn't using the points. (8-b-558)

> I am not convinced that the bargains you get are really good bargains. (14-b-245)

> At Douglas' I get a five-Euro voucher on my birthday. I like that; they are really investing in me. (11-b-656)

According to the identified lines of reasoning in regard to loyalty cards, all three quotes can be categorised as arguments that stress the aspect of rewards. One of the major ideas within this category is that loyalty cards enable "good deals"—this was stated in several interviews. These quotes refer to a calculable deal and paying more attention to the outcome than to a possible relationship that might have been established. However, all of them can be interpreted on another level.

The first statement refers to the card as a piece of material that can be thrown away, as part of the exchange—the points—are not used. This may be read as a breaking of the relationship. The second statement voices scepticism about the nature of the "deal" or relationship that comes with the loyalty card. The third interviewee sees the voucher she receives as an investment in herself by the company—a gift that has to be returned. None of these quotes can be categorised distinctively as either gift or commodity oriented. This can be said about almost all statements that fall into this line of argument. It remains unclear what kind of exchange actually takes place and how the role of loyalty cards can be described unequivocally. As a marketing tool that aims to tie customers to a shop or brand, loyalty cards clearly belong to the world of commodities. However, it is the exchange of bargains against loyalty—"investments" against the felt "obligations" to continue shopping at particular shops because of the constructed community—that is of more importance than the actual card. Hence loyalty cards make use of certain features of gift exchanges and their power of constructing social relations, obligations and a wider network that may resemble a community.

It is not surprising that many loyalty card schemes promote websites where the user may engage with a community of shoppers, thus pretending to be more than a mere economic exchange. Loyalty cards seem to mediate commodity exchanges and to attach further meanings to the relationships between shoppers and shops. Gifts are never free (cf. Gudeman, 2007:80) and the bargains that may be gained by the use of loyalty cards are nothing other than an initial gift in an ongoing exchange of obligations and reciprocity (positive or negative), at once or much later.

Gifts as Intermediaries

If I follow the argument that Komter (cf. 2007:98) highlights from the readings of Mauss, then the spirit of the gift is what counts in primitive as well as in contemporary societies. But what would be the spirit of the gift, if it takes on the form of a loyalty card? In order to understand why loyalty cards work as gifts, in the sense that they establish a social relationship between a person and a corporation, it is important to look at the practices and procedures that the gift initiates (cf. Därmann, 2010:165).

According to the interview material already presented in this paper, it is rarely the card as a material item that is of prime importance, but rather the activities, practices or advantages (and disadvantages) that are attached to the exchanges associated with a card. Loyalty card schemes, as systems of exchange, communicate a sense of belonging, community, reciprocity, obligation or social bonds (e.g., investment in an individual). As part of an economic exchange, loyalty cards disguise the act of commodity exchange, while at the same time supporting its efficiency.

When Marilyn Strathern (1997:293) writes that "person" can be replaced by "gift," she asks whether this idea, which is fitting to describe rituals and relationships among pre-modern Melanesian people, still describes what happens in contemporary consumer societies. She concludes that gifts in consumer culture establish a relationship between individuals who choose to engage in this exchange. While in Melanesian society, the gift always indicates a larger context, in which the gift giver and the receiver participate and that shapes their whole identity as group members and indeed as human subjects. Consumer culture, on the other hand, is based upon choices, which, in her reading, alters the nature of gifts altogether, and makes them less binding and, following her argument, implies no obligation at all. However, in consideration of the spirit of the gift, I want to argue that loyalty cards are also seen to represent corporations issuing gifts and offering bargains in return for some form of (consumer) loyalty. The following quotes may illustrate how loyalty cards, as part of the gift exchange, become what they represent and mediate something more than the exchange itself.

> Erdkorn [local health-food chain in Hamburg] has a loyalty card that will not be scanned, which I find better. (9-d-706/726)

> I flirted with Budni [short for Budnikowsky, drugstore, see above], because it was sympathetic. (2-b-331)

> Karstadt card—I would not want to have, they have no positive image. (11-a-670)

The reasons for owning a loyalty card or for refusing one in these cases is not reduced to the economic value of the exchange but based upon the perceived reputation of the issuer. The first quote cites the issue of data protection, the second suggests that the issuer portrays a general image of sympathy, while the third cites a negative image as a basis for a refusal; i.e., the interviewee does not want to form part of an exchange with that particular business. These statements support the view that loyalty cards, as gifts that represent a system of exchanges and obligation between consumers and businesses, mediate more than purely economic transaction of commodities. These transactions appear as personalised relationships between actors that are involved in a wider frame of exchange, involving the image (spirit) of the business, community and obligations that are usually not thought to be of relevance for economic actions. It is exactly this quality of mediation that helps us to understand why and how surveillance may be consumed as part of these exchanges.

Conclusion: Consuming Surveillance

Loyalty cards are part of a global economy of personal information. They are used to monitor and profile customer behaviours as part of a business model of economic growth. Although, analytically, the pervasive mode of data gathering can be seen as consumer surveillance in the everyday practice this does not constitute a problem to most consumers. My analyses have shown that the setting these cards are used in provides a context where surveillance itself becomes part of the exchange and hence can be described as "being consumed," which expresses an ambiguity, as loyalty cards are integral to surveillance at a systemic level, they are not conceived and experienced in such a way.

So far in this chapter, the analyses have shown how shopping, as a social and mundane practice, involves aspects beyond its economical purpose. Consumption is more than economics and encompasses issues of lifestyle, distinction or identity. The person as well as the group are reproduced through a form of consumption (cf. Strathern, 1997:295)—thus consumption becomes a mode of social formation. Life itself becomes "consumption" in the consumerist sense of the concept (cf. Bauman, 2009). The use of loyalty cards is embedded in the practices of shopping, which are also concerned with social relationships, the narratives of everyday life, family and friends, and peoples' position in society. Based on my interviews, data protection and surveillance issues play a marginal role within this practice. From the analyses, it can be stated that loyalty cards are less part of a system of consumer surveillance and more a part of shopping and the everyday life.

By applying theories of gift exchange to loyalty cards, I have been able to highlight that the seemingly commodity-oriented transaction has some deeper aspects including the felt obligation to engage in a reciprocal exchange—in this case, to continue shopping at a particular shop. As with other gifts, loyalty cards are not about the object, but about the meanings they carry. They often invoke the reputation ("the spirit") of the chain or brand, so that the relationship that has been established becomes the actual focus of the exchange. However, this can be said about consumerism as well: it is not concerned with the object as an object but with the image the object represents. Thus loyalty card transactions reconstitute identities in the process of the gift exchange in both a Maussian and a consumerist reading (cf. Algazi, Jussen, & Groebner, 2003:17).

In terms of what is literally exchanged, the consumer's data may be read as identity, which is lent to the corporation and has to be returned—not necessarily as data, but as bargains, discounts or as other investments (cf. Maurer, 2012:479). In light of this, it is possible to conceptualise these kinds of relationships as forms of embedded surveillance. Consumer profiling is made possible through the social practice of shopping. Surveillance is not only attached to the practices in a disguised form, but is also itself part of the exchange. As gifts incorporate the memories of those involved in the exchange, because they involve moving—objects, persons, relations in time and space (cf. Algazi Jussen, B., & Groebner, 2003:7)—the collected data may serve as the objectified memory; in the case of loyalty cards, together with the obligation and the modes of reciprocity initiated. Loyalty cards highlight the stated ambivalence of such exchanges in consumer culture, where surveillance or the practices of profiling become a gift, a commodity, but definitely part of the exchange, indistinguishable from the context in which it takes place.

Surveillance is part of the social relationships that have been made possible through exchanges. In this regard, surveillance is mediated through loyalty cards, not from a malign intention, but because of the nature of exchanges as modes of social formation. Surveillance is consumed. To differentiate between a thing, person, relationship, subject or object becomes irrelevant, as exchanges render gifts into intermediaries (Därmann, 2010:167) and thus the gift conceals the commodity (cf. Strathern 2012:402). The logic of consumer culture has extended its logic into social relations, but not completely. In this way, consumer surveillance is made possible and invisible at the same time. For a consumer, providing data is not only part of the "deal," but also part of a wider social context of community, everyday life and the establishment of links and relationships.

Acknowledging this connection helps us to understand why data protection is not an issue for many consumers and why the loss of privacy is not necessarily a problem. It is seen as part of an obligation in a consumer culture.

Notes

1. The study was funded by the German Research Council (DFG) and was conducted between 2008 and 2010. Its main part consisted of qualitative and focused group interviews (17 with 49 respondents, 23 male, 26 female, 40 had at least one loyalty card). In addition, seven interviewees kept a diary on their consumption behaviours over a period of two weeks, with a conclusive second interview. The interviews focused on shopping discounts and the issue of loyalty cards was not addressed as a primary topic to avoid possible preoccupation with public discussions on data protection and surveillance. Interviews lasted 1–2 hours each and generated narrations of everyday practices circling around shopping, but very often took off from there into other fields of social life.

2. Code for group interviews statements: *4* = 4th interview; *a/b* = Person in interview; *463* = line in transcript, other interviews accordingly, all quotes are translated from German by the author.

References

Algazi, G., Jussen, B., & Groebner, V. (Eds.). (2003). *Negotiating the gift: Pre-modern figurations of exchange*. Göttingen: Vandenhoeck & Ruprecht.

Arvidsson, A. (2005). Brands: A critical perspective. *Journal of Consumer Culture, 5*(2), 235–258. doi:10.1177/1469540505053093

Bauman, Z. (2009). *Das leben als konsum*. Hamburg: Edition HIS.

Beckett, A., & Nayak A. (2008). The reflexive consumer. *Marketing Theory, 8*(3), 299–317.

Ben-Porath, Y. (1980). The F-connection: Families, friends, and firms and the organization of exchange. *Population and Development Review, 6*(1), 1–30.

Berking, H. (1996). *Schenken. Zur Anthropologie des Gebens*. Frankfurt am Main/New York: Campus.

Bogard, W. (2006). Welcome to the society of control: The simulation of surveillance revisited. In K. D. Haggerty & R. V. Ericson (Eds.), *The new politics of surveillance and visibility*. Toronto: Toronto University Press.

Callon, M. (Ed.). (1998). *The laws of the markets*. Oxford: Blackwell.

Capizzi, M. T., & Ferguson, R. (2005). Loyalty trends for the twenty-first century. *Journal of Consumer Marketing, 22*(2), 72–80.

Därmann, I. (2010). *Theorien der Gabe zur Einführung*. Hamburg: Junius.

Gómez, B. G., Arranz, A. G., & Cillán, J. G. (2006). The role of loyalty programs in behavioral and affective loyalty. *Journal of Consumer Marketing, 23*(7), 387–396.

Gregory, C. A. (2004). *Savage money: Studies in anthropology and history*. London: Routledge.

Gregory, C. A. (1982). *Gifts and commodities: Studies in political economy*. London: Academic.

Gudeman, S. (2007). *The anthropology of economy*. Malden, MA: Blackwell.

Haggerty, K. D. (2006). Tear down the walls: On demolishing the panopticon. In D. Lyon (Ed.), *Theorizing surveillance: The panopticon and beyond*. Cullompton: Willan.

Hellmann, K. U. (2005). Soziologie des Shopping: Zur Einführung. In K. D. Hellmann & D. Schrage (Eds.), *Das Management des Kunden: Studien zur Soziologie des Shopping* (pp. 7–36). Wiesbaden: Verlag für Sozialwissenschaften.

Hénaff, M. (2009). *Der Preis der Wahrheit*. Frankfurt am Main: Suhrkamp.

Komter, A. (2007). Gifts and social relations: The mechanisms of reciprocity. *International Sociology, 22*(1), 93–107.

Komter, A. (Ed.). (1996). *The gift: An interdisciplinary perspective*. Amsterdam: Amsterdam University Press.

Langman, L. (1992). Neon cages: Shopping for subjectivity. In R. Shields, *Lifestyle shopping*. London: Routledge.

Lim, K. S., & Razzaque, M. A. (1997). Brand loyalty and situational effects. *Journal of International Consumer Marketing, 9*(4), 95–115. doi:10.1300/J046v09n04_06

Marx, G. T. (2006). Soft surveillance: The growth of mandatory volunteerism in collecting personal information—"Hey Buddy, can you spare a DNA?" In T. Monahan, *Surveillance and security: Technological politics and power in everyday life* (pp. 37–56). New York: Routledge.

Maurer, B. (2012). Late to the party: Debt and data. *Social Anthropology, 20*(4), 474–481.

Mauss, M. (1989). *Soziologie und Anthropologie* (ungek. Ausg.). Frankfurt am Main: Fischer.

Miller, D. (1998). *A theory of shopping*. Cambridge: Polity.

Monahan, T. (2011). Surveillance as cultural practice. *The Sociological Quarterly, 52*(4), 495–508.

Osteen, M. (2002). Gift or commodity? In M. Osteen, *The question of the gift*. London: Routledge.

Pridmore, J. (2008). *Loyal subjects: Consumer surveillance in the personal information economy*. (Unpublished doctoral dissertation). Queens University, Kingston, Ontario.

Prus, R. (1987). Developing loyalty: Fostering purchasing relationships in the marketplace. *Journal of Contemporary Ethnography, 15*(3–4), 331–366. doi:10.1177/089124168701500303

Rosenbaum, M. S., Ostrom, A. L., & Kuntze, R. (2005). Loyalty programs and a sense of community. *Journal of Services Marketing, 19*(4), 222–233.

Rundle-Thiele, S. (2006). Look after me and I will look after you! *Journal of Consumer Marketing, 23*(7), 414–420.

Samatas, M. (2004): *Surveillance in Greece. From anticommunist to consumer surveillance*. New York: Pella.

Scanlon, J. (2005, Fall). Making shopping safe for the rest of us: Sophie Kinsella's Shopaholic series and its readers. *Americana: The Journal of American Popular Culture (1900–present), 4*(2).

Schrage, D. (2009). *Die Verfügbarkeit der Dinge*. Frankfurt am Main: Campus Verlag.

Slater, D. (1997). *Consumer culture and modernity*. Cambridge: Polity.

Slater, D., & Miller, D. (2007). Moments and movements in the study of consumer culture: A discussion between Daniel Miller and Don Slater. *Journal of Consumer Culture, 7*(1), 5–23.

Staples W. G. (1997). *The culture of surveillance: Discipline and social control in the United States*. New York: St. Martin's.

Strathern, M. (2012). Gifts money cannot buy. *Social Anthropology, 20*(4), 397–410.

Strathern, M. (1997). Partners and consumers: Making relations visible. In A. D. Schrift (Ed.), *The logic of the gift*. New York: Routledge.

Sykes, K. (2005). *Arguing with anthropology*. London: Routledge.

Turow, J. (2006). Cracking the consumer code: Advertisers, anxiety, and surveillance in the digital age. In K. D. Haggerty & R. V. Ericson, *The new politics of surveillance and visibility* (pp. 279–307). Toronto: Toronto University Press.

Ullrich, W. (2006). *Haben Wollen*. Frankfurt am Main: S. Fischer.

Vannini, P. (2009). Material culture and the sociology and anthropology of technology. In P. Vannini (Ed.), *Material culture and technology in everyday life: Ethnographic approaches*. New

York: Peter Lang.

Warde, A. (2005). Consumption and theories of practice. *Journal of Consumer Culture, 5*(2), 131–153. doi:10.1177/1469540505053090

Zurawski, N. (2011a). Local practice and global data: Loyalty cards, social practices, and consumer surveillance. *The Sociological Quarterly, 52*(4), 509–527.

Zurawski, N. (2011b). "Budni, Ist doch Ehrensache!": Kundenkarten als Kontrollinstrument und die Alltäglichkeit des Einkaufens. In N. Zurawski (Ed.), *Überwachungspraxen—Praktiken der Überwachung: Analysen zum Verhältnis von Alltag, Technik und Kontrolle.* Opladen: Budrich.

Zureik, E., Harling Stalker, L., Smith, E., Lyon, D., & Chan Y. E. (Eds.). (2010). *Surveillance, privacy, and the globalization of personal information: International comparison.* Montreal: McGill-Queen's University Press.

Zureik, E., & Mowshowitz, A. (2005). Consumer power in the digital society. *Communications of the ACM, 48*(10), 46–51.

3

Social Networking Sites in the Surveillance Society [1]

Critical Perspectives and Empirical Findings

Thomas Allmer, Christian Fuchs,
Verena Kreilinger, & Sebastian Sevignani

Introduction

The social networking site (SNS) Facebook became a public company on February 1, 2012. As part of this process, financial data required for the registration as public company was published.[2] Facebook says that it generates "a substantial majority" of its "revenue from advertising": 98.3% in 2009, 94.6% in 2010, 85% in 2011.[3] It says that the "loss of advertisers, or reduction in spending by advertisers with Facebook, could seriously harm our business."[4] Facebook's self-assessment of this risk shows that it is coupled to the broader economy; an advertising-based business model depends on influx of investments into advertising and the belief of companies that specific forms of advertisement on specific media can increase their profits. A general economic crisis that results in decreasing profits can result in a decrease of advertisement investments.

Figure 3.1 shows the development of Facebook's profits in the years 2007–2011. Since 2007, the company's annual profits have increased by a factor of 7.2 from US$138 million in 2007 to US$1 billion in 2011. There was a slump in 2008 (US$56 billion, 60% in comparison to 2007), which was due to the economic crisis that took effect in that year all over the world. Since 2009, Facebook's profits have almost exploded. At the same time, there was a large increase of users: the number of monthly active users was 197 million in March 2009, 431 million in March 2010, 680 million in March 2011, and 845 million in December 2011.[5]

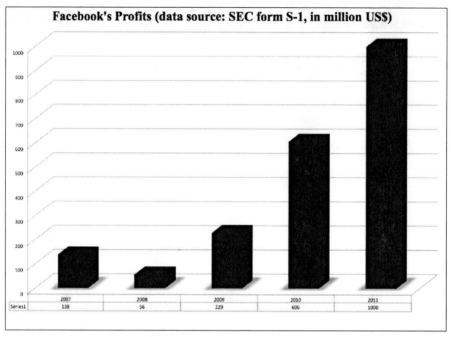

Figure 3.1. The development of Facebook's profits, 2007–2011 (data source: SEC Filings, Form-S1 Registration Statement: Facebook, Inc.)

"Social Networking Sites in the Surveillance Society" is a 30-month research project funded by the Austrian Science Fund (FWF) (see: http://www.sns3.uti.at) that aims to study how information processing works on Facebook and what the broader implications of Facebook are for contemporary societies that are shaped by power asymmetries and complex information flows.

The task of this chapter is to outline theoretical foundations as well as selected empirical results of the project. The next section outlines how we have conceived the notions of privacy, surveillance and digital labor that are at the core of the project's theoretical foundations.

Theoretical Foundations: Privacy, Surveillance, Digital Labor

Three notions form the core of the theoretical foundations of the research project "Social Networking Sites in the Surveillance Society": privacy, surveillance and digital labor.

Privacy is a contested concept. The criticisms include the following points (see Allmer, 2011a; Fuchs, 2011b):

a. Privacy is a form of individualism that neglects the common good.
b. The privacy concept separates public from private life, which can result in problems, such as privacy as a patriarchal value that legitimates violence in families.
c. Privacy can shield the planning and carrying out of illegal or antisocial activities and can be deceptive by concealing information in order to mislead others or misrepresent the character of individuals.
d. The privacy concept advances a liberal notion of democracy that can be opposed by the idea of participatory democracy.
e. Privacy is a Western-centric concept.
f. The notion of privacy is bound up with the idea of private property and can shield the rich and powerful from public accountability and wealth and power structures from transparency.

Partly responding to the criticism that privacy is an individualistic Western-centric concept that harms the public good, some authors have conceptualized privacy in an alternative way and have stressed its social and societal aspects (Nissenbaum, 2010; Solove, 2011. Our own theoretical discussions in our project have revolved around the question of whether privacy is necessarily a liberal and individualistic concept and needs to be abandoned for a critical theory of society, or if there can be a critical concept of privacy. Although the four of us are critical of the privacy concept to various degrees, our basic conclusion was that we need a socialist concept of privacy that protects users, workers and consumers from the power of capitalism, exploitation and the neoliberal state (Fuchs, 2012c, 2012d, 2011b; Allmer, 2011b; Kreilinger, 2010; Sevignani, 2011).

We argue for going beyond a bourgeois notion of privacy and to advance a socialist notion of privacy that tries to strengthen the protection of consumers and citizens from corporate surveillance. Economic privacy is therefore posited as undesirable in those cases where it protects the rich and capital from public accountability, but as desirable where it tries to protect citizens from corporate surveillance. Public surveillance of the income of the rich and of companies and public mechanisms that make their wealth transparent are desirable for making visible the wealth and income gaps in capitalism, whereas privacy protection for workers and consumers from corporate surveillance is also important. In a socialist privacy concept, existing liberal privacy values have therefore to be reversed. Whereas today we mainly find surveillance of the poor and of citizens who are not capital owners, a socialist privacy concept focuses on surveillance of capital and the rich in order to increase transparency and privacy protection of consumers and workers. A social-ist privacy concept conceives privacy as a collective right of dominated and exploited groups that need to be protected from corporate domination that aims at gather-ing information about workers and consumers for accumulating capital, disciplin-ing workers and consumers and for increasing the productivity of capitalist production and advertising. The liberal conception and reality of privacy as an individual right within capitalism protects the rich and the accumulation of ever more wealth from public knowledge. A socialist privacy concept as a collective right of workers and consumers can protect humans from the misuse of their data by com-panies. The question therefore is: privacy for whom? Privacy for dominant groups in regard to secrecy of wealth and power can be problematic, whereas privacy at the bottom of the power pyramid for consumers and normal citizens can be a protec-tion from dominant interests. Privacy rights should therefore be differentiated according to the position people and groups occupy in the power structure. The dif-ferentiation of privacy rights is based on the assumption that the powerless need to be protected from the powerful. Example measures for socialist privacy protection in the area of internet policies are legal requirements that online advertising must always be based on opt-in options, the implementation and public support of cor-porate watchdog platforms and the advancement and public support of alternative non-commercial internet platforms (Fuchs, 2012d). Given the power of companies in the capitalist economy, economic privacy needs to be contextualized in a way that protects consumers and workers from capitalist control and at the same time makes corporate interests and corporate power transparent.

It is time to break with the liberal tradition in privacy studies and to think about alternatives. The Swedish socialist philosopher Torbjörn Tännsjö (2010) stresses that liberal privacy concepts imply "that one can not only own self and personal things, but also means of production" and that the consequence is "a very closed society, clogged because of the idea of business secret, bank privacy, etc." (Tännsjö, 2010:186). Tännsjö argues that power structures should be made transparent and not be able to hide themselves and operate secretly protected by privacy rights. He imagines an open society based on utopian socialist ideas that is democratic and fos-ters equality, so that (Tännsjö, 2010:191–198) in a democratic socialist society, there is, as Tännsjö indicates, no need for keeping power structures secret and therefore no need for a liberal concept of privacy. However, this does in our view not mean that in a society that is shaped by participatory democracy, all forms of privacy van-ish. There are some human acts and situations, such as defecation (Moore, 1984), in which humans tend to want to be alone. Many humans would both in a capital-ist and a socialist society feel embarrassed having to defecate next to others, for example by using toilets that are arranged next to each other without separating walls. So solitude is not a pure ideology, but to a certain desire also a human need that should be guaranteed as long as it does not result in power structures that harm others. This means that it is necessary to question the liberal-capitalist privacy ideology, to struggle today for socialist privacy that protects workers and consumers, limits the right and possibility of keeping power structures secret and makes these structures transparent. In a qualitatively different society, we require a qualitatively different concept of privacy, but not the end of privacy. Torbjörn Tännsjö's work is a reminder that it is necessary not to idealize privacy, but to think about its contradictions and its relation to private property. At the same time, we question Tännsjö's idea that all forms of privacy have to be abolished in a socialist society.

To speak about surveillance instead of the liberal and individualistic concept of privacy is often presented as a more critical alternative. However, what we found in our project is that the mainstream of surveillance theory treats surveillance as a quite administrative notion and that based on what we term a "neutral concept" of surveillance (Fuchs, 2011a; Allmer, 2012a; 2012b), surveillance studies is just as uncritical and administrative as liberal privacy concepts.

Neutral concepts of surveillance make one or more of the following assumptions (Fuchs, 2011a):

- There are positive aspects of surveillance.
- Surveillance has two faces; it is enabling and constraining.
- Surveillance is a fundamental aspect of all societies.
- Surveillance is necessary for organization.
- Any kind of systematic information gathering is surveillance.

Max Horkheimer says that neutral theories "define universal concepts under which all facts in the field in question are to be subsumed" (Horkheimer, 1937/2002:224). Neutral surveillance concepts see surveillance as ontological category; it is seen as being universally valid and characteristic either for all societies or all modern societies. In our opinion, there are four reasons that speak against defining surveillance in a neutral way (Fuchs, 2011a):

1. Etymology
    Surveillance stems etymologically from the French "surveiller," to oversee, watch over, which implies a hierarchic power relation between the watcher and the watched.

2. Theoretical Conflationism
    Neutral concepts of surveillance analyze phenomena, as, for example, taking care of a baby or the electrocardiogram of a myocardial infarction

patient on the same analytical level as for example pre-emptive state-surveillance of personal data of citizens for fighting terrorism or economic surveillance of private data and online behavior by internet companies such as Facebook, Google, etc. for accumulating capital by targeted advertising. If surveillance is used as a neutral term, then the distinction between non-coercive information gathering and coercive surveillance processes becomes blurred; both phenomena are amassed in an undifferentiated unity that makes it hard to distinguish or categorically fix the degree of coercive severity of certain forms of surveillance (see Lyon, 2007:54). The double definitional strategy paves the categorical way for trivializing coercive forms of surveillance.

3. Unclear Difference Between Information Gathering and Surveillance
   If surveillance is conceived as the systematic gathering of information about a subject population, as many surveillance scholars do, then the difference between surveillance and information processing is unclear and surveillance becomes synonymous with information processing.

4. The Ideological Normalization of Surveillance
   If almost everything is defined as surveillance, then it becomes difficult to criticize repressive forms of surveillance politically because surveillance is then a term that tends to be used in everyday language for all sorts of harmless information processes that do not inflict damage on humans.

Our view is that we need to overcome the neutral concept of surveillance and substitute it by a critical concept and theory of surveillance (Fuchs, 2011a; Allmer, 2012a; 2012b). We see information as a more general concept than surveillance, and that surveillance is a specific kind of information gathering, storage, processing, assessment and use that involves potential or actual harm, coercion, violence, asymmetric power relations, control, manipulation, domination, disciplinary power. It is instrumental and a means for trying to derive and accumulate benefits for certain groups or individuals at the expense of other groups or individuals. Surveillance is based on a logic of competition. It tries to bring about or prevent certain behaviors of groups or individuals by gathering, storing, processing, diffusing, assessing and using data about humans so that potential or actual physical, ideological or structural violence can be directed against humans in order to influence their behavior. This influence is brought about by coercive means and brings benefits to certain groups at the expense of others. Surveillance is in our view therefore never cooperative and never an expression of solidarity—it never benefits all. Establishing a critical concept of surveillance is, in the contemporary situation of new imperialistic capitalism, global crisis and neoliberalism, in our view most fruitful based on Marxist theory that is combined with Foucauldian concepts (such as the panopticon, governmentality and Foucault's critique of the political economy of neoliberalism; see Allmer, 2012b; Fuchs, 2011a; 2012c). Surveillance can also be carried out by the state. As the modern state is entrenched with capitalist interests, this surveillance most of the time hits the underclass, such as welfare recipients and the unemployed. At the same time, if there were a communist government aiming at abolishing capitalism, there could be more efficient surveillance of the dominant class, i.e., capitalists and the rich in order to better ensure they pay taxes. As the state is predominantly a class state, this critical reality of the state hardly exists today.

Digital labor is a concept that has become a crucial foundation of discussions within the realm of the political economy of the internet (see Burston, Dyer-Witheford, & Hearn, 2010; Fuchs & Dyer-Witheford, forthcoming; Scholz, 2012). The basic argument is that the dominant capital accumulation model of contemporary corporate internet platforms is based on the exploitation of unpaid labor by users, who engage in the creation of content and the use of blogs, social networking sites, wikis, microblogs, content sharing sites for fun and in these activities create value that is at the heart of profit generation (Fuchs, 2010b). Online activity creates content, social networks and relations, location data, browsing data, data about likes and preferences, etc. This online activity is fun and work at the same time—play labor. Play labor (playbour) creates a data commodity that is sold to advertising clients as a commodity. They thereby obtain the possibility of presenting advertisements that are targeted to users' interests and online behavior. Users employ social media because they strive for a certain degree to achieve what Bourdieu (1986a, 1986b) terms social capital (the accumulation of social relations), cultural capital (the accumulation of qualification, education, knowledge) and symbolic capital (the accumulation of reputation). The time that users spend on commercial social media platforms for generating social, cultural and symbolic capital is in the process of prosumer commodification transformed into economic capital. Labor time on commercial social media is the conversion of Bourdieuian social, cultural and symbolic capital into Marxian value and economic capital. Surveillance plays a special role in the exploitation of digital labor (Allmer, 2012a; Andrejevic, 2012; Fuchs, 2012a; Sandoval, 2012): Corporate social media platforms continuously monitor all activities of all users on their own sites and receive monitoring data about the users' behavior on other sites (collected by targeted ad servers such as Google's DoubleClick) that they process, store, analyze, compare and assess in order to target advertisements on the interests and online behavior of the users. Targeted advertising is at the heart of the capital accumulation model of many corporate social media platforms. It is legally enabled by terms of use and privacy policies. In the digital labor debate, the application and development of the Marxian labor theory of value and Marxist labour theories of advertising (Smythe, 1977; Jhally & Livant 1986/2006) has played an important role. Dallas Smythe's Marxist political economy of the media and communication has in this context been revived and further developed (for an overview, see Fuchs, 2012b, forthcoming). A debate about the use of Marx's theory and the Marxist labor theory has emerged in this context (see Fuchs, 2010b; Arvidsson & Colleoni, 2012; Fuchs 2012e).

The research project "Social Networking Sites in the Surveillance Society" deals with the topic of digital labor and the role of privacy and surveillance in the context of the political economy of social networking sites. In the next two sections, we will present some of the obtained empirical research results that deal with the perception of targeted advertising and digital labor.

Targeted Advertising and Digital Labor on Social Networking Sites: Survey Results

We conducted an online survey (Batinic, Reips, & Bosnjak, 2002; Johns, Chen, & Hall, 2004; Couper, 2000; Schmidt, 1997; Sills & Song, 2002; Zhang, 2000; Hewson, Laurent, & Vogel, 1996) that focused on Austrian students. We identified how important students consider the topic of surveillance in relation to SNS by analyzing their answers to our questions with the help of PASW Statistics 18 (formerly SPSS Statistics) for the quantitative data (Field, 2009) and SPSS Text Analytics for Surveys 4 for the open questions. Our questions focused on the most frequently used SNS in Austria, namely Facebook (according to alexa.com, Top 100 sites in Austria). We constructed a questionnaire that consisted of single and multiple choice, open-ended, interval-scaled, matrix and contingency questions. The survey was conducted in German. Depending on the contingency level, students had to answer at least three questions and no more than 78 questions. Filling out the whole questionnaire took about 20 minutes. The questionnaire was thematically grouped into different subsections. We strived to achieve two main objectives in the survey: On the one hand, we tried to figure out which major advantages and disadvantages of social networking platforms Austrian students see and if privacy is considered an extrinsic or intrinsic value. On the other hand, we made an effort to find out if knowledge and attitudes towards surveillance and privacy of Austrian students and their information behavior on social networking platforms are connected. In the last part of the questionnaire, we collected data on socio-demographic factors (gender, age, number of studied semesters, level of study and field of study), socio-economic status (monthly income, highest education achievement of parents and main occupation of parents), and the respondents' usage of social networking sites. The questionnaire was implemented as an electronic survey with the help of the online survey tool SurveyMonkey (Gordon, 2002; Babbie, 2010:286). The research was carried out during the time period June 20 to November 23, 2011. Our potential respondents were male and female students at all Austrian universities. In order to reach students at Austrian universities, we asked vice-chancellor's offices, offices of public relations at universities and student unions to send our email invitation to their students. In total, 5,213 participants started and 3,558 students completed (63.8% women, 36.2% men; these are 1.31% of the Austrian student population) our survey.

Along with asking about the greatest advantages of social networking sites such as Facebook and MySpace, we also asked the students about their greatest concerns (open question). We received N=3,534 qualitative answer texts to the question that addressed disadvantages. We identified 14 categories for the concerns and analyzed the answers to the questions by employing content analysis (Krippendorff, 2004; Berg, 2001). The categories were adopted from theoretical and empirical studies about social networking sites (Fuchs, 2010a; Livingstone, 2008) on the one hand, and were revised and expanded regarding the provided answers by summarizing, paraphrasing, abstracting and generalizing groups of answer texts to categories on the other hand; that is, a combination of inductive and deductive methods (Berg, 2001:248–249; Babbie, 2010:339). Our respondents tended to list more than one major disadvantage. Many answers are therefore mapped with more than one category (Berg, 2001:247–248). Here are some characteristic examples of answers that were given to the question of what the major disadvantages of social networking platforms are [authors' translations from German to English]:

> That employers are able to receive private information (respondent ID 1519050546)

> That pictures, comments etc. are seen by people, who should not see them [such as an employer]....difficulties in finding a job (respondent ID 1567729690)

> Unlawful usage of data, forwarding, personalized advertising, algorithm of face recognition, alienation of the term "friend," meanwhile group pressure and social pressure to join in (respondent ID 1559706802)

> That personal information, which I often expose unconsciously, is used against me. Besides I am annoyed by personalized advertising (respondent ID 1559719051)

> Transparent individual, commercial usage of user data (respondent ID 1566130533)

> ... [prospective] increasing usage of all collected data, user details for market research; that is profit maximization....a further step towards "global police state," in which the people/politicians will no longer rule, but corporations and lobbies...opaque, non-user-friendly privacy settings (respondent ID 1525388777)

What are your greatest concerns of social networking platforms such as Facebook, Myspace, LinkedIn, etc? N=3534

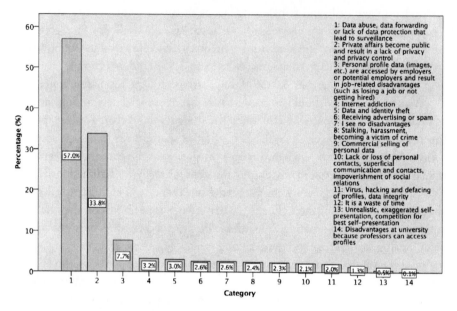

Figure 3.2. Major perceived disadvantages of SNS.

These examples indicate that targeted advertising and the commercial selling of personal data are considered a disadvantage of social networking sites. The next figure shows our respondents' major concerns about social networking sites.

Figure 3.2 shows that surveillance is considered the greatest concern of social networking sites. Almost 60% of our respondents stress that surveillance as a result of data abuse, data forwarding or a lack of data protection is the main threat of SNSs. One-third (33.8%) say it is problematic that personal affairs that would be better kept private tend to become public. Of concern to 7.7% is the risk that current and potential employers could access profiles and that could result in job-related disadvantages. In addition, 3.2% mention internet addiction, and 3.0% of the participants stress data and identity theft as greatest risks of social media. Advertising or spam is a concern for 2.6%. Also interesting is that 2.6% of the students do not see disadvantages in the usage of commercial social networking platforms. As a result, although the general surveillance threat (category 1) is considered as the major disadvantage, it can be argued that economic surveillance (category 3, 6 and 9) also plays an important role as perceived concern and risk of SNSs, because it is the third-most-mentioned major concern (12.6%). It is likely that many answers subsumed under category 1 are also directly or indirectly linked to targeted advertising and commercial selling of personal data, but brief responses such as "surveillance" or "data forwarding" do not expose whether it is meant in a political, economic or cultural sense. For reasons of impartiality, we put the open-ended questions about advantages and disadvantages of social networking sites at the very beginning of the survey. Although the above figure already indicates the importance of economic surveillance, students obviously tend to be more concerned about targeted advertising if they are confronted with closed-ended questions, as the following analysis will show.

We gave special attention to targeted advertising in our study: how much students know about it, which attitudes they have towards it, what their concerns are and how they actually behave in the context of targeted advertising.

Knowledge

In order to test students' knowledge about advertising on Facebook, we asked them if the presented statement was true or false. Also, an "I don't know" answering option was provided. Findings show that respondents know that Facebook employs targeted advertising. A clear majority of 83.2% was aware that the statement "On Facebook all users see the same advertisements" (Q41) is false. When asked if it is true that Facebook is allowed to give personal data (e.g., contact information, interests, activities, friends, online behavior) to third parties/other companies for advertising purposes, respondents were not sure about their answers; 31.8% answered "I don't know." Another third (32.6%) thought it was true (which is the right answer), and a relative majority of 35.6% answered with " No, that's false." Huge uncertainty also determined the answers to the question of whether advertisements, commercial sites and paid services on social networking sites such as Facebook must be explicitly marked as such. In its terms, Facebook clearly states "You understand that we may not always identify paid services and communications as such." Only 19.4% knew the correct answer (false); 46.5% gave the wrong answer; and 34.1% of the respondents said that they don't know the answer.

Attitude/Concerns

Asked if they actually want websites to tailor ads to personal interests, an overwhelming majority of 82.1% opposed this practice. Judging from these results, it is even more questionable why there is no opt-out possibility on Facebook. Or expressed in other terms: these results make it very clear why Facebook—from a profit-oriented point of view—has no interest in offering such an option. Another example for user concerns about targeted advertising is their distinct rejection of advertisements that are tailored based on location data. A huge majority of 71.1% stated their disapproval of such advertising practices when we asked "Would it be OK if these ads were tailored for you based on your location (e.g., location-based data via mobile internet, pictures, you've uploaded, or the Facebook application 'Places')?"

Behavior

It is often questioned if people actually read targeted ads, like those displayed on the right side of a Facebook profile. Our results show that though a majority never or hardly ever read these ads, 23.1% do read them at least once a month (or even more often). Twenty-two percent of the respondents have clicked on any ads. How much value targeted advertising methods actually have for Facebook becomes even more obvious when taking into account the results of another question we asked to the study participants: "Have you ever joined a group or site that has been established and is run by a commercial actor (e.g., local restaurants or shopping malls, brand communities such as Starbucks, Nike, etc...)?" Brand sites are quite present on Facebook and are attempts by companies to market their commodities on social media. They aim at establishing deep and long-lasting relationships and an intensified and ubiquitous brand presence in the lives of customers (Illobre, 2008). Brand networking capitalizes on social interactions and human relationships as a marketing tool. Over 60% of our respondents stated that they have joined such groups or sites.

Comparing knowledge, attitudes and behavior, one can observe some contradictions. Although most respondents do know that Facebook employs targeted advertising and clearly reject targeted advertising, they don't critically act upon their concerns. Another example is Facebook's "social ads": if a user likes any commercial site, product or service, advertisements can be linked with his/her picture and may even be displayed in the form of a "personal recommendation among friends." Although this is a highly targeted form of advertising, nearly half of our respondents have not opted out of the social ads (the settings, of course, are default active). Reasons may be the default setting of this option and Facebook's lack of transparency in its privacy policy.

Targeted Advertising and Digital Labor on Social Networking Sites: Results from Qualitative Interviews

Critical theory has stressed that research always fails to be neutral and that the positivist assumption that research is value-free is itself a value (Adorno, 1976:2–3; Horkheimer, 1937/2002:242). Is critical research more about critical interpretation than critical methods, or is research itself a part of emancipation? We concluded from these discussions that our qualitative research should include participatory aspects. After exploring users' attitudes towards advertising on SNSs, we provided them with information about economic surveillance within the interviews. This information was retrieved from a content analysis of Facebook's terms of use and privacy policies. The underlying hypothesis is that there is a lack of awareness and knowledge about economic surveillance as it is less visible and shows less direct consequences for the users. The idea was to receive a more accurate image about users' attitudes towards advertising once they are informed about this issue.

The research methods employed were semi-structured interviewing (N=30) and qualitative content analysis (Kracauer, 1952; Ritsert, 1972; Mayring, 2004) informed by thematic coding (C. Schmidt, 2004). We included a group of interviewees who are especially critical of (economic) surveillance and have a high knowledge about privacy issues, as well as a group of less concerned (standard) users. The sample consisted of 30 Austrian students between the ages of 20 and 34 (mean = 24.9 years; standard deviation = 3.33 years; two-thirds women, and one-third men), who used or are using SNSs. The participants came from a broad range of academic disciplines and study at a university in Salzburg.

How do the interviewees perceive targeted advertising in general? Thirteen interviewees agreed with advertising on SNSs, 10 interviewees disagreed, and 7 interviewees held an ambiguous attitude. We identified three lines of argumentation that characterize positive attitudes towards advertising on SNSs. First, interviewees say that advertising and advertisements pose no negative consequences for them because they are not forced to notice advertisements, to click on them and to buy the advertised products. Moreover, they also say they are not forced to participate in the use of SNSs. Second, interviewees made clear that advertisements on SNSs have positive consequences for them, such as providing useful product information and interesting offers, and that it's fun to watch them. The most important positive consequence identified by the interviewees, however, was that advertising makes the usage of SNSs "free" for them. Third, the interviewees also argued that advertising is a common and societally recognized funding model, to which we are all accustomed.

We were able to discern four strands of arguments opposing advertising on SNSs. First, interviewees pointed to negative consequences of advertising. A relatively frequently occurring argument in this context is that advertising on SNSs is pressing, manipulating and creates (unwanted) new needs. The most frequently mentioned negative consequences that our interviewees pointed out are annoyance and deflection. Second, interviewees frequently argued that advertising brings no positive consequences for them and that it is unnecessary and a waste of time. Third, interviewees argued that advertising contradicts SNSs' inherent and genuine goal that they are about maintaining and establishing social relations. Hence the argument was that SNS should not be about advertising for profit purposes. Interviewee 16 stated:

> My claim to a SNS is that it is a social network, and that it provides me with the opportunity to organise and exchange with others, etcetera. That is what matters for a SNS and advertising is not necessary for a social network. That is a feature which is necessary for a company. . . .

In this context, the interviewees also expressed their fear or actual observation that advertising determines or influences SNSs' content and structure. Fourth, interviewees argued that there is no alternative to the advertising funding model. Here, the identified arguments were similar to the third positive strand of argumentation, but the interviewees interpreted this argument negatively. Interviewee 1, for instance, argued that advertising is "a necessary evil" and interviewee 10 explained:

> I think there is no alternative choice. I think it is not OK. . . . I am bothered that my data is sold for economic purposes, that someone is making a profit with it and I do not agree with that.

> Interviewer: One could argue that you have already agreed when you accepted the terms of use in the beginning.

> Interviewee 10: I have the decision to exclude myself or to agree to be in. I have to decide, there is nothing in between.

We asked then more specifically whether or not advertising is perceived as a privacy invasion? Again, the distribution was nearly balanced, but the number of interviewees holding an ambiguous attitude towards this question was less high: 14 interviewees said that advertising is not problematic in this respect; 12 said that it is a privacy invasion; 4 held ambiguous views. Arguments neglecting advertising as a problematic, privacy invasive form of surveillance could be clearly grouped into two major strands of argumentation. First, it was argued that there was an informed consent by the user to the SNSs' terms of use, which also includes the acceptance of targeted advertising. Therefore, the knowledge of how advertising works on SNSs is accessible to everyone. Second, and similar to a strand of argument described above, was that advertising on SNSs has no negative consequences for users. The particular argument in this context is that third parties cannot personally identify users.

Interviewees who think that advertising on SNSs is a privacy invasion employed the following strands of arguments. First, interviewees challenged that there was an informed consent to advertising. They thought that it is a problem that the privacy settings do not apply to advertising and the SNS provider is allowed to use and sell information marked as "private" for advertising purposes. Interviewees also held the opinion that advertising is problematic because it has negative effects. Second, interviewees argued (referring to direct consequences) that advertising on SNSs is a problematic form of surveillance as the SNS provider conducts it excessively and disproportionally. This applies in particular when surveillance is performed on other sites than the genuine SNS. Interviewee 21 said in this context:

> As I said, this bears no proportion. The whole system, how Facebook is financed and works, makes it understandable from Facebook's perspective. They need certain information and process them. However that does not justify the multitude of data [that is collected] because, in my view, an incredible portion of it is not needed at all.

Another argument was that the SNS provider itself invades users' privacy. Interviewee 23 explained:

> That is a kind of distortion. They say that they pass it away anonymously, but it comes back to me.... When it comes back to me with the advertisement that is targeted to me, then that is not anonymous.

Third, interviewees argued that advertising on SNSs has indirect consequences because third parties, such as state authorities or hackers, can access the collected data later on. Fourth, the interviewees were uncertain about the exact use of their data and they linked this uncertainty to potential negative consequences. In this context, they were also afraid that SNS would collect and use ever more data in the future, which results in a surveillance creep.

As part of our participatory research approach, we confronted the interviewees with information about how advertising on SNSs works, that it is targeted and demands a wide range of various data categories in order to be performed. We first asked them about their attitudes towards targeted advertisements on SNSs. Then we provided information about how targeted advertising works on Facebook. Third, having in mind the provided information, they were asked again about their views on targeted advertising. We were able to observe a significant number of interviewees who switched to a negative perception of targeted advertising on social media. These results allow us to assume that users' knowledge and awareness of economic surveillance plays a key role in the assessment of targeted advertising. Hence the assumption that there is an informed consent becomes quite questionable: many users would not agree with advertising on SNSs if they knew exactly how it works.

Do users think that their digital labor is exploited while using SNSs? We assume that one aspect of feeling exploited is that one wants to receive compensation in return for others taking advantage from the foreign efforts. We mainly identified one influential line of argumentation among those who want compensation for their digital labor: interviewees see a bad or exploitative ratio between the SNSs' profits and their own benefits of using the SNS. Interviewee 12 expressed this clearly:

> Facebook is earning so much money; therefore it is my opinion that one should receive something extra for using the site for free.

Among those who do not want compensation in exchange for the usage of their data, we found an interesting line of argumentation. It is interesting because at the same time it is problematic and offers an emancipatory perspective. The interviewees argued that personal data should not be traded at all and receiving compensation will not stop this trade. They said that any compensation payment is based on such a trade. For instance, interviewee 24 argued:

> Because my privacy means a lot to me, I think it cannot be compensated with material goods. Privacy is about my decision and my freedom so that I do not lose my self-control. They should not [be allowed to] exercise so much power over me.

Interviewee 9 said that receiving compensation would "basically be a form of selling myself." Those interviewees resist the ongoing "reconceptualization of privacy in the consumer's mind from a right or civil liberty to a commodity that can be exchanged for perceived benefits" (Campbell & Carlson, 2002:588; see also Comor, 2011). To argue that privacy should not at all be traded means that it cannot become a commodity, which to a certain degree also questions SNSs' capital accumulation. These interviewees conceive privacy as the need to protect internet prosumers from the interests of capital. That these interviewees perceive privacy as non-alienable persona right may have to do with their European cultural background. However, this emancipatory argument brings us back to the discussion of privacy and its liberal and individualistic connotations. The struggle for privacy tends to frame the problem of surveillance and exploitation in individual terms, instead of recognizing it as a structural societal problem (Nock, 1993:1; Lyon, 2005:27; Stalder, 2002; Andrejevic, 2002).

Conclusion

Although the general surveillance threat is considered as the major disadvantage of social networking sites, economic surveillance such as targeted advertising and the commercial selling of personal data also plays an important role. Users employ a wide range of supportive and challenging arguments when it comes to advertising on SNSs. We found strong resistance against the surveillance-based business model that was particularly based on two lines of argumentation: users think that personal data should not be for sale at all or they feel exploited by the SNSs and therefore want something back in return for the usage of their data. Even though most respondents of our study do know that Facebook employs targeted advertising and clearly reject targeted advertising, they don't automatically critically act upon their concerns. Therefore we can observe some contradictions when comparing knowledge, attitudes and behavior.

Our study indicates that most users do know that SNSs such as Facebook collect and store huge amounts of personal information and use it for targeted advertising. However, our results also show that there is a great lack of knowledge when it comes to details about the actual process of the data collection, storage and sharing. Respondents of our study were quite uncertain or even misinformed about what exactly Facebook is allowed to do with their personal data and which personal data, browsing data and usage data is actually used for the purpose of targeted advertising. This may partly be explained by the fact that privacy policies and terms of use are often lengthy, complicated and confusing (Fuchs, 2011c; Fernback & Papacharisi, 2007; Sandoval, 2012). SNSs often argue that users give their informed consent to targeted advertising. In the light of our findings, this argument is questionable.

We see structurally induced reasons for the gap between users' attitudes and their behavior. The SNS realm is highly monopolized. On the one hand, Facebook has accumulated immense capital power and is therefore able to mobilize a broad range of resources, such as investments in research and development and the acquisition of rival or complementary enterprises, to keep its dominant position. On the other hand, network effects play a crucial role as the use value of any SNS increases in relation to its users. Although critical of surveillance, users are facing sink-or-swim opportunities: Today, they only can benefit from SNSs when they accept surveillance and privacy threats.

Economic surveillance is inherent to the capitalist character of corporate SNSs like Facebook. It is neither just a technical issue nor an individual problem, but a societal problem. The embeddedness of social media surveillance into societal phenomena such as capitalism, neoliberalism, imperialism and state power implies that overcoming social media surveillance requires the sublation of domination, asymmetric relations of power and capitalist society as well as the creation of a commons-based information society and a commons-based internet. The question that arises is which political steps can be taken for fostering such developments.

- Support is needed for critical privacy movements in order to develop counter-hegemonic power and advance critical awareness of surveillance (Lyon, 1994:223; Lyon, 2001:127). Good instances in this context are initiatives against the leading SNS, Facebook, such as the complaints by the Electronic Privacy Information Center (EPIC) addressed to the U.S. Federal Trade Commission (FTC); the complaints by Austrian students addressed to the Irish Data Protection Commissioner (Europe versus Facebook, 2011); or the investigation by the Nordic data inspection agencies (Datatilsynet, 2011).

- Parliamentary and regulatory means can drive back exploitation on SNS. On the one hand, data protection laws could be internationalized and sharpened. On the other hand, as the users commonly produce relationship and interactions that are sold by commercial SNS to the advertising industry, "capital should in return give something back to society" (Fuchs, 2010b:193). For instance, a particular tax on internet companies is imaginable in this context.

- Cyberactivism and "counter-surveillance" (Lyon, 1994:159) can watch the watchers "and document instances where corporations and politicians take measures that threaten privacy or increase the surveillance of citizens" (Fuchs, 2009:116).

- Parenti (2003:212) suggests civil disobedience, rebellion and protest: "It will compel regulators to tell corporations, police, schools, hospitals, and other institutions that there are limits. As a society, we want to say: Here you may not go. Here you may not record. Here you may not track and identify people. Here you may not trade and analyze information and build dossiers."

- The creation and support of non-profit and non-commercial social networking platforms can help advance an alternative internet. For instance, Diaspora* is a distributed SNS that operates on behalf of free software protected by copy law (Sevignani, 2012). Unlike Facebook that processes user data in huge server parks, Diaspora* consists of a potentially unlimited number of interoperating servers that are locally distributed and not controlled by a single organization. Theoretically, it is possible for everyone to operate such a "pod." Diaspora* protects its users and their personal data from exploitation and practically provides an alternative concept of privacy: "Yet our distributed design means *no big corporation will ever control Diaspora*. Diaspora* will never sell your social life to advertisers, and you won't have to conform to someone's arbitrary rules or look over your shoulder before you speak" (Diaspora, 2011; emphasis in original).

Notes

1. Acknowledgement: The research presented in this paper was conducted for the project "Social Networking Sites in the Surveillance Society," funded by the Austrian Science Fund (FWF): project number P 22445-G17. Project co-ordination: Christian Fuchs.
2. Form-S1 Registration Statement: Facebook, Inc. http://www.sec.gov/Archives/edgar/data/1326801/000119312512034517/d287954ds1.htm, accessed on March 26, 2012.
3. Ibid., pp. 12, 50.
4. Ibid., p. 12.
5. Ibid., p. 44.

References

Adorno, T. W. (1976). Introduction. In T. W. Adorno, H. Albert, R. Dahrendorf, J. Habermas, H. Pilot, & K. R. Popper (Eds.), *The positivist dispute in German sociology* (pp. 1–67). London: Heinemann.

Allmer, T. (2012a). Critical internet surveillance studies and economic surveillance. In C. Fuchs, K. Boersma, A. Albrechtslund, & M. Sandoval (Eds.), *Internet and surveillance: The challenges of Web 2.0 and social media* (pp. 124–143). New York: Routledge.

Allmer, T. (2012b). *Towards a critical theory of surveillance in informational capitalism.* Frankfurt am Main: Peter Lang.

Allmer, T. (2011a). A critical contribution to theoretical foundations of privacy studies. *Journal of Information, Communication and Ethics in Society, 9*(2), 81–101.

Allmer, T. (2011b). Critical surveillance studies in the information society. *tripleC: Communication, Capitalism & Critique. Open Access Journal for a Global Sustainable Information Society 9*(2), 566–592.

Andrejevic, M. (2012). Exploitation in the data mine. In C. Fuchs, K. Boersma, A. Albrechtslund, & M. Sandoval (Eds.), *Internet and surveillance: The challenges of Web 2.0 and social media* (pp. 71–88). New York: Routledge.

Andrejevic, M. (2002). The work of being watched: Interactive media and the exploration of self-disclosure. *Critical Studies in Media Communication, 19*(2), 230–248.

Arvidsson, A., & Colleoni, E. (2012). Value in informational capitalism and on the internet. *The Information Society, 28*(3), 135–150.

Babbie, E. (2010). *The practice of social research* (12th ed.). Belmont: Wadsworth Cengage Learning.

Batinic, B., Reips, U.-D., & Bosnjak, M. (Eds.).(2002). *Online social sciences.* Seattle: Hogrefe & Huber.

Berg, B. (2001). *Qualitative research methods for the social sciences* (4th ed.). Boston: Allyn & Bacon.

Bourdieu, P. (1986a). *Distinction: A social critique of the judgement of taste.* London: Routledge.

Bourdieu, P. (1986b). The (three) forms of capital. In J. G. Richardson (Ed.), *Handbook of theory and research in the sociology of education* (pp. 241–258). New York: Greenwood.

Burston, J., Dyer-Witheford, N., & Hearn, A. (Eds.). (2010). Digital labour: Workers, authors, citizens. *Ephemera: Theory & Politics in Organization, 10*(3).

Campbell, J. E., & Carlson, M. (2002). Panopticon.com: Online surveillance and the commod-ification of privacy. *Journal of Broadcasting & Electronic Media, 46*(4), 586.

Comor, E. (2011). Contextualizing and critiquing the fantastic prosumer: Power, alienation and hegemony. *Critical Sociology, 37*(3), 309–327.

Couper, M. (2000). Web surveys: A review of issues and approaches. *Public Opinion Quarterly, 64*(4), 464–494.

Datatilsynet (2011). Questions to Facebook from the Nordic DPA's. http://www.datatilsynet.no/upload/Dokumenter/utredninger%20av%20Datatilsynet/Letter%20with%20questions%20to%20Facebook%20from%20nordic%20countries%20endellig.pdf

Diaspora (2011, September 21). Diaspora* means a brighter future for all of us. http://blog.diaspora foundation.org/2011/09/21/diaspora-means-a-brighter-future-for-all-of-us.html

Europe versus Facebook (2011). Legal procedure against "Facebook Ireland Limited." http://www.europe-v-facebook.org/EN/Complaints/complaints.html

Fernback, J., & Papacharisi, Z. (2007). Online privacy as legal safeguard: The relationship among consumer, online portal, and privacy policies. *New Media & Society, 9*(5), 715–734.

Field, A. (2009). *Discovering statistics using SPSS* (3rd ed.). London: Sage.

Fuchs, C. (Forthcoming). Dallas Smythe reloaded: Critical media and communication studies today. In V. Manzerolle & L. McGuigan (Eds.), *The audience commodity in a digital age: Revisiting a critical theory of commercial media.* New York: Peter Lang.

Fuchs, C. (2012a). Critique of the political economy of Web 2.0 surveillance. In C. Fuchs, K. Boersma, A. Albrechtslund, & M. Sandoval (Eds.), *Internet and surveillance: The challenges of Web 2.0 and social media* (pp. 31–70). New York: Routledge.

Fuchs, C. (2012b). Dallas Smythe today: The audience commodity, the digital labour debate, Marxist political economy, and critical theory. *tripleC: Communication, Capitalism & Critique. Open Access Journal for a Global Sustainable Information Society, 10*(2).

Fuchs, C. (2012c, April 2). Political economy and surveillance theory. *Critical Sociology.*

Fuchs, C. (2012d). The political economy of privacy on Facebook. *Television & New Media, 13*(2), 139–159.

Fuchs, C. (2012e). With or without Marx? With or without capitalism? A rejoinder to Adam Arvidsson and Eleanor Colleoni. *tripleC: Communication, Capitalism & Critique. Open Access Journal for a Global Sustainable Information Society, 10*(2), 633–645.

Fuchs, C. (2011a). How to define surveillance? *MATRIZes, 5*(1), 109–133.

Fuchs, C. (2011b). Towards an alternative concept of privacy. *Journal of Information, Communication and Ethics in Society, 9*(4), 220–237.

Fuchs, C. (2011c). *What is Facebook's new privacy policy all about? More complexity, more intrans-parent data storage, continued internet prosumer commodification, ideological pseudo-participa-tion, and a reaction to the privacy complaints filed by "Europe versus Facebook."* http://fuchs.uti.at/699/

Fuchs, C. (2010a). Social networking sites and complex technology assessment. *International Journal of E-Politics, 1*(3), 19–38.

Fuchs, C. (2010b). Labour in informational capitalism. *The Information Society, 26*(3), 176–196.

Fuchs, C. (2009). *Social networking sites and the surveillance society: A critical case study of the usage of studiVZ, Facebook, and Myspace by students in Salzburg in the context of electronic surveillance.* Salzburg: Research Group Unified Theory of Information.

Fuchs, C., & Dyer-Witheford, N. (Forthcoming). Karl Marx@Internet Studies. *New Media & Society*.

Gordon, A. (2002). Surveymonkey.com: Web-based survey and evaluation system. *Internet and Higher Education, 5*, 83–87.

Hewson, C., Laurent, D., & Vogel, C. (1996). Proper methodologies for psychological and sociological studies conducted via the internet. *Behavior Research Methods, Instruments, & Computers, 28*, 186–191.

Horkheimer, M. (1937/2002). Traditional and critical theory. *Critical theory: Selected essays* (pp. 188–243). New York: Continuum.

Illobre, N. (2008): Brand networking: Social media ownership, return on involvement and open social networks. http://www.spoig.com/l.c.bin/F/15045097/20080828_BrandNetworking.pdf

Jhally, S., & Livant, B. (1986/2006). Watching as working. The valorization of audience consciousness. In S. Jhally, *The spectacle of accumulation: Essays in culture, media, and politics* (pp. 24–43). New York: Peter Lang.

Johns, M., Chen, S.-L., & Hall, J. (Eds.). (2004). *Online social research*. New York: Peter Lang.

Kracauer, S. (1952). The challenge of qualitative content analysis. *The Public Opinion Quarterly, 16*(4), 631–642.

Kreilinger, V. (2010). *Remarks on theoretical foundations of privacy studies* (SNS3 Research Paper Number 6). UTI.

Krippendorff, K. (2004). *Content analysis: An introduction to its methodology* (2nd ed.). Thousand Oaks: Sage.

Livingstone, S. (2008). Taking risky opportunities in youthful content creation: Teenagers' use of social networking sites for intimacy, privacy and self-expression. *New Media & Society, 10*(3), 393–411.

Lyon, D. (2007). *Surveillance studies: An overview*. Cambridge: Polity.

Lyon, D. (2005). *Surveillance society: Monitoring everyday life*. Buckingham: Open University Press.

Lyon, D. (2001). *Surveillance society: Monitoring everyday life*. Maidenhead: Open University Press.

Lyon, D. (1994). *The electronic eye: The rise of surveillance society*. Minneapolis: University of Minnesota Press.

Mayring, P. (2004). Qualitative content analysis. In U. Flick, E. von Kardorff, & I. Steinke (Eds.), *A companion to qualitative research* (pp. 266–269). London: Sage.

Moore, B. (1984). *Privacy: Studies in social and cultural history*. Armonk: Sharpe.

Nissenbaum, H. (2010). *Privacy in context: Technology, policy, and the integrity of social life*. Stanford, CA: Stanford Law Books.

Nock, S. (1993). *The costs of privacy: Surveillance and reputation in America*. New York: de Gruyter.

Parenti, C. (2003). *The soft cage: Surveillance in America: From slavery to the war on terror*. New York: Basic Books.

Ritsert, J. (1972). *Inhaltsanalyse und Ideologiekritik: Ein Versuchüberkritische Sozialforschung*. Frankfurt am Main: Athenäum Fischer.

Sandoval, M. (2012). A critical empirical case study of consumer surveillance on Web 2.0. In C. Fuchs, K. Boersma, A. Albrechtslund, & M. Sandoval (Eds.), *Internet and surveillance: The challenge of Web 2.0 and social media*. New York: Routledge.

Schmidt, C. (2004). The analysis of semi-structured interviews. In U. Flick, E. von Kardorff, & I. Steinke (Eds.), *A companion to qualitative research* (pp. 253–258). London: Sage.

Schmidt, W. (1997). World-wide web survey research: Benefits, potential problems, and solutions. *Behavior Research Methods Instruments & Computers, 29*(2), 274–279.

Scholz, T. (Ed.). (2012). *Digital labor. The internet as playground and factory.* New York: Routledge.

Sevignani, S. (2012). The problem of privacy in capitalism and the alternative social networking site Diasproa*. *tripleC: Communication, Capitalism & Critique. Open Access Journal for a Global Sustainable Information Society* (Special Issue. *Marx Is Back: The Importance of Marxist Theory and Research for Critical Communication Studies Today,* C. Fuchs & V. Mosco, eds.), *10*(2), 600–617.

Sevignani, S. (2011). *A contribution to foundations of a critical theory of privacy* (SNS3 Research Paper Number 7). UTI.

Sills, S., & Song, C. (2002). Innovations in survey research: An application of web-based surveys. *Social Science Computer Review, 20*(1), 22–30.

Smythe, D. W. (1977). Communications: Blindspot of Western Marxism. *Canadian Journal of Political and Social Theory, 1*(3), 1–27.

Solove, D. J. (2011). *Nothing to hide: The false tradeoff between privacy and security.* New Haven, CT: Yale University Press.

Stalder, F. (2002). Opinion: Privacy is not the antidote to surveillance. *Surveillance & Society, 1*(1), 120–124.

Tännsjö, T. (2010). *Privatliv.* Lidingö: Fri Tanke.

Zhang, Y. (2000). Using the internet for survey research: A case study. *Journal of the American Society for Information Science, 51*(1), 57–68.

4

The Emerging Surveillance Culture

David Lyon

People who research and write about surveillance often have an axe to grind or at least some concerns about the world of personal data: online snooping, over-reaching security checks, police wanting warrantless access to information, companies using details to make consumer profiles, schools using video cameras to keep order, employers reading staff emails or social media posts. But the world out there has mixed responses. Some are still anxious about what they call "Big Brother" but others seem indifferent to such concerns. Some may object to intrusive airport screening, find certain kinds of internet stalking spooky or worry that their customer profile may be inaccurate, but for others surveillance is a fact of life that we have to get used to, at worst an annoyance that has to be negotiated.

We can be more specific. One way to diagnose a culture is to look at those afflicted with extreme anxieties about it. For the culture of surveillance perhaps this would be "The Truman Show delusion." In the movie *The Truman Show*, the main character discovers that he has been inescapably filmed for a documentary since before birth. He is under the gaze of permanent surveillance. Psychiatrists in the U.S. and the U.K. encounter a small but growing number of people suffering from a psychosis whose symptoms are the belief that everything one does is being recorded like a reality TV show. And in a related scenario are "internet delusion" patients who believe that their lives are intimately being monitored by the "web" (Gold & Gold, 2012; Kershaw, 2008). What are mild worries for some, are treatable conditions for others.

At the opposite end of the spectrum, however, are today's social media users who, it seems, have few qualms about uploading all kinds of messages, images and footage for the world to see. Most young people—so-called digital natives in particular—enjoy and believe they benefit from using social media despite the fact that these sites exist by selling users' data to others. Keeping up with acquaintances and friends through visiting social media sites such as Facebook is an integral part of daily life (Kang, 2012). Of course, the stories of indiscriminate posting to social media sites are often overblown but frequent embarrassing or spectacular situations do indicate that some feel free to "share" in fairly uninhibited ways. This also reflects today's culture.

Why is this? The study of surveillance provides evidence that people's lives are affected, sometimes in profound ways, by surveillance. It can positively or negatively affect life-chances, close down or open up potential opportunities, permit or deny legitimate access, circumscribe or broaden choices, ensure rights are respected or reinforce negative discrimination, expose people to desired or unwanted visibility and speed up or slow down straightforward processes. A lack of surveillance can make people vulnerable to harm, deflect attention from genuine risks or introduce unfairness into economic relationships. So why don't people seem to care about surveillance? Why isn't caution with personal information more pronounced?

Part of the problem is that while surveillance scholars may know about new technologies or organizations that probe people's lives, or about policies, laws and regulations designed to curb excessive or inappropriate surveillance, they don't necessarily know that much about the people themselves. That is, we may understand some specific cases—especially, as I say, the notorious or even the exemplary cases—but we know far less about the ordinary patterns of everyday life and how surveillance is woven into them. What we do know, however, is that, extraordinary though it may seem to those bothered about Big Brother breathing down our necks or the panoptic gaze penetrating personal lives in new ways, people comply with surveillance. We get used to it. It becomes natural, normal. It may be a minor irritant but we lose no sleep.

We live within what I call an emerging culture of surveillance. It is time to stop thinking of surveillance merely as a top-down phenomenon where "they" monitor "us." Surveillance has become an everyday social experience, from a serious security issue to an incessant demand for data from numerous organizations to a playful part of mediated relationships. We comply with surveillance to an unprecedented extent and if asked why, often have reasons for doing so. Many inhabitants of the global north as well as an increasing number in the global south are not only subject to complex and intense form of surveillance, but they also participate knowingly (or less knowingly) in surveillance. They may even enjoy it.

Once, surveillance was something you could consider evading, escaping. Now, it's in the air we breathe, the buildings where we work, the streets we walk, the stores where we shop, the cars we drive, the phones we use to connect with each other and of course in social media. Surveillance is not simply something done by police and security officials, nor is it merely mimicked by merchants and marketers. Once feared as the surveillance state or worried about as a surveillance society, surveillance is now increasingly normal. We enjoy the benefits of security or convenience but also put up with intrusions, accept a pinched form of privacy, concede that control is lost over personal information, fit into the fishbowl, not to mention keep an electronic eye on others as well. We may speak of surveillance culture.

Take the issue of identification, for example. Not much more than a generation ago, people in Europe and North America had a fairly fixed sense of their identity and did not expect to have it constantly checked. Today, identification is a basic requirement for living in modern society; we are asked for "ID" for numerous purposes. My university recently issued new ID cards for faculty, pieces of plastic that can be used to work out at the gym, pay at campus cafeterias, check out books from the library and soon, possibly, enter offices and laboratories. Increasingly, IDs are associated with complex databases in which we have overlapping profiles and where surveillance is a given. Yet many ID cards offer only a slippery sense of who we are, one that changes depending on what sort of verification is involved. Even the apparently strong sources of data, such as biometric or "body-related" information—such as facial recognition—can fail (Magnet, 2011; Gates, 2011). "Who we are" may have to be traced back to the classic "breeder document," the birth certificate, that may or may not be available or accurate. And if our self-identification depends on recalling yet another password, say, for online access, "who we are" becomes notoriously dependent on our mutable memories.

Being "asked for ID" is often regarded as part of the price we pay for living in a digital society. It is something we take for granted, a mundane reality of everyday life. The fact that it is also, historically, a major innovation in the way we conduct our lives does not readily occur to us. For most of human history only a select few—often disadvantaged or deviant populations—have had to "show ID" to negotiate daily living. Today, showing ID is a condition of our freedom, a means of participating in "normal" life (Rose, 1999:240ff; Lyon, 2009). The very fact that we show ID, often without questioning why, is evidence that we participate in a culture of surveillance. We expect to have to carry tokens of legitimate identity (IDs) and we fish them out of our wallets on demand. We comply, we cooperate. It's part of our culture.

From Experience to Engagement

Compared to the recent history of many countries, the idea that we participate in a surveillance culture is striking. In what follows I want to draw attention to this key feature of a culture of surveillance: people are surprisingly compliant. From classics such as George Orwell's *1984*, many in the global north assumed that surveillance could easily be negative if not malign, and resistance to surveillance was seen as a challenge. This is the struggle that consumed and in the end overwhelmed Winston Smith, the novel's harried hero. In the same vein, Franz Kafka's *The Trial* leaves one with a strong sense that who knows what about us is significant, especially when they clearly have connections with powerful policing organizations. These classic treatments focus the mind on care with disclosing personal data and wariness about watchers. The same outlook has been encouraged by privacy commissions, privacy laws and data protection regimes around the world.

The willing cooperation of individuals with surveillance is driven by many cultural currents. But in the 21st century, two key factors have fostered this growing compliance. One, I call the fear factor (especially following 9/11) (Lyon, 2003), and the other, the fun factor (consequent on social media) (Trottier, 2012). The first has been analyzed at length since 9/11 and as I write an anti-surveillance campaign is happening in the streets of Brussels, Belgium, under the banner "Freedom from Fear." Surveillance equipment may be installed to allay fears of attack, especially from terrorists, but the effect is often to ratchet up levels of fear. As David Altheide observes, installing cameras or creating urban fortresses can "reaffirm and help produce a sense of disorder that our actions precipitate" (Altheide, 2006). Thus surveillance spirals, fostered by fear. Because of a generalized fear, and more particularly because many believe they are safer with surveillance in place, many cooperate with it.

At the other end of the emotional spectrum, however, the fun factor also operates. That is, the excitement and enjoyment of engaging with social media also prompts participation in surveillant activities. This is perhaps most pronounced with younger users, but it seems to be a general phenomenon, too. As danah boyd finds, teens turn to social media for entertainment and, more seriously, to "perform identity" and to find "community" (boyd, 2007). As she says, they "(heart) social media." A 2012 survey of social media users in Canada, the U.S. and the U.K. indicated that although such users are aware of the avid interest of social media sites in gathering and processing personal data for profit, few consider this a reason to moderate their online activities (VisionCritical Survey, 2012).

The two factors to which I draw attention sound very recent; each belongs in the 21st century. But in fact each also has a crucially important pre-history stretching back well into the 20th century. In the present century, each factor has mushroomed rapidly, giving the appearance of novelty and indeed, accentuating the sense of fluidity and volatility of the times. For other reasons it is vital to acknowledge the mutating movement of the pulsating present; the concept of "liquid surveillance" helps here (Lyon, 2010; Bauman & Lyon, 2013). But the fear factor and the fun factor make no sense without looking beneath them to sift the soil in which they grew.

The fear factor existed well before 9/11, fostered especially by the rise of risk discourses. After the first flush of post-war optimism about industrial progress in the 1950s and 1960s, awkward questions were posed—and eventually were articulated most clearly in the social sciences by Ulrich Beck (1992)—about the unintended consequences of rapid development. Rachel Carson's *Silent Spring* (1962) sounded a timely alarm about environmental risks, but by the end of the century the concept of risk had made inroads into numerous areas of life, increasing the sense of general precariousness and of the profound uncertainties of everyday life. Nevertheless the idea that human beings could remain in control did not die but each effort to demonstrate this tended to produce new insecurities, new fears (Garland, 2001). The aftermath of 9/11 demonstrates this clearly: the securitization of everything, including, obviously, airports, simultaneously generates insecurities and fears, particularly, in the west, for groups such as Arabs and Muslims (Aas, Oppen Gundhus, & Lomell, 2008).

The "fun factor," on the other hand, while it refers in unmistakable ways to social media surveillance, also harks back to a key feature of 20th-century life, namely, the expansion of many forms of electronic media. While an older generation may express astonishment at the extent to which a younger seems willing to expose all manner of intimate and revealing details online, along with identifying tags from real names to photos, such "publicness" was nourished in the soil of radio and, especially, television cultures. As Joshua Meyrowitz observes, mass television helped prepare the way for surveillance in more interactive media, such as social networking. It helped blur public and private, weakened links between location and experience and fostered tolerance for pervasive government and corporate surveillance (Meyrowitz, 2009). Similarly, and building on Hannah Arendt's ideas on "mediated visibility," John Thompson points out that ordinary visibility is always situated, whereas in the 20th and 21st centuries, emerging media enable visibility to break free of temporal, spatial and reciprocal limits. What is deemed public and private now relates to a fluid context of communication technologies where boundaries are ineluctably porous and contested (Thompson, 2011).[1]

These two factors, fear and fun—apparently very different—are both implicated in encouraging cooperation with surveillance. But at the same time they also help to normalize surveillance, making it seem natural, necessary, unremarkable. The perceived need for surveillance to maintain secure borders or safe streets seems to suggest a tradeoff operates: more security demands less liberty or privacy (a sentiment amplified by many promoting security-surveillance expansion). So however reluctantly or regretfully, intensified surveillance is accepted. But benefits are also available from online surveillance; Facebook can suggest suitable "friends" just as Amazon offers relevant reading and much more. Here a seductive convenience, not to mention a fascinating force field of the lives of others, once again renders surveillance as at worst a necessary evil and at best a source of convenience and efficiency.

But not only compliance and cooperation with surveillance is evident today. A newer trend is that people seem more and more ready to undertake what I call "shadow surveillance," from checking their own health and fitness with monitoring devices to finding out about others without their knowledge on Facebook. New terms are heard, describing these phenomena as they appear in online media. Mark Andrejevic speaks of "lateral surveillance" (Andrejevic, 2005) and Anders Albrechtslund of "participatory surveillance" (Albrechtslund, 2008). Shadow surveillance includes both, but serves to distinguish surveillance by individuals—even reliant on gargantuan databases, like Facebook's tag-suggestion—from that which characterizes large-scale organizational monitoring. In Albrechtslund's account, surveillance may now be viewed, not as disempowering, disciplinary and controlling, but as empowering, subjectivity-building and playful. Here is the fun factor again, now drawing users into what in other contexts might be described as snooping or stalking. But equally, safety and security may have a role, as when crib monitors, nanny-cams or other devices are used to monitor infants or toddlers.

Exploring Surveillance Culture

Showing ID may be part of our cultural experience, but is this really surveillant? Surveillance is often seen as hazy, hidden and thus somewhat sinister. We also assume, too easily, that it is something unusual that is unlikely to affect us personally or negatively. We have nothing to hide; why would "they" be interested in us? In fact, surveillance today is less something undertaken by undercover agents and more likely to happen in the routines of everyday life. It has not only become normal but ordinary people cheerfully engage in surveillance practices, online for example (Albrechtslund, 2008). Far from being a remote possibility, surveillance is constant, unavoidable and, sometimes, a source of fun.

However, surveillance *is* hidden in the sense that its presence is less easy to discern and its impact does vary with different groups in the population. The hiddenness of surveillance has to do in part with its increasingly technological character, or rather with the ways that technology itself is disappearing from sight even as it becomes more powerful. Sometimes this is called "ubiquitous computing" or "ambient intelligence" as high-tech is literally part of the furniture. Secrecy may also be a factor, especially in regard to national security or marketing methods. Which is not to say that surveillant forces do not seek seclusion if not secrecy; they often do. Concealed cameras are not only in movies. And Facebook tells you how to "protect your privacy" only from other users like you, not from the corporations to whom they sell your data.

The concept of a culture of surveillance points to an emerging reality that surveillance is becoming, for many, a whole dimension of daily life.[2] Even calling this phenomenon a culture of surveillance gives it a kind of fixity and apparent solidity that it does not possess. Raymond Williams' term "structures of feeling" tries to capture the sense of the actively lived and felt; things that are emergent, developing and that cannot be pinned down (Williams, 1977:Chapter 9). Zygmunt Bauman stresses fluidity rather than fixity in his concept of "liquid modernity" and it's that volatile mix of forces, feelings and fluidity that I have in mind in considering the culture of surveillance (Bauman & Lyon, 2013).

Surveillance practices are experienced and engaged by ordinary people in everyday life as they participate in and negotiate surveillance, informed by what I call "surveillant imaginaries." These are constructed both through everyday involvement in surveillance and through popular media such as film, television and the internet. To use a double-edged metaphor, surveillance is not merely a spectator sport. We know how to act the part when performing for airport security, we purchase surveillance cameras for "home security" and we use social media to check on others in multiple ways.

However, the emergence of surveillance culture does not mean that somehow other descriptors—the surveillance state or surveillance society—are less important or have been superseded. Far from it. One key issue here is the way we interact on the internet and for that matter in front of street cameras. Such digitally mediated relationships mean that we are increasingly involved, not merely as the "objects" and "bearers" of surveillance but as active participants, adopting surveillance mentalities and practices.

A much more complex cultural landscape is emerging and the old binaries of power/participation, in/visibility, privacy/publicness give us less purchase on what's happening. As Miyase Christiansen notes, while people strive to become more flexible, connected and mobile through the use of new media, they also become subject to various forms of surveillance. While new media enable geographically extended experiences and deepened senses of social community, security and control, they also tie the individual to abstract systems that enable tracking and monitoring of their consumption habits, mobility and private interests (Christensen, 2009).

To think about our activities within surveillance cultures and to answer the questions about surveillance history, global trends and local realities will take us to the heart of a dimension of modernity that has mushroomed in recent decades. Only if we have some answers to these questions can we speak in an informed way about current surveillance trends, about what we can expect in the next few years and, importantly, about what can be done to benefit from the best and weaken the worst effects of living in surveillance cultures.

What are some of the key issues in understanding emerging surveillance cultures? Here I offer some important clues about context—to do with history, culture, technology and power. First, cultures of surveillance have developed over several centuries: how does today's surveillance culture relate to previous ones? Second, how does surveillance fit with life in modern cultures generally? If, as I stress, surveillance is not a distinct dimension of our lives, then how is it interwoven with other cultural threads and patterns? Third, surveillance is decreasingly visible; it's smart. Technologies are slipping into the background, often literally becoming "part of the furniture." Frequently we're surveilled without knowing it. Fourth, positive aspects of surveillance are promoted while the downsides are often unknown. We may be participants in surveillance culture, but I contend we're under-informed participants.

These dimensions of surveillance culture confront us with some new questions. First, shadow surveillance shows how monitoring others has become participatory, connected with consumption and with play—the "fun factor." So does the emergence of a culture of surveillance mean that expanding surveillance is more palatable or that we can be less vigilant? I respond with a decisive no. The patterns of power are often reinforced even though discrimination may be less visible. Privacy may be diminished even though we may not grasp the consequences of this. If these things are true, what can be done? Though space is lacking to expand on this here, my view is that we need a new politics of personal information, based on a fresh ethics, focusing on the human face and on human flourishing. Cultures of surveillance could be transformed.

Beyond State and Society

It is tremendously important to have a strong sense of history when considering surveillance. The field is all too often littered with ahistorical comments and a concomitant over-emphasis on new—read "digital"—technologies. While the role of digital technologies is unavoidably significant, earlier developments in surveillance, along with their own technological innovations and popular responses to them also throw light on today's surveillance situations. What follows tells us more about how scholars have understood surveillance than exactly how surveillance has developed.

The so-called information state developed in Europe over the past 400 years. In England, for example, state gathering of information on individuals has occurred since the 16th century for a number of administrative reasons. These practices have evolved and increased steadily over time such that government is engaged in the collection and manipulation of personal information for both benign and repressive purposes (Higgs, 2004; Weller, 2012).

For example, individual registration and identification of citizens grew tremendously from the late-19th and early-20th centuries, with many experimental systems trialed not in Europe but in colonial settings such as India, Egypt, Argentina and Palestine. Both democratic participation and policing were enabled by such practices, in differing ways depending on the context.

From the start, then, state power was enhanced by its surveillance capacities and those capacities were associated with new technologies, from bureaucratic file records to photography, the phonograph and telephone (Lauer, 2011). Indeed, there is a reciprocal relation between state surveillance and technology that has been part of the dynamic of what I am now calling surveillance cultures. While ordinary people were always aware of state surveillance, it was a dimension of life that could be considered in distinction from others. You could escape state surveillance or at least you could limit its impact on your life by attending to government requests only when necessary.

By the later 20th century, with the growing influence of computerized systems for administration in production and consumption as well as in government, the idea of the surveillance *society* started supplanting the earlier emphasis on the information state and government surveillance. Everyday life was touched by surveillance systems as never before, as, for example credit cards were introduced, along with social insurance, driver's license and other systems depending on the computerized processing, storage and retrieval of information.

Such systems were developed in many countries, including newly industrializing ones, the then "emerging economies" of India, China and Brazil. Thus a new globalization, beyond the colonial, also entailed new surveillance practices. And although the body had been implicated in surveillance before, particularly in policing contexts, it now became increasingly important as a source of surveillance data (Lyon, 2001). And because alterations in the patterns of space and time are essential constituents of social change, these developments, from their global to their local, body-based manifestations, helped shape fresh social formations.

At the same time, awareness of surveillance grew in many ways, from the development of data protection and privacy policy through to popular evocations of surveillance in film, TV, music. Surveillance is now a common theme and trope of popular culture. When it appeared in 2002, few failed to note the uncanny relevance of *Minority Report* to the aftermath of the attacks of 9/11. The "pre-crime" approach seemed to echo exactly what the new Department of Homeland Security was attempting with its anticipatory and preemptive initiatives. Equally, when in 2010 an episode of *The Simpsons* aired, called "To surveil with love," a new surveillance awareness had reached a very broad audience.

Just as state surveillance was an element of surveillance society, so many features of each are also part of surveillance cultures. Now, however, some older ideas of surveillance being carried out by "them" over "us" is giving way to a much more nuanced state of affairs where surveillance develops horizontal as well as vertical dimensions, where the categories of public and private are smudged by new digitally enabled relationships and where data gathered for one purpose (such as marketing) may readily be used for another (say, policing).

In each of these contexts, what were once referred to in policy documents as "data subjects" are often actively involved in the production of surveillance data. This triggering through transactions is not new, of course, but with increasing dependence on digital media and especially now social media, ordinary individuals generate surveillance data in ever-growing proportions. Individuals also interact more knowingly with surveillance systems, recognizing that their ubiquity makes them inescapable and thus that forms of negotiation are an indispensible dimension of daily existence. They become aware that the machines and environments with which they interact are surveillant, that "logjects" (such as smartphones) (Kitchin & Dodge, 2011) record and report their usage continuously. They may also adopt strategies of resistance or alternatively, develop their own surveillance practices. Parents use cell phones to keep track of their children; employers use Facebook to check on workers. Not only is surveillance a basic organizational tool; being surveilled and doing surveillance is the new normal.

One of the keys to understanding surveillance cultures is the variety of mediated relationships that are apparent today. While globalization and mobility and the restructuring of political economy are vital components of this, the new forms of mediation seem complicit in all. From Google maps to MySpace and from Twitter to Foursquare, the world of surveillance cannot now be conceived without reference to new media. State surveillance is dependent on new media; the ever-spreading surveillance society likewise. So how may surveillance cultures be analyzed and understood?

The dominant conventional focus of surveillance studies is on surveillance agencies and technologies and on their impacts on ordinary people. But much may also be learned about surveillance by focusing on the activities of those "ordinary people" like you and me. In particular, the concept of *surveillant imaginaries* helps us to see how surveillance is understood in all ways from repressive and constraining to enabling and playful. Such imaginaries are constructed from experiences of surveillance, popular treatments of surveillance in the mass media and from online and offline discussions of surveillance. They are also generated by surveillant practices, often in conjunction with new media, that inform the imaginaries in a constant feedback loop.

The idea is not to substitute one kind of surveillance studies for the other, however. Rather, in the manner of the famous French theorist Pierre Bourdieu, to consider the "habitus" of surveillance, those habits of being and behaving that produce the "necessary improvisations" of everyday life (Bourdieu, 1977:72ff). Those necessary improvisations today include many ways in which surveillance finds an everyday response—avoiding cameras, paying with cash or, for that matter, giving out postcodes or allowing a range of users to see one's Facebook page. But they are also visible in ways that we check on others and ourselves, often using high-tech means such as online searches or audio monitors.

At the same time, surveillance cultures have to be considered across several dimensions; technical, political, economic and so on. For instance, the emerging imaginaries and practices occur in a world of codes and networked searchable databases that may be prompting some genuinely novel developments. Clearly, surveillance is facilitated by the shift to the digital—greater capacity for data gathering, storage, manipulation and exchange is readily available at decreasing cost. One aspect of this is that surveillance entails less friction[3] today. It's simply easier to do surveillance without being noticed, and this is true for corporations, governments and ordinary individuals such as social media users.

Take Facebook. High privacy settings are available but nothing indicates to Facebook users just what can still be known about them to others. Facebook helps to alter our perceptions about many things—notoriously, such as how "friend" is defined—so that at the level of design our imaginaries, our ways of thinking about and responding to the social world, are affected. "Timeline," the biographical Facebook feature, contains old information but packaged in a new way; it subtly shifts the default of who may know what about you and in how much detail. Facebook may also stress your brag list of friends while saying nothing about those with whom your data may be shared. And of course it's far from obvious that even Facebook knows the outcome of the innovations it launches. It's left to coding and databases to self-augment.

Is there something basically different about digital surveillance that we're only just beginning to perceive? The world of analogue information was full of friction. Time and space were required in much larger quantities in order to make surveillance happen. Operators had to watch the screens for camera images, police had to make manual checks to discover if the speeding motorist had previous convictions or was driving a stolen car. Marketers had to hire researchers to pore over government ledgers to discover what price had been paid for that house, and public transit users had to be checked at the gate for valid tickets. Facial recognition technologies, automated license plate recognition, consumer record data-mining and radio frequency identification techniques reduce the friction tremendously.

Surveillance: Liquefying but Not Evaporating [4]

If surveillance is such a central dimension of modernity that it makes sense to speak of surveillance culture, then we also have to ask, what sort of modernity? As suggested above, one contribution to this debate comes from Zygmunt Bauman, who suggests that modernity has *liquefied* in some new and different ways (beyond Marx and Engels' insight that "all that is solid melts into air"). This is partly seen in the move beyond enclosed places of panopticon into control spaces of everyday life, as access points are opened and closed. But it's also seen in its shifts beyond, into algorithmic and coded spaces of empowerment and control on larger scale. Two features stand out.

First, all social forms melt faster than new ones can be cast. This notion seems to resonate with the world of social media in particular and as we have seen, social media is structurally and economically predicated on surveillance. Among the theorists whose work could be thought of as precursors to the liquidity theorem in surveillance is Gilles Deleuze whose observations on the "society of control" are a prominent and oft-cited example (Haggerty & Ericson, 2000). Shifting patterns of social life are seen neatly in the processes of surveillance as control, where above all movement is monitored.

Today, security is less about constraint and much more, in a neo-liberal world, about freedom. It is about how information, things and people circulate freely around the globe. The new surveillance technologies appearing everywhere are intended to maintain mobility and thus they often police at a distance and attempt to pre-empt the future (Bigo, 2008). Airports and border-crossing practices are a case in point. Novel approaches tie security to discipline in both space and time. This connects with themes of fluidity and mobility in Bauman. Surveillance as a border triage helps to keep valued things and persons moving while at the same time slowing down and even excluding those at the margins.

Bauman's other key theorem is that power and politics are splitting apart. Power now exists in global and extraterritorial space; but politics, which once linked individual and public interests, remains local, unable to act at the planetary level.

Power becomes a source of great uncertainty and frustration because it's out of reach, while politics seems parochial and irrelevant to many people's real-life problems and fears. Surveillance power, as exercised by government departments, police agencies and private corporations, matches well this depiction. Even national borders, that once had geographical locations—however arbitrary—now appear in airports distant from the "edge" of the territory and, more significantly, in databases that may not even be "in" the country in question (Lyon, 2007).

The apparent social fragmentation featured in Bauman's liquid modernity is blamed by some on new media, but for Bauman it's as much cause as effect. Power must be free to flow, and barriers, fences, borders and checkpoints are a nuisance to be overcome or circumvented. Mobility is vital to what Manuel Castells calls today's "spaces of flows" (Castells, 1992). As Bauman would say, for liquid modernity, dense and tight networks of social bonds, especially based in territory, should be cleared away. It's the brittleness of those bonds that allows the powers to work in the first place.

Beyond these trends, of course, are others that push surveillance more and more into the tissues of everyday life. Several are obvious to anyone: many increases in security awareness produce surveillance outcomes, not just in airports and on borders, but in downtown streets, buildings, public transit, schools and so on. Security threats, it seems, are legion. But who deals with these is another interesting question, because security seems successively to involve more players, both public and private. Surveillance, far from being only a "state-run" business, is more often than not a business, a for-profit enterprise.

As we have just noted with regards to liquidity, surveillance is also expanding its reach beyond an interest in individuals' identities and activities to their locations. This is facilitated by the growth of GPS and related technologies such as cellular telephony and again reflects interests both public (for instance, emergency services) and private (think geographical advertising for Starbucks or The Gap). But it also emerges from the fact that environments are more and more sensitive; that is, with computing embedded in all sorts of everyday environments, the capacity to check on where who does what enlarges constantly. Nigel Thrift calls this the "technological unconscious" (Thrift, 2005) where technical processes simultaneously become less visible and more consequential. Technological unconscious is the world of code, which, through instructions and algorithms, not only mediates but also constitutes social interactions and associations.

And even if the general environment does not contain sensors, at specific points data associated with our bodies is available for checking—we carry cards that can be read at a distance or, at certain entry points, may have to pass through biometric scanners of some sort. This is the fluid surveillance of mobilities: keeping track of increasingly shifting populations and individuals in everyday life. Kitchin and Dodge's "logjects"—self-logging objects such as smart phones—record their own status and usage, thus adding surveillance utility (2011). Reporting real-time user location becomes part of people's life-paths and thus helps to constitute the activities of users but also makes them more vulnerable to social sorting.

So surveillance may be liquefying in some respects (as with all metaphors its illumination is real but limited), but it is certainly not evaporating. The solid shapes may melt but the fluid forms are no less powerful for their loss of concreteness. Indeed, as a cultural phenomenon, it is likely that surveillance will be experienced more, not less strongly in its liquid phase. Time will tell whether or not the term "surveillance" will be sufficient to capture all that is experienced or whether what is experienced is described as surveillance. But surveillance as defined here will help to define social and cultural life as never before.

Environments that are mediated by new modes of information and communication could once be thought of in terms of place; now, increasingly, they must also be considered in terms of flows. Among the emergent properties of this is rampant, multi-directional, powerful surveillance. But not only is mediation in question. Social associations and interactions are now not only mediated by software and code; more and more they are, in part at least, constituted by it. As several prominent theorists—such as Nigel Thrift, above—have argued, information may no longer be merely epistemological, it is becoming increasingly ontological (Beer, 2009). Information is now not only a means by which we come to understand the world; it is also an active agent in constructing it (Lash, 2002); a new "new media" ontology (Lash, 2007), in which many of the essential underpinnings of social life—the operation of power in particular—are becoming ever more "algorithmic" (Beer, 2009). In surveillance terms, our data image helps constitute who we are. Yet as we have also seen, in the culture of surveillance we also comply with and contribute to those data images through our quotidian involvement in the routines of life.

Surveillance: Critical Cultural Analysis

The foregoing just starts to scratch the surface of how we might understand surveillance culture, though I hope that at least its contours are clear. Let me say three things by way, not of concluding, but of suggesting lines of inquiry that should inform our consideration of these emerging phenomena. One is a caution about surveillance power. Whatever may be said about surveillance culture, it should not deflect attention from the realities of the ways that ordinary people's opportunities, life chances and choices may be opened or constrained through contact with surveillance. Indeed, investigating surveillance culture should lead right into such realities.

It is quite clear that ordinary people contribute to their data image, for example by using credit cards, cellphones or social media. But the data images themselves, along with their associated profiles, are primarily the product of large organizations. Government departments, police and intelligence agencies and competing corporations all use personal data to perpetuate their power. The result is that even though we all contribute to our data images, they are often taken to be more reliable than our personal narratives. The culture of surveillance emerges in the context of political economies that valorize personal data and seek control, fluidly and flexibly, by manipulating and mining those data for their ends. The work of surveillance theorists such as Mark Andrejevic (2007), in his book *iSpy*, who see the structural, political and economic aspects interacting with the cultural dimensions, should be heard here.

The second line of inquiry for the analysis of the culture of surveillance stresses the varieties of practices and experiences involved in this emerging arena. The culture of surveillance is not monolithic in the sense that it appears everywhere with the same frequency and in the same formats. I chose the term "culture of surveillance" to indicate that new shared dimensions of a whole way of life have been subtly emerging in recent decades and that this culture has clearly identifiable features in many countries around the world. At the same time, as David Garland indicates in his similarly titled *The Culture of Control* (2001), this phenomenon varies by country and culture. Histories and even personalities make a difference. Local filters produce recognizable but different cultures of surveillance despite the major themes in common.

Take surveillance cultures in Japan for instance. David Murakami Wood observes while many familiar kinds of surveillance operate, especially in Tokyo, the local culture of surveillance is distinctive. Deep-seated tendencies to comply, even to "desire to be controlled," cannot be reduced to Foucault's "docile bodies" but rather to hierarchy and sameness in Japanese culture. Equally, door-to-door police family surveys, unheard of in most other countries, play a basic role in Japanese surveillance. In the same vein, willingness to accept ID cards in Japan may have much to do with traditional fears of the non-Japanese other (Murakami Wood, 2009).

A third line of inquiry worth pursuing in relation to the culture of surveillance has to do with the opportunities for engaging creatively and politically with surveillance in the 21st century. Even though the available avenues for such engagement are bound to depend on local situations, and sometimes on time-constrained opportunities, and despite the fact that large, often global corporations or coalitions of governmental influence do much to control the sluices and channel the flows of surveillance power, struggles over information slanted to surveillance are still just that—struggles.

The forms that such struggles take in digital times are bound to vary from antecedent cultural struggles of the 20th century, but some of their features will nonetheless persist. It is worth invoking Raymond Williams' work (1977) in this context. His analyses of culture emphasized both the need to see the complex interrelations among different aspects of the contemporary world and the imperative to consider the dynamics of cultural struggle—for him, this meant for self-determination—in each context. Today, he would note both the hegemonic and surveillant features of developments such as social media. But following his robust resistance to technological determinism, he would also seek to probe the democratic and participatory potentials opened by them.

Surveillance today still entails state-sponsored attempts to keep tabs on citizens, but to limit ourselves to considering this fails to appreciate the vast array of commercial and marketing surveillance that has in many respects overtaken even state surveillance. For instance, the facial recognition capacities of the largest police and intelligence agencies in the world pale before the scope and power of Facebook's tag-suggestion databases. But state surveillance and the surveillance society tell only part of the story. The experiences of surveillance, the rise of surveillant imaginaries and practices and the engagement of ordinary people in surveillance as compliant or complaining "data subjects" and as active users of new surveillance techniques suggests that exploring the growth of surveillance culture is a rich new source of understanding. Surveillance culture is symbiotic with surveillance state and surveillance society; it is likely to both add force to the flows and simultaneously to stimulate more to swim against the stream.

Notes

1. Consider this, for example: "The reconstitution of the public and the private as spheres of information and symbolic content that are largely detached from physical locales and increasingly interwoven with evolving technologies of communication and information flow has created a very fluid situation in which the boundaries between public and private are blurred and constantly shifting, and in which the boundaries that do exist at any point in time are porous, contestable and subject to constant negotiation and struggle" (Thompson, 2011: 68).
2. Raymond Williams' well-known definition of culture is that it refers to a "whole way of life."
3. I'm indebted to Christopher Parsons for this insight.
4. See Zygmunt Bauman & David Lyon (2013), *Liquid Surveillance: A Conversation.* Cambridge: Polity Press.

References

Aas, K. Franko., Oppen Gundhus, H., & Lomell, H. Mork (Eds.). (2008). *Technologies of InSecurity: The surveillance of everyday life*. London: Routledge.

Albrechtslund, A. (2008). Online social networking as participatory surveillance. *First Monday*, *13*(3). http://firstmonday.org/article/view/2142/1949/

Altheide, D. (2006). *Terrorism and the politics of fear*. New York: Altamira.

Andrejevic, M. (2007). *iSpy: Surveillance and power in the interactive era*. Lawrence: University Press of Kansas.

Andrejevic, M. (2005). The work of watching one another: Lateral surveillance, risk, and governance. *Surveillance & Society*, *2*(4), 479–497.

Bauman, Z., & Lyon, D. (2013). *Liquid surveillance: A conversation*. Cambridge: Polity.

Beck, U. (1992). *Risk society: Towards a new modernity*. London: Sage.

Beer, D. (2009). Power through the algorithm? Participatory web cultures and the technological unconscious. *New Media and Society*, *11*(6), 985–1002.

Bigo, D. (2008). Security: A field left fallow. In M. Dillon & A. Neal (Eds.), *Foucault on politics, security and war*. London: Palgrave Macmillan.

Bourdieu, P. (1977). *Outline of a theory of practice*. Cambridge: Cambridge University Press.

boyd, d. (2007). Why youth (heart) social network sites: The role of networked publics in teenage social life. In D. Buckingham (Ed.), *Youth, identity, and digital media volume* (MacArthur Foundation Series on Digital Learning). Cambridge, MA: MIT Press.

Carson, R. (1962). *Silent spring*. Boston, MA: Houghton Mifflin Harcourt.

Castells, M. (1992). *The informational city:Economic restructuring and urban development*, Oxford: Wiley-Blackwell.

Christensen, M. (2009, October). Watching me watching you. *Le Monde Diplomatique*. http://mondediplo.com/2009/10/02networking/

Garland, D. (2001). *The culture of control*. Chicago: University of Chicago Press.

Gates, K. (2011). *Our biometric future: Facial recognition technology and the culture of surveillance*. New York: New York University Press.

Gold, I., & Gold, J. (2012). The "Truman Show" delusion: Psychosis in the global village. *Cognitive Neuropsychiatry*, *17*(6), 455–472. Oakstone Medical Publishing.

Haggerty, K. D., & Ericson, R. V. (2000). The surveillant assemblage. *British Journal of Sociology*, *51*(4), 605–622.

Higgs, E. (2004). *The information state in England: The central collection of information on citizens, 1500–2000*. London: Palgrave Macmillan.

Kang, C. (2012, June 26). Teens in survey paint positive picture of social media's effect on their lives *Washington Post*. http://www.washingtonpost.com/business/technology/teens-in-survey-paint-positive-picture-of-effect-of-social-media-on-their-lives/2012/06/26/gJQAOszA5V_story.html

Kershaw, S. (2008, August 29). Culture of surveillance may contribute to delusional condition. *New York Times*. www.nytimes.com/2008/08/30/arts/30iht-truman.1.15737640.html?pagewanted=all

Kitchin, R., & Dodge, M. (2011). *Code/space: Software and everyday life*. Cambridge, MA: MIT Press.

Lash, S. (2007, September). *New New Media Ontology*. Presentation at Toward a Social Science of Web 2.0, National Science Learning Centre, York, UK.

Lash, S. (2002). *Critique of information*. London: Sage.

Lauer, J. (2011). Surveillance history and the history of new media: An evidential paradigm. *New Media & Society, 14*(4), 566–582.

Lyon, D. (2010). Liquid surveillance: The contribution of Zygmunt Bauman to surveillance studies. *International Political Sociology, 4*, 325–338.

Lyon, D. (2009). *Identifying citizens: ID cards as surveillance*. Cambridge: Polity.

Lyon, D. (2007). The border is everywhere: ID cards, surveillance, and the other. In E. Zureik, & M. Salter (Eds.), *Global surveillance and policing*. Collumpton: Willan.

Lyon, D. (2003). *Surveillance after September 11*. Cambridge: Polity.

Lyon, D. (2001). *Surveillance society: Monitoring everyday life*. Buckingham: Open University Press.

Magnet, S. (2011). *When biometrics fail: Gender, race and the technology of identity*. Durham: Duke University Press.

Meyrowitz, J. (2009). We liked to watch: Television as progenitor of the surveillance society. *Annals of the AAPSS, 625*, 32–48.

Murakami Wood, D. (2009). The "surveillance society": Questions of history, place and culture. *European Journal of Criminology, 6*(2), 179–194.

Rose, N. (1999). *Powers of freedom*. Cambridge: Cambridge University Press.

Thompson, J. (2011). Shifting boundaries of public and private life. *Theory, Culture and Society, 28*(4), 49–70.

Thrift, N. (2005). *Knowing capitalism*. London: Sage.

Trottier, D. (2012). *Social media as surveillance*. London: Ashgate.

VisionCritical Survey (2012, July). Made in conjunction with the Surveillance Studies Centre, Queen's University. To be deposited in the Queen's Data Archive 2013.

Weller, T. (2012). The information state: A historical perspective on surveillance. In K. Ball, K. Haggerty, & D. Lyon (Eds.), *Routledge Handbook of Surveillance Studies*. London: Routledge.

Williams, R. (1977). *Marxism and literature*. London: Oxford University Press.

PART II

Practices

5

The Infinite Debt of Surveillance in the Digital Economy

Mark Andrejevic

Freedom's Just Another Word for Indirect Payment

In the 1990s, when the television industry faced the challenge posed by digital video recorders that allowed viewers to skip ads with a flick of a button, its representatives made explicit the terms of their implicit pact with audiences: viewers get "free" programming in exchange for doing the "work" of watching the advertisements. That is, the commercial pact entailed an implicit obligation or responsibility on the part of viewers: in return for not having to pay directly for free-to-air programming, viewers owed something to producers—an obligation variously described in terms of viewers' time, their attention, or their "eyeballs." Of course, even by the mid-1990s, free-to-air TV was a thing of the past for the majority of U.S. households, which were already paying for their TV directly through payments to their cable company (and indirectly via the advertising, whose costs were built into the products they consumed). This fact did not stop television producers from bemoaning the desire of viewers to shirk their responsibilities—a desire that helped frame the act of watching ads as a form of labor: something inherently undesirable undertaken in order to receive compensation. Political economists may have wrangled over the niceties of describing watching as labor, but the television executives did not, decrying the desire of viewers to obtain something for nothing: to get television programming without *earning* it.[1] In 2002, for example, the CEO of Turner Broadcasting described TiVo's ad-skipping capability as a form of theft: "Your contract with the network when you get the show is you're going to watch the spots.... Any time you skip a commercial...you're actually stealing the programming" (Kramer, 2002:32).

The form of "payment" required of viewers, then, takes the form of the responsibility to perform a value-generating activity for programmers. If viewers are not going to pay production costs directly (as in other models that rely on license fees or pay-per-view), they must do something to earn the content. As one news account at the time put it, "Executives have all but said it's the patriotic duty of American viewers not to skip commercials, even if they can, so Hollywood can continue to afford to make their favorite programs" (Chonovic, 2002:6). It was only against the background of the threat that viewers might withhold their value-generating activity—via a technologically facilitated "general strike"—that the need emerged to find new ways of enforcing the pact, and thus of making it explicit.

The structure of the pact is a suggestive one, not least because, as I will argue, it carries over into the realm of the online economy: the fact that a good or service is provided "freely" comes with a form of obligation or responsibility. By watching the programming or using the service, we incur a debt to those who have provided it. "Free-to-air" it turns out, is a misnomer: the "gift" comes with an obligation enforced by the practical constraints imposed on viewers. As technology worked around those constraints, the pact had to be spelled out more explicitly: "If you watch our programming, than you owe us your time and attention." Indeed, the more one watches, the more one owes—and the opportunities to pay off this debt are distributed throughout the programming.

This logic of ongoing obligation has become a central feature of the online economy with its "free" content and services. As awareness grows regarding the increasingly comprehensive and intrusive forms of monitoring that characterize the commercial internet, these come to be framed in terms of the cost of convenience and access. In addition to watching the ads, willing submission to monitoring is what we owe to our benevolent internet overlords for the wealth of resources they have provided us. The formulation is a familiar one: when, for example, a study reveals that commercial entities are gathering detailed information about children in order to more effectively target them with advertising appeals and marketing strategies, right-wing policy wonks at the Cato Institute tell us not only that we needn't worry, but that we have already given our tacit consent to this state of affairs: "Judging by their behavior, though, most people regard the trade-off of personal information for access to content and communication as a good one" (Harper, 2012). This argument is a familiar one in the era characterized by critical amnesia— a forgetting of the point of critical theory, which was precisely to call into question the social and economic relations that structure allegedly "free" exchange.

This chapter draws on the notion of the ongoing "debt" assumed by those who avail themselves of the services, information and convenience on offer in the digital economy to interrogate the structured terms of access and the injunction to submit to commercial forms of monitoring. It argues that we need to do more than simply judge the implicit pact that underlies the commercial online economy by the fact of its existence—that is, that people accept the terms on offer. I draw on research conducted in Australia to argue for the importance of exploring the gap between people's behavior and their words; between their stated concerns about the personal information economy and the fact that they avail themselves of the conveniences on offer despite these concerns. Along the way, I explore some aspects of the relationship between debt and surveillance, drawing on Richard Dienst's observation that, "The two great abstract machines that define our era—the market and the media—are two faces of this inscriptive-projective process, the organization of lived temporality around the interminable working-up and working-off of an imperishable indebtedness (2011:125).

Surveillance and Debt

The defining feature of debt—its temporal form as a yet-to-be discharged obligation—goes hand in hand with its relationship to monitoring and surveillance. Immediate exchanges such as cash purchases need not be monitored exchanges, but debt always entails some level of recording and supervision. The obligation must be recorded, the debtor evaluated, the terms of payment supervised. Long before governments monitored populations for the purposes of security, health and other forms of intervention and management, they collected data for the purposes of taxation— that is, for the collection of a particular kind of debt obligation. Similarly, the attempt to secure a loan (to incur another type of debt) opens applicants up to detailed forms of information collection that ascertain their ability to pay or, failing that, the available assets that can be used as security in case of default. Simply put, a regime of debt is simultaneously and necessarily one of surveillance even if different regimes are associated with different modalities of monitoring. As Dienst (2011) puts it, "Each of these [societal] systems produces its own visibility of debt, its own kind of social 'eye.'…In every case, the social 'eye' would be a kind of collective inscription of memory that keeps track of filiations and alliances, imposes duties, and records payments" (124). The tracking of this eye is backed up by various modalities of power; that is, it does more than watch, serving as the basis for inclusion and exclusion, and for the exercise of strategies of guidance and enforcement.

Thus, as Steven Shaviro (2010) has argued, debt and its associated forms of surveillance might be understood as a vector of social control, one well-suited to an era in which social relations are increasingly enfolded into the terms of the marketplace. Following Deleuze's observations in the "Postscript on the Societies of Control" (1992), Shaviro describes debt as a flexible strategy of control tailored to an era in which the institutional boundaries of industrial society give way to the convergent logic of the information era, one in which interactive, networked devices span and de-differentiate realms of production and consumption, education, domesticity and incarceration. As Deleuze (1992) puts it, "In the disciplinary societies one was always starting again (from school to the barracks, from the barracks to the factory), while in the societies of control, one is never finished with anything—the corporation, the educational system, the armed services being metastable sites coexisting in one and the same modulation, like a universal system of deformation" (3).

Crucially, for our purposes, Deleuze makes explicit the connection between debt and the flexible control associated with spatial and functional de-differentiation: because the debt obligation follows debtors across these realms, conditioning their opportunities and constraining their activity (thanks in part to increasingly sophisticated monitoring mechanisms): "man is no longer man enclosed, but man in debt" (5). In other words, debt lends itself to logics of flexible and pervasive control characteristic of the forms of convergence envisioned by Deleuze. As Shaviro puts it, "The objective function of the market [in the control society] is that it 'forces us to be free,' forces us to behave 'rationally' and 'efficiently,' forces us to act concertedly in our own individual interests....The 'price system' continually forces us into debt. And thereby it confines, restricts, and channels our behavior . . ." (2010:8). Following the recent work of Maurizio Lazzarato (2012) on indebtedness, Mark Cote (2012) emphasizes the way in which debt enables market-based strategies of control in the digital era because of the way it "breaks down the binaries producer-consumer and working-nonworking....Debt is a strategy of control, a command of encumbrance: 'become productive.'"

In this regard, the sporadic moral panics surrounding high levels of personal and household debt in the U.S. (and elsewhere) can be deceptive: economists see the willingness of consumers to incur new debt as a positive sign for the economy. After the staggering recession triggered by the 2008 collapse of the sub-prime lending market in the U.S., for example, financial analysts welcomed Americans' increased willingness to take on debt as a healthy sign of recovery. As one press account put it, "For the first time since the Great Recession hit, American households are taking on more debt than they are shedding, an epochal shift that might augur a more resilient recovery" (Lowrey, 2012). One of the key indicators of economic growth in the U.S. is new housing starts—an indicator that, in the majority of cases, refers to the incurrence of debt in the form of long-term mortgage obligations. During a period of significant economic growth in the U.S.—from 1997 to 2007, "household debt ballooned from 66% of economic output to 98%" and was knocked back down to 89% by the recession" (Hilsenrath & Simon, 2011). The figures are striking: economists and pundits describe a shift toward debt levels that equal the nation's entire domestic output as a step in the right direction. Alternatively, foregoing consumption in order to pay down existing bills rather than continuing to carry high debt levels is seen as a drag on the economy: "Paying off bills slows consumer spending on appliances, travel and a slew of other products and services . . ." (Hilsenrath & Simon, 2011). Thrift has fallen a long way since the days of Ben Franklin: "During the Great Depression, economist John Maynard Keynes warned of a so-called paradox of thrift: When everyone turns frugal, everyone suffers. Synchronized thrift slows the economy....Some experts worry that is happening now" (Hilsenrath & Simon, 2011).

The relationship of monitoring to debt, then, takes place in several registers: as a precursor to the imposition of an obligation (background checking and census data collection); as a means of monitoring and accounting for outstanding obligations; and as a population-level indicator of economic growth. Given the close relationship between monitoring and surveillance, it is no coincidence that credit card companies and credit rating agencies helped pioneer the forms of economic surveillance that are becoming an increasingly important part of the commercial online economy. Along with loyalty cards, they are a key player in the attempt to bridge the realms of online and offline data collection by linking an online consumer with past patterns of purchase behavior and preferences. Credit card companies are one of the most comprehensive assemblers of the consumer archive.

It turns out that the type of information lenders have generated over the years about borrowing behaviour and patterns is more than a transactional by-product or a record-keeping necessity. Thanks to the development of techniques and technologies for putting the data to work, the captured information becomes an additional asset on top of and in addition to the economic value of the loan. The latest soundbite wisdom of the economic pundits at places like *Forbes* and the World Economic Forum is that "data is the new oil"—a "natural" resource, that, if properly processed and refined can serve as an important source of value in the information economy: "Indeed, data is the next big thing....The real impetus is the potential insights we can derive from this new, vast, and growing natural resource" (Rotella, 2012).

Data mining, predictive analytics and sentiment analysis are the economic watchwords of the emerging big-data economy. The ability to collect, sort and correlate data on a hitherto unprecedented scale promises to generate useful patterns that are far beyond the ability of the human mind to detect or even explain. As data-mining consultant Colleen McCue puts it, "With data mining we can perform exhaustive searches of very large databases using automated methods, searching well beyond the capacity of human analysts or even a team of analysts" (2007:23). In short, the promise of data mining is to generate patterns of actionable information that outstrip the reach of the unaided human brain. In his book *Too Big to Know*, David Weinberger describes this "new knowledge" as requiring, "not just giant computers but a network to connect them, to feed them, and to make their work accessible. It exists at the network level, not in the heads of individual human beings" (2011:130). Typically such forms of knowledge can be described in terms of their instrumental power. We know what we need to know even if we don't understand it.

Viewed as a data-generating activity, then, the lending process contributes to what William Bogard (1996) describes as the "simulation of surveillance": forms of data-driven modeling that seek to displace the uncertainty of the future by modeling it. Simulation stands in for a kind of knowledge about the future that exerts control in the present. The fantasy of simulation is that total information capture in the present might saturate the possibilities of the future. As Baudrillard puts it in his discussion of the virtualization of reality via simulation, "It seems that it would be the radical effectuation, the unconditional realization of the world, the transformation of all our acts, of all historical events, of all material substance and energy into pure information. The ideal would be the resolution of the world by the actualization of all facts and data" (1995:97).

Debt, of course, is also future-oriented in the sense that its present value is predicated on an anticipated payoff. But its information-generating role in the digital era adds another layer of significance to Shaviro's claim that, "Ultimately, financial debt is a way of colonizing and pre-empting…the future, of pricing its unknowability according to a measure that is graspable and controllable in the present" (2010:9). However, the reach of predictive analytics and data mining extends far beyond financial information—and even beyond the growing range of data collected by creditors about debtors. The ambition of commercial data mining is to monetize as much of the available information as possible. Viewed through the right lens, all types of data have the potential to be leveraged as assets. By definition, in other words, there is no category or amount of data that is ruled out a priori from the perspective of those who seek to mine it for unknowable and unpredictable patterns.

This infinite appetite for information is one way of approaching the infinite or limitless data-debt obligation that has come to characterize the digital economy: the fact that the increasing range of available services and applications with which we are provided is the obverse of the process of monitoring without limits. The exchange on offer is one in which the development of new information services and products goes hand in hand with the widening and deepening of the scope of data collection.

Debt and the Database

If, once upon a time, services like Google, Gmail and Facebook might have been thought of as "free" services provided by commercial entities whose motives remained obscure, we are gradually arriving at a less romanticized and mysticized understanding of the exchange that supports them: we "pay" for access to these services not simply with our attention (as in the case, for example, of commercial free-to-air broadcasting), but with our data. This data is not a "found" asset, something that marketers simply stumbled across because it was lying around cluttering the information landscape. Rather it is a resource generated by user activity and deliberately captured by an infrastructure developed for the express purpose of creating useful databases. If, once upon a time, user data collected by so-called cookies permitted monitoring and tracking as an inadvertent by-product (generated by the attempt to make websites more convenient by allowing them to "remember" and "recognize" users), now the production of this data is deliberate and increasingly comprehensive. As in the case of commercial broadcasting, online companies see submission to both advertising and data collection as a consumer obligation—something owed to them in return for the services, convenience and information they provide.

Thus, when it comes to ad-blocking software, we hear much the same refrain from the commercial sector as we did about TiVo. As an executive of one online company put it, ad-blocking is, "like a shoplifter coming in and stealing your money" (Flynn, 1999). By the same token, attempts to limit online tracking and targeting of consumers, such as "Do Not Track" legislation, are described as grave threats to the future viability of the online economy. As one advertising executive put it, "this may sound like a good idea to online privacy absolutists, but the practical implications of such regulations would be devastating—not just for advertisers and the online publishers who depend on their money, but for the technology industry and economy as a whole" (Wheeler, 2012). There is a somewhat circular aspect to such arguments: once you build a commercial economy predicated on the comprehensive monitoring of consumers, then the economy itself becomes an argument in favour of comprehensive monitoring. However, such arguments also reiterate the value proposition on offer: consumers owe something in return for the services they receive. As these services multiply indefinitely, that consumer debt correspondingly increases. At the limit we are offered total convenience, complete automation, in exchange for willing submission to comprehensive monitoring.

The emerging commercial architecture of the internet, then, can be construed in terms of a certain type of indebtedness, not simply in its technological configuration, such as the development of new and more sophisticated capabilities for data capture built into the hardware and the software, but also in the implicit message: "we built this for you and in return you owe us your submission to the forms of tracking that sustain it." Such architecture is neither unprecedented nor limited to the "virtual" realm. The wholesale privatization of public space that has come to characterize suburban and small-town USA might be described in related terms. The private sector has, in a sense, taken on the duties of the provision of publicly available facilities for sociality, conviviality and popular forms of diversion. The commercial shopping mall is a "free" space, in the sense that we do not need to pay to enter into a costly enclosure or to benefit from many of the facilities there: spacious promenades, lounge areas and even landscaping and play facilities for children. Much has been written about the ways in which commercial spaces displace public, civic ones, furthering the mall-ification of America, the displacement of Main Street by the food court and the attendant displacement of forms of public life by consumerism (see, for example, Kohn, 2004; Mitchell, 1995; Voyce, 2006).

Although they are open to the public, commercial spaces like malls are not public spaces in the civic sense. They are not governed, for example, by protected freedoms of assembly and speech that obtain in truly public spaces. Rather they are private spaces governed by the commercial imperatives of their owners and operators who have the discretion to limit speech, commerce, social intercourse and access as they see fit. In his discussion of shopping malls, Richard Dienst has suggested that insofar as such spaces impose a certain sense of obligation upon their users, they embody, "the global sprawl of an indebted world within the terms of a single building" (2011:129). The huge investment in commercial infrastructure carries with it a certain imperative, perhaps even an implied obligation toward those who have supplied the "public" space: "the sheer proliferation of shopping spaces should be seen as the physical extension of the regime of indebtedness where individual subjects are empowered to enact their own fidelity to the reigning powers of money" (129). Once such a physical infrastructure is created, it carries with it its own set of imperatives built into both the spaces themselves and the social and economic logics that sustain them. Empty or underused malls become yet another economic indicator: the sign of an ailing economy, an admission of weakness, a public concern.

Spaces of Debt: From the Physical to the Virtual

Echoing the transformation of physical space, the internet rapidly transformed from a publicly supported infrastructure to a commercial one—a digital mega-mall of sorts—and continues to construct an information-intensive system of commerce that carries with it not simply the injunction to consume, to interact and pay attention, but also to submit to its monitoring logics. Typically this obligation is framed in terms of an individual exchange of proprietary forms of privacy for a particular service or convenience. As one commentator put it, "The average American finds a very healthy acceptable balance between privacy and convenience, they give up some privacy and get a lot of convenience" (Oppmann, 2010). This framing of the exchange is open to several challenges: it assumes informed consent (that people have read and really understood the terms of the exchange insofar as these are made available), and it takes acquiescence to prestructured terms of access as an enthusiastic embrace of these terms. It is all too easy to speak on behalf of the monitored public, equating the apparent interest in public self-expression with a general willingness to submit to data collection and monitoring.

On closer examination, however, such claims fall short. The notion of informed consent is surely a vexed one in the online context, in part because so few people read the terms of the contract to which they are agreeing when they join or sign in. For example, our nationwide representative telephone survey of 1,100 Australians indicated that fewer than one in five people say they read privacy policies always or most of the time.[2] The survey was followed up by an ongoing series of person-on-the-street interviews conducted in three major Australian cities (Brisbane, Sydney and Melbourne). Well over one-third of the survey respondents (36%) indicated that they never read privacy policies. In the structured interviews (N=40, as of this writing) conducted subsequent to the survey, people said, unsurprisingly, that they often did not read privacy policies because they had already decided to use a particular service and knew they had no choice but to accept the policy or go without the service. Some respondents said they did not read privacy policies because they are long, boring and difficult to understand. The follow-up interviews were skewed toward younger, urban respondents, who were recruited in public spaces in Sydney, Melbourne and Brisbane, and were thus not statistically representative the way the survey was. We deliberately focused on active internet users (people who went online at least several times a week) in order to get responses from those who might be considered relatively experienced and savvy internet users.

These findings suggest the obvious but often overlooked point that there is a big difference between the form of consent indicated by clicking "accept" on a website and *informed* consent. It is worth adding that privacy policies change often, and that users who sign up under one set of terms often find themselves subject to an entirely new set of terms on sites into which they have already invested large amounts of time and energy. You can quit Facebook if the terms of use change in ways that irritate you, but you can't take your network and all the comments, posts and interactions with you. Finally privacy policies often present their terms of use in such general terms that it is difficult to extrapolate to concrete uses of the data. It is one thing to agree in general terms to have one's data used for marketing purposes, but quite another to sign off on a system of targeting that will allow a retailer to know, for example, if someone is pregnant before that person has told her family (as reportedly happened to a Target customer, according to a widely circulated article in the *New York Times*) (Duhigg, 2012).

In an environment in which data miners are continually finding new uses for the data collected by commercial sites and applications, consumers cannot be expected to anticipate any and all uses to which their information might be put. Thus, the implicit claim that users have a clear, informed understanding of what they are signing up for when they agree to have their data collected and mined is absurd. Typically, the claim that users are happy with the terms on offer is inferred from user behaviour, because when they are asked, the vast majority of respondents express concern over the collection and use of their personal information for customization and targeting. This response is quite consistent in the available research. For example, a 2012 Pew study revealed that the majority (65%) of people who use search engines do not approve of the use of behavioral data to customize search results. More than two-thirds of all internet users (68%) in the study did not approve of targeted advertising based on behavioral tracking (Purcell, Brenner, & Rainie, 2012). Another nationwide survey in the U.S. found that 66% of respondents opposed ad targeting based on tracking users' activities (Turow, King, Hoofnagle, Bleakley, & Hennessy, 2009). A U.S. study of public reaction to proposed "Do Not Track" legislation found that 60% of respondents said they would opt out of online tracking if given the choice. My own survey in Australia revealed strong support for "Do Not Track" legislation (95% in favor). Well over half of the respondents (56%) said they opposed customized advertising based on tracking, and 59% said they felt websites collect too much information about users.

The overall picture, then, is very different from one in which users happily agree to the capture and use of their personal information. The majority of internet users surveyed do not approve of the tracking and targeting practices that comprise the dominant commercial model for providing access to "free" services and information. There is a split between what people say and what they do; that is, they may not like the available model, but they submit to it anyway. That is a far cry, however, from claiming that users embrace this commercial model, that they are happy with the available choices or that they find the balance between "privacy and convenience" to be a healthy one. On the contrary, what emerges from the research is a world in which people submit to the available model because they do not see any alternative way of accessing the services and conveniences on offer. For the commercial service providers, the mere fact of acceptance is certainly enough, but the need to push the further claim that people like and embrace the terms on offer is a telling one. Perhaps this attempt to equate acquiescence with enthusiastic embrace reflects the desire to re-assert the claim that the market always provides what people want (in a context in which it clearly does not—at least insofar as the majority of users say they do not approve of the commercial model on offer).

This conflicted response to online tracking came out clearly in our structured interviews about the survey findings. The common reaction to the apparent split between behavior and stated preferences was a sense of helplessness in the face of the prestructured alternatives: if you want access to the services on offer, you have to submit to the terms set by those who own and control the platforms. If you do not accept these terms, then you have to go without access to services that are becoming an increasingly important part of contemporary social, personal and, in some cases, professional life. As one respondent put it,

> If you ask people about whether they want anyone going through their information, they'll say 'I don't want you to read my things.' On the other hand we don't do anything, because we think that we can't. What can I do? Lose my Gmail account? I don't want to. All my contacts are there, all my emails, everyone has my address. You feel like you can't do anything. (male, 32)

Suggestively, what emerged from the interviews was not so much a concern about privacy invasion in the conventional sense, as a strong reaction to a feeling of powerlessness in the face of the structured conditions that shape access to online resources. By privacy in the conventional sense, I mean a concern over whether someone in particular (or the public more generally) knows intimate secrets about users. This is the sense invoked by Google CEO Eric Schmidt when he admonished people concerned about online privacy by observing, "If you have something that you don't want anyone to know, maybe you shouldn't be doing it in the first place" (Dvorak, 2009). Perhaps the most recent high-profile example of this version of "privacy invasion" was the widespread public revelation about former CIA director David Petraeus's affair with his biographer. The revelation triggered an avalanche of stories about the fate of "privacy" in the internet era, with pundits wondering, breathlessly (and worriedly), whether the fact that the CIA director couldn't keep his private life secret meant that no one could any more. This notion of privacy equates concern over the fate of one's personal information with an attempt to keep a secret. However, as common sense and our interviews suggest, these are not necessarily the same thing. One need not have any secrets per se—nefarious or otherwise—to be concerned about the ways in which the use of personal information can be turned back upon oneself for the purposes of sorting, filtering, inclusion or exclusion, and various forms of targeting. In an era when details about one's personal life can, often in seemingly random ways, influence whether or not one has access to financial credit, health insurance or various benefits and opportunities, people who register concern about data collection are not necessarily trying to "hide" something about themselves. Rather they may be reasonably concerned about the various nontransparent uses to which their data can be put. As one respondent said, "We really don't know where things collected about us go—we don't understand how they interact in such a complex environment" (female, 22). This observation neatly summed up the survey's finding that people feel they do not know enough about how their information is collected and used; that is, we seem to have reached the point where people are starting to get a sense of just how much they do not know about what is taking place.

In this regard, our respondents' observations seem to parallel developments in the data-mining techniques to which their data is being subjected. One of the central tenets of data mining large databases is that the mining process is an "emergent" one in the sense that patterns cannot be discerned, predicted or modeled in advance. That is to say, the explicit goal is to discover indiscernible and perhaps even inexplicable correlations in the data. If, for example, a person's political preference can be reliably predicted based on the model of car he or she drives or the brand of toothpaste he or she uses (or vice versa), this is actionable information in the sense that it can facilitate targeted forms of political campaigning or marketing, but it is not necessarily comprehensible information. There may be no clear underlying explanation for why people who drive a Mercury vote Republican. To put it somewhat differently, we do not know what type of predictive power particular types of data might bestow upon those who can access it. Do habits that seem completely unrelated lump us in with groups who are stigmatized (or privileged) in one way or another? In the "small-data" era, it was relatively simple to reverse engineer the forms of sorting that resulted in various forms of discrimination. In the "big-data" era, this might be much more difficult: are we turned down for a job because other people who share some similar, seemingly random trait have not had success in the past? As the algorithms get increasingly complex, we may not even know what combination of traits conspired to include or exclude us, or to turn us into a target of one kind or another. The question becomes not so much whether we want to hide some aspect of our private lives, but rather how data, once it is sorted and mined, might be used to influence decisions that impact our lives but remain profoundly opaque to us. As one respondent put it, "you end up accepting having no privacy without knowing the consequences" (male, 32).

In keeping with such observations, many of our respondents were worried about the unanticipated ways in which information about them might be used. I interpret this not as concern that their secrets would be publicized (by, for example, someone revealing details of their personal lives on a public website), but rather that information collection and processing might double as a form of control, exacerbating the inequality between those who control the data and those who generate it. Many respondents criticized the asymmetry of online monitoring: the fact that even as companies collected more and more data about them, they did not have a clear idea about how this was being used. As one respondent put it, in a conversation that touched on email and social networking, "It's not fair, it's not transparent. It's funny because Facebook is supposed to be all about transparency, and they're the ones who aren't transparent at all" (female, 31). This concern over asymmetry translated into a perceived sense of subjection to unequal power relations. As one respondent stated in a discussion of privacy policies:

> I just click agree, because what else can I do? I think that frustration sometimes just translates into: "I won't even think about it, because what can I do?" It [the internet] becomes part of how you connect with people. It's really useful for your career, for your choice in life. It doesn't mean you can't live without it, but living with it becomes important. (female, 29)

These people aren't particular interested in hiding anything in particular, *pace* Eric Schmidt. They are more concerned with the possibility that information might be used about them in ways that impact their lives but that remain obscure, nontransparent or incomprehensible to them. They are also frustrated by the choices on offer: either submit to monitoring or go without. There is a sense, at least on the part of some respondents, that they are being mined for data that corporations can turn to their advantage, and that the appetite for this data is bottomless: "It's not just what you want—it's where you are, what you do. It's everything. You're not free any more. You're just a slave of these companies" (male, 22). If this comes across as hyperbolic, it's interesting to reflect on the stark contrast between such a response and the rhetoric of freedom and convenience that underpins the online economy. I would speculate that this discrepancy is, at least in part, a result of the relatively recent widespread news coverage that has started to explore the ways in which companies like Facebook and Google are putting the large amounts of data they collect to use. Such responses also start to press against the claim that there is a clear categorical distinction between work—commonly the realm associated with forms of structural exploitation—and forms of activity that take place online and are often treated as non-work—leisure, entertainment, and so on. Several of our respondents indicated the importance of social networking sites and other online resources for their professional lives as well as for their social lives. At least in some quarters, withdrawing from social networking and email services amounts to a social or professional handicap.

Beyond Privacy

The disconnect between what people had to say about the collection and use of their personal information and the framing of privacy as a form of secrecy or conceal-ment suggests that we may not yet have an adequate lexicon to address the chang-ing information landscape. The notion of privacy on offer is inadequate to many of the concerns raised by our respondents, and, we imagine, to the concerns expressed by respondents to our nationwide survey. One of the pressing challenges facing those who write about surveillance and "privacy" in the digital era is to unpack the dimen-sions of this concern and to develop a critical lexicon appropriate to it. Based on the admittedly preliminary findings introduced here, I would suggest the need to move beyond the notion of privacy as control over personal secrets and, conversely, of dis-closure as another human's conscious registration of the secret. Google, for exam-ple, likes to point out that no humans actually see people's Gmail messages: the process is automated and thus, in some restricted sense "private." That is, it's not like someone reading through your mail or your diary (this, of course is precisely what did take place in the Petraeus case, which is what made it so amenable to dominant privacy discourses). Most of the forms of targeting and sorting associated with data mining in the private sector can function perfectly smoothly without any particu-lar individual knowing the personal details that enter into the database to be processed by the algorithm. That is, the data can be used to shape economic, edu-cational, professional and even health prospects of individuals without being "pub-licized" (in the way the details, say, of Petraeus's love life were). Moreover, proprietary conceptions of privacy as something we own—and therefore as something that we might trade in order to gain access to goods and services—miss the mark. The value of data is not directly linked to any individual user but to the broader information context in which this information fits. Individual data becomes valuable when it can be pooled and mined for patterns by those who control the infrastructure to sort, store and process large amounts of data. Perhaps one of the points of confusion in contemporary discussions of privacy has to do with a misunderstanding of the focus of concern. The paradox of the fate of personal information in the digital era is that it often involves mundane information that, in general, people are not particularly concerned about revealing. Indeed, several of our respondents emphasized that they had nothing that they particularly wanted to hide, before going on to express some level of concern over not knowing how their information was being used. These responses reflected an emerging public concern over how seemingly mundane information might be leveraged into forms of control and manipulation, thanks in no small part to the types of claims marketers (and others) are making about the power of data mining. Admittedly, the interview findings are preliminary—and the project is scheduled to continue for another two years subsequent to this writing—but in combination with the survey, they suggest the need to approach with a healthy dose of scepticism the recurring refrain that people are happy with the terms of exchange on offer. Legislators, corporate spokespeople and advocates of various types have a tendency to speak on behalf of a public that, paradoxically, while increasingly monitored, has received insufficient scrutiny regarding its preferences and concerns about the shape the online economy is taking. What was most surprising to me about the interviews—an admittedly relatively small sample as of this writing—was how few people evinced the lack of concern over the fate of their information so often attributed to them by pundits and corporate spin doctors. There were respondents who initially responded that they didn't have anything to hide, but in the vast majority of cases they went on to express some level of frustration with having to submit to forms of data monitoring that remained opaque to them.

To return to the concerns with which this chapter opened, the notion of debt gets us to the related question of how this personal data is extracted. What intrigues me about the responses to our interviews is the frustration exhibited in the face of a seemingly inescapable obligation. In order to access what is good and useful about the internet, we need to rely upon a commercial infrastructure that sets the terms of access. We do not need to pay—in fact we cannot pay directly for services such as Facebook or Gmail—but we are told we owe something to them in return for access and use. In this regard, the notion of debt (and various forms of resistance to the obligations it imposes) refers directly to the political economy of the commercial internet; the fact of its commercialization and the ways in which privatization begets privatization or, as Marx suggested, in which separation begets separation (De Angelis, 2002). When you separate people from (control over) the means of sociability, communication and information storage and access, you can then separate them from their own data—and extract further data about them in exchange for allowing them to access what they have created (their email, Facebook account, Tweets and so on). The notion of debt also speaks to the forms of resignation evinced by our respondents—an understanding that, as in the case of broadcasting before it, the huge private infrastructure must be financed somehow. Once we accept this commercial model, we find ourselves beholden to the logics that support it. Finally the notion of debt invokes the character of the current commercial arrangement as an ongoing relationship. This is a defining element of debt as a form of social control: it designates an ongoing relationship between debtor and creditor, one that can be extended indefinitely given the right combination of interest and payment rates. The debt obligation envisioned by the online economy is similarly open-ended; there is no point at which Facebook decides it has collected enough data, that we have, in a sense, fulfilled our obligation to it. As new commercial conveniences and capabilities continue to develop, the appetite for data is as infinite as the ongoing obligation to supply it.

Notes

1. With respect to the theoretical discussions about the "work" of watching, see: Smythe, 1977; Murdock, 1978; Livant, 1979; Jhally & Livant, 1986; Maxwell, 1991.
2. The findings presented here are based on a national telephone survey conducted with N=1,106 adults across Australia between November 17 and December 14, 2011. The project was managed by the Social Research Centre, with respondents sourced through random-digit phone number generation for landlines and mobile phones. The final sample consisted of 642 surveys through landline numbers and 464 through mobile numbers. Reported data was proportionally weighted to adjust for design (chance of selection), contact opportunities (mobile only, landline or both) and demographics (gender, age, education and state). A complete summary of the findings and methodology is available online at http://cccs.uq.edu.au/personal-information-project. As of this writing, 40 structured interviews have been conducted at three sites across Australia (Melbourne, Sydney, Brisbane). Interviewees were recruited randomly in public spaces for 20- to 40-minute sessions.

References

Baudrillard, J. (1995). The virtual illusion: Or the automatic writing of the world. *Theory, Culture & Society, 12*, 97–107.

Bogard, W. (1996). *The simulation of surveillance: Hypercontrol in telematic societies.* Cambridge: Cambridge University Press.

Chonovic, L. (2002, November). Next stop: On-demand ads. *Television Week, 11*, 6.

Cote, M. (2012, November). *Data motility: Life, labour and debt in the age of Big Social Data.* Plenary paper for the Media, Games and Art Conference, Swinburne University, Melbourne (cited with permission). http://www.academia.edu/3123022/Data_Motility_Life_Labour_and_Debt_in_the_Age_of_Big_Social_Data.

De Angelis, M. (2002, September 2). Marx and primitive accumulation: The continuous character of capital's "enclosures." *The Commoner.* http://www.commoner.org.uk/02deangelis.pdf

Deleuze, G. (1992, Winter). Postscript on the societies of control. *October, 59*, 3–7.

Dienst, R. (2011). *The bonds of debt.* New York: Verso.

Duhigg, C. (2012, February 16). How companies learn your secrets. *New York Times.* http://www.nytimes.com/2012/02/19/magazine/shopping-habits.html?pagewanted=all &_r=0

Dvorak, J. (2009, December 11). Eric Schmidt, Google and privacy. *Wall Street Journal: Market Watch.* http://articles.marketwatch.com/2009–12–11/commentary/30712576_1_privacy-advocates-chief-executive-eric-schmidt-cnet-article

Flynn, L. (1999, June 7). Battle begun on internet ad blocking. *New York Times*, 1.

Harper, J. (2012, December 12) Get over your "privacy" concerns. *New York Times.* http://www.nytimes.com/roomfordebate/2012/12/11/privacy-and-the-apps-you-down load/get-over-your-privacy-concerns-about-the-web

Hilsenrath, J., & Simon, R. (2011, October 22). Spenders become savers, hurting recovery. *Wall Street Journal.* http://online.wsj.com/article/SB10001424052970204294504576614942937855646.html

Jhally S., & Livant, B. (1986). Watching as working: The valorization of audience consciousness. *Journal of Communication, 36*(3), 124–143.

Kohn, M. (2004). *Brave new neighborhoods: The privatization of public space.* New York: Routledge.

Kramer, S. (2002, April 29). Content's king. *Cable World*, 32.

Lazzarato, M. (2012). *The making of the indebted man.* Cambridge: MIT Press.

Livant, B. (1979). The audience commodity: On the blindspot debate. *Canadian Journal of Political and Social Theory, 1*(3), 91–106.

Lowrey, A. (2012, October 26). Rise in household debt might be sign of a strengthening recovery. *New York Times.* http://www.nytimes.com/2012/10/27/business/rise-in-household-debt-might-be-sign-of-a-strengthening-recovery.html?_r=0

Maxwell, R. (1991). The image is gold: Value, the audience commodity, and fetishism. *Journal of Film and Video, 43*(1/2), 29–45.

McCue, C.. (2007). *Data mining and predictive analysis: Intelligence gathering and crime analysis.* Burlington, MA: Butterworth-Heinemann.

Mitchell, D. (1995). The end of public space? People's Park, definitions of the public, and democracy. *Annals of the Association of American Geographers, 85*(1), 108–133.

Murdock, G. (1978). Blindspots about Western Marxism: A reply to Dallas Smythe. *Canadian Journal of Political and Social Theory, 2*(2), 109–119.

Oppmann, P. (2010, April 14). In a digital world, we trade privacy for convenience. *CNN.com.* http://www.cnn.com/2010/TECH/04/14/oppmann.off.the.grid/index.html

Purcell, K., Brenner, J., & Rainie, L. (2012, March 9). *Search engine use, 2012.* Pew Internet and American Life Project. http://pewinternet.org/Reports/2012/Search-Engine-Use-2012.aspx.

Rotella, P. (2012, April 4). Is data the new oil? *Forbes.* http://www.forbes.com/sites/perry-rotella/2012/04/02/is-data-the-new-oil/

Shaviro, S. (2010, May 1). *The "bitter necessity" of debt: Neoliberal finance and the society of control.* Unpublished manuscript. http://ftp.shaviro.com/Othertexts/Debt.pdf

Smythe, D. (1977) Communications: Blindspot of Western Marxism. *Canadian Journal of Political and Social Theory, 3*(1), 91–106.

Turow, J., King, J., Hoofnagle, C. J., Bleakley, A., & Hennessy, M. (2009, September 29). *Americans reject tailored advertising and three activities that enable it.* Annenberg School of Communication, University of Pennsylvania. http://papers.ssrn.com/sol3/papers.cfm?abstract_id=1478214

Voyce, M. (2006). Shopping malls in Australia: The end of public space and the rise of "consumerist citizenship"? *Journal of Sociology, 42*(3), 269–286.

Weinberger, D. (2011). *Too big to know.* New York: Basic Books.

Wheeler, E. (2012, September 20). How "do not track" is poised to kill online growth. *CNET.com.* http://news.cnet.com/8301-1023_3-57516422-93/how-do-not-track-is-poised-to-kill-online-growth/

6

Mobile Social Networks and Surveillance

Users' Perspective

Lee Humphreys

It is predicted that by 2020, most people in the world will access the internet through mobile devices (Anderson & Rainie, 2008). This means social networking sites will primarily be used and accessed through a mobile device. Like other social networks, mobile social networks incorporate, rely on and broadcast personal and locational information of users (Albrechtslund, 2008, 2012; Humphreys, 2007). This chapter explores how people think about privacy issues and personal information when using mobile social networks. Drawing on a year-long qualitative field study, this chapter examines how mobile users manage expectations, norms and understandings about privacy and surveillance when broadcasting personal and locational information. More specifically, I argue that three kinds of surveillance manifest in and around mobile social network use, but not all raise privacy concerns on the part of users.

Privacy and Surveillance

The rise of information technology brings about many issues with regards to privacy and surveillance. Privacy and surveillance are often presented as counterpoints when discussing issues of personal information and new technology. Privacy has been defined as the ability to control what information about oneself is available to others (Westin, 2003). When one cannot control what information about one-self others know, one may be open to surveillance by others. Lyon defines surveil-lance as "any collecting or processing of personal data, whether identifiable or not, for the purposes of influencing or managing those whose data have been gathered" (2001:2). Inherent to the definition of surveillance is the power or influence over others. Asymmetry is an important differentiating factor between monitoring or watching and surveillance (Andrejevic, 2006). Part of the power of surveillance is that people whose personal data is collected or observed may not know when or if they are being watched.

Twenty years ago, Oscar Gandy (1989) argued that the use of new information technologies by corporate and state bureaucracies leads to increased surveillance in society. Like Poster (1990), Gandy suggests that information technology and the growth of databases create an asymmetrical monitoring of behavior. Drawing on Bentham's concept of the panopticon (Foucault, 1977), Gandy (1993) demonstrates how information technology facilitates the surveillance by an unseen corporate and bureaucratic observer who can not only commodify the personal information of those observed, but also use such information to inform practices of social control and dis-crimination. Such information technology "involves the collection, processing, and sharing of information about individuals and groups that is generated through their daily lives as citizens, employees, and consumers and is used to coordinate and con-trol their access to the goods and services that define life in the modern capitalist economy" (Gandy, 1993:3). Thus the monitoring of individuals through information technology allows for people and groups to be sorted into categories based on their presumed economic or political value and those deemed more and less valuable may be given differing economic and political opportunities.

As Lyon (2001) argues, the information society is a surveillance society. Information and computing technologies both facilitate but also necessitate the col-lection of personal information. Information technology databases allow for the inte-gration and layering of different kinds of information from different sources. The most important aspect of this point is that it allows those who control the databases (often corporate or government entities) to know more about individuals than they may know about themselves. This coupling of information highlights behavioral and cognitive tendencies that people may not be aware of. This information can also be commoditized and potentially used for discriminatory activities (Gandy, 1993).

Privacy and surveillance have long been concerns of scholars of interactive media. Previous studies have explored privacy concerns when using particular inter-active technologies such as cable television (Kay, 1978; Vidmar & Flaherty, 1985), electronic banking (McLuhan & Powers, 1980; Poster, 1990), TiVo (Elmer, 2003; Andrejevic, 2007), and the internet (e.g., Elmer, 1997; Fox et al., 2000). These studies suggest the use of interactive digital technologies leads to a decrease in personal privacy because people do not have control over their personal information. Interactive technologies rely on people disclosing personal information in order to provide them with services. People willingly share their personal information because they derive some sort of benefit from these interactive, information-based services, thus reinforcing the notion that the information society is a surveillance society (Lyon, 2001).

Three Kinds of Surveillance

In addition to the traditional notion of surveillance, characterized by its nontransparency by an authority such as the government, three other kinds of surveillance have been identified in the literature: voluntary panopticon, lateral surveillance, and self-surveillance. Voluntary panopticon refers to the voluntary submission to corporate surveillance or what Whitaker (1999) calls the "participatory panopticon." A voluntary or "participatory" panopticon differs from older systems of surveillance in that it is consensual (Whitaker, 1999). The voluntary panopticon is based on a consumer society where information technology allows for the decentered surveillance of consumptive behavior. Participatory panopticon is very similar to participatory surveillance (Albrechtslund, 2008; Poster, 1990) in that people willingly participate in the monitoring of their own behavior because they derive benefit from it.

Lateral surveillance is the asymmetrical, nontransparent monitoring of citizens by one another (Andrejevic, 2006). With the advent of the internet and interactive media, people have similar technological capabilities previously held exclusively by corporate and state entities. As such, citizens can monitor other citizens' behavior through nonreciprocal forms of watching. Everyday people can search for information about other citizens without their knowledge or permission. The advent of social media has given rise to other forms of lateral surveillance such as "social surveillance" (Marwick, 2012), which suggests a mutual surveillance among actors using social media. Like lateral surveillance, social surveillance involves nonhierarchical forms of monitoring (i.e., not involving the state or corporate entities) among everyday people. Unlike lateral surveillance, social surveillance suggests that people engage in permissible and reciprocal forms of watching.

The last kind of surveillance is self-surveillance. Meyrowitz (2007) defines self-surveillance as "the ways in which people record themselves (or invite others to do so) for potential replaying in other times and places" (p. 1). Technologies such as video cameras and cameraphones allow people to capture aspects of their lives to replay later. The ability to record oneself can lead to the scrutiny of mundane behavior, which can fundamentally change one's understanding of that behavior or event. The recorded behavior has power over the lived experience because exposure to the recorded behavior can replace or alter one's understanding of the event based on one's lived experience of it. Therefore power implicitly functions within Meyrowitz's concept of self-surveillance insomuch as new interactive technologies, such as mobile social networks, allow users to "see" things about their behaviors they previously could not perceive and changes their understanding of their own tendencies and behavior.[1]

Case Study

Dodgeball was a mobile service owned by Google that distributed location-based information of users so that people could meet up at venues within cities. Similar to a social network site, Dodgeball allowed users to set up publicly articulated social networks of friends so that they could broadcast their location to these individuals' mobile devices. For example, when users got to a bar or cafe, they could "check in" by sending a text message to Dodgeball such as "@ Irish Pub." Dodgeball then broadcasted their location via text message to people in their Dodgeball network. The system also allowed members to send "shouts" or general text messages broadcasted among Dodgeball friends, such as "Roof party tonight my place 9pm 'til whenever." Shouts could be used like a check-in to facilitate meeting at places not in Dodgeball's venue database or for whatever other reason users might want to broadcast messages to their Dodgeball network of friends (such as jokes, celebrity sightings, etc.).

Founded in 2000, Dodgeball was one of the first commercial mobile social networks and was available in 22 cities in the U.S. It was free to use, however, users were charged by their mobile carriers for each text message they sent and received through Dodgeball (unless they had signed up for an unlimited text messaging plan, which in 2000 was relatively uncommon). Dodgeball did not use GPS but required users to actively text message their location to Dodgeball.

Dodgeball was officially shut down by Google in January 2009; however, its co-founder, Dennis Crowley, left Google and in March 2009 co-launched Foursquare, which allows members to "note their locations with a mobile phone and can find out where friends are" (foursquare.com). Like Dodgeball, Foursquare offers users the ability to share their locations with friends via their mobile phones. As a mobile service, Dodgeball relied on text messaging to send locational information to and from users. Foursquare is an app-based service that allows users to share their locations based on GPS.

There are two primary differences between Foursquare and Dodgeball. The first is that Foursquare has a formal, competitive game element that Dodgeball did not. Although Dodgeball did officially recognize the user with the greatest number of check-ins in each city per month, it did not offer badges or mayorships of locations to incentivize people to use the system. The top users in a city would occasionally compete but only informally. Additionally, Dodgeball did not offer a merchant platform like Foursquare does, which allows businesses to claim and manage locations and promote their businesses and brands. Despite these differences, there are many similarities between the services.

Methodology

Based on a year-long study (2005 to 2006) using participant observation, user observations and in-depth interviews, this chapter explores Dodgeball use and how it relates to privacy and surveillance. Twenty-one in-depth interviews were conducted with Dodgeball users from seven cities throughout the U.S.[2] Because the Dodgeball system did not allow users to easily send messages to people who are not "Dodgeball friends," I initiated contact with Dodgeball's founder, Dennis Crowley, to ask if he would help recruit informants. Crowley sent recruitment emails to top users in several cities. In addition, I used snowball sampling based upon those interviews. In total, I interviewed 13 users through an introduction from Crowley and eight users with a snowball sample from the original 13. While I was originally interested in the issue of privacy on Dodgeball when collecting data, the various conceptions of surveillance did not emerge as a salient topic until after the data collection had been completed. Therefore I was not able to probe the topic directly with most of the study participants. In addition, I analyzed messages sent among a group of Dodgeball users sent during a week-long period in October 2006 in order to explore trends in timing, language and proximity. I also interviewed Crowley to understand the background and context of Dodgeball as a mobile social network service.

The demographics of my Dodgeball informants varied by several characteristics. I interviewed 9 women and 12 men, ranging in age from 23 to 30. Geographically, they lived in Chicago (n=1), Los Angeles (n=2), Minneapolis (n=4), New York City (n=9), Philadelphia (n=3), San Francisco (n=1), and Seattle (n=1). I conducted fieldwork in Philadelphia, New York City and Minneapolis and therefore was able to interview more users in these cities. Other interviews were conducted over the phone. My informants' Dodgeball networks ranged in size from one friend to 149 friends. The mean number of Dodgeball friends for my sample was 40.38 (sd=37.41) and the median was 24 friends.

Most of my interviewees (18 of the 21) considered themselves highly active Dodgeball users. Five of the 13 informants recruited through Crowley had been top user with the most check-ins in their respective cities within a particular month. This sample is not a representative sample of Dodgeball users, but a sample of mostly enthusiastic early adopters. Nevertheless, studying the activities of this group of users is an important first step in exploring the ways in which people embed social meaning in mobile social network use.

Results

Privacy

When I asked informants if they had any thoughts or concerns about privacy when using Dodgeball, they all implicitly defined privacy as privacy from other users or people and not privacy from state, corporate or bureaucratic entities. Informants were generally not concerned about privacy for one of two reasons: (1) because they felt they had control over their information and to whom it was sent, (2) because they believed themselves to be experienced and savvy internet users.

Some Dodgeball informants suggested that they actively controlled their privacy because they controlled when, where and to whom this information is sent. Because Dodgeball users had the power to choose when to communicate and to whom through Dodgeball, informants were not concerned about privacy. Some participants felt they had control because they would only check in when out socializing and only close friends would receive their check-ins. The Dodgeball website also explicitly suggested that one way users could control their privacy was by carefully selecting the composition of their Dodgeball network of friends. A line from the 2005 Dodgeball privacy statement indicated this: "You can control how certain information is displayed by selectively choosing your friends."[3] Many participants in the study felt that they maintained a sense of privacy and control through careful friending practices.

Other informants, such as Deirdre, were not concerned about privacy on Dodgeball because they believe they are good judges of character after having been online for many years. Dierdre believed she has learned how to be savvy online and therefore was not concerned about privacy on Dodgeball. Because of her experience interacting with others online, she was not concerned about scary situations that might have arisen through her Dodgeball use. As Deirdre described her online savviness and good judge of character, she implicitly defined privacy on Dodgeball as privacy from dangerous or scary users.

There was one informant who suggested that Dodgeball could raise privacy concerns for some people and that Dodgeball may not be for everyone. Kirk, from Seattle, acknowledged that the amount and kind of information collected and disseminated through Dodgeball could be scary, but because such information was only going to "friends," it was not worrisome. However, such information could be shared with strangers. Because Dodgeball catalogued all check-in messages, it offered RSS (Rich Site Summary) feeds of members' check-ins so that members could share their check-in information on their blogs or elsewhere. While most Dodgeball users did not use the RSS feeds, Kirk did use this on his personal website and suggested that it was not that different from strangers in public knowing where you are because they are there with you. Kirk argued, "Just because no one ever has been able to tell strangers where people are, [doesn't] make it a private matter." Just like any stranger could see him in the public spaces he checked into, anyone could also read his website and see his check-ins. Kirk felt if you are engaging in public spaces, that information is also public.

Voluntary Panopticon

As much as Dodgeball members were telling their friends where they were, they were also telling Google where they were. Every time a Dodgeball member sent a check-in message or a shout message, they sent it to Google. Such behavior illustrates a voluntary submission to corporate surveillance or what Whitaker (1999) calls the "participatory panopticon."

Like other participatory panopticons, the benefits of using Dodgeball were tangible. For the Dodgeball members I interviewed, it facilitated sociality. Informants indicated that Dodgeball made it easier to coordinate meeting up. Communication on the system also reinforced social bonds (Humphreys, 2007). Additionally, some members felt Dodgeball was a cheaper, more efficient way to communicate with groups of friends than to contact each friend individually. The benefits of using Dodgeball were apparent and immediate to these active members.

Some Dodgeball informants suggested that one of the reasons they liked Dodgeball over other services was because it was an opt-in system. Users had to actively submit their social-location information to Dodgeball rather than being tracked by GPS. For example, Dean, a computer programmer, liked Dodgeball because it was not automated and thus afforded him a sense of privacy. He liked feeling as if he had control over his information; he liked volunteering his personal information when he found it beneficial to do so. Despite this sense of privacy, however, by participating in an interactive system where one's behaviors and interactions are mediated through a central server that can then be linked to other databases, Dean's participation on Dodgeball feeds into what Andrejevic (2007) has termed the "digital enclosure," "an interactive realm wherein every action and transaction generates information about itself" (2). The promise of interactivity leads to the participation by everyday people in a system where the traditional work of marketers is replaced through the data mining of transaction-generated information. Within this digital enclosure, Andrejevic (2007) argues that participation in interactive media is an "invitation to participate in one's own manipulation by providing increasingly detailed information about personal preferences, activities and background to those who would use the knowledge to manage consumption" (242). By volunteering his personal information in order to coordinate meeting up with friends, Dean submitted personal and locational information to Google. Dodgeball users like Dean were doing the work of an interactive surveillance society.

While some Dodgeball informants enjoyed the autonomy of having to proactively contribute to the system, other Dodgeball informants would rather give up this autonomy of interactive participation. These Dodgeball informants suggested that they would rather submit to automated tracking of their movements so they wouldn't have to be bothered to check in. For example, both Irwin and Taylor thought that automating the Dodgeball check-in process would make it easier for users. This is part of the reason why a voluntary panopticon is so powerful. People willingly submit to surveillance for the sake of convenience.

It is important to note that the Dodgeball members I interviewed did not express any concerns about surveillance when using a mobile social network. Nor did they bring up issues of surveillance at all. No one mentioned state or corporate surveillance during any of the interviews. As Whittaker (1999) points out, this is not terribly surprising since such concerns are generally intangible. This kind of surveillance, however, could potentially lead to discrimination and social control as has been demonstrated with other examples of interactive technology (Andrejevic, 2007; Gandy, 1993). Nevertheless, it is unclear how exactly Google used the information collected through Dodgeball.

A potentially relevant factor that may help to interpret this finding is the degree to which Dodgeball was actually integrated into Google. When Google first acquired Dodgeball, there was plenty of speculation that Google would integrate Dodgeball into their other services, and thus its many forms of targeted advertising (e.g., Shirky, 2005); however, there was little actual evidence of this. Besides the replacement of the Dodgeball log-in with a Google log-in and the replacement of the Dodgeball privacy statement with Google's official privacy statement, there was little evidence of any strategic integration of Dodgeball with the rest of Google products and services. For example, Dodgeball was not cross-promoted on any of Google-owned webpages, nor was it featured on the primary product webpage of Google. Additionally, the founders of Dodgeball eventually quit Google two years after their acquisition because they felt that Google bought them and then did nothing with them (Crowley, 2007). This, coupled with the disintegration of Dodgeball in January of 2009, leads me to believe that Google did not strategically integrate Dodgeball or the consumer information collected through Dodgeball into their other services. That said, Dodgeball was technologically integrated via the log-in and legally integrated into Google through its privacy statement. Therefore while it is unclear the degree to which Google strategically used Dodgeball data, according to their privacy statement Google and all Google's partners had access to all Dodgeball user social-locational information. In addition, in 2009 Google's mobile privacy statement indicated that mobile battery life and location information of Google Latitude users was collected, stored, and merged with other Google Account information. While Google's privacy policy has since changed, at the time such customer information was used to "process and personalize" users' requests.[4] This suggests that search results may have been influenced by where your location is tracked.

Lateral and Social Surveillance

Dodgeball also facilitated a kind of lateral and social surveillance where network members monitored the communication and behavior of other network members (i.e., their friends). As a communicative system, Dodgeball relied on mutual monitoring—friends telling each other where they are through Dodgeball so they can meet up. However, not all members of the network used the system in the same way. Sometimes there was asymmetrical use of Dodgeball where one member checked in on Dodgeball and another member would not. This asymmetry is the difference between surveillance and monitoring (Andrejevic, 2006). Elicia in New York suggested that there were people in her network who generally do not check in on Dodgeball, but still receive the messages. "There's also a group of people who are more like the eavesdroppers who never send out ever, but they always want to know where people are.... They still find it interesting to observe, but they don't want to participate." (Elicia, New York City).

When people observe each other's mediated behaviors in an asymmetrical manner, such as Elicia describes, Dodgeball could become a tool, not for social interaction and coordination, but for lateral surveillance. "Interpersonal interaction always contains an element of mutual monitoring, but the deployment of interactive networked communication technology allows individuals to avail themselves of the forms of asymmetrical, nontransparent information gathering modeled by commercial and state surveillance practices" (Andrejevic, 2006:398).

Continued lateral surveillance on a mobile social network like Dodgeball may ultimately weaken the network. If there are too many people "eavesdropping," then there may be little value for other people to use it and the network can break down. If people did not actively contribute to their Dodgeball networks, the value of it decreases for those who did contribute. This may ultimately hurt the growth and sustainability of the mobile network. For example, two members I interviewed in

Philadelphia were in each other's Dodgeball network. They had each checked in a couple times, but no one ever was able to meet up. Eventually they stopped using the network altogether because they were never able to leverage its benefits. Overall, however, this kind of eavesdropping was the exception rather than the rule among participants' experiences with Dodgeball.

In addition to eavesdropping, lateral surveillance could potentially lead to stalking. In the last 15 years, cyberstalking has become a societal concern (McFarlane & Bocij, 2003). Overall, however, the Dodgeball informants I interviewed were not concerned about stalking on the network. In addition to careful friending practices, Dodgeball also allowed users to "block" other users from "seeing" them, communicating with them and interacting with them through the service. Dodgeball also allowed members to block a person who had been in their friend network from sending and receiving messages without letting that other person know he or she had been blocked. Only four of the 21 informants had blocked anyone on Dodgeball. They blocked another user not because of stalking or privacy concerns, but to manage awkward or annoying social situations such as when a friend was sending too many messages through Dodgeball or they had had a falling out.

Most of the Dodgeball informants were not concerned about lateral surveillance in the form of stalking or eavesdropping, but expressed that they enjoyed using Dodgeball to learn where their friends hung out socially. They benefited from the social surveillance that Dodgeball facilitated. This mutual monitoring in some ways could become asymmetrical, because (1) not all people broadcasted personal information at the same rate, and (2) users did not always know when or if people accessed the information they broadcast over Dodgeball. While people may not know exactly who sees what, participation in Dodgeball suggested an expectation and desire to watch and be watched, like other forms of social media (Marwick, 2012).

Self-Surveillance

There were a number of technological features on Dodgeball that facilitated a form of self-surveillance through the ability to record one's behavior for viewing at a later time. For example, when users logged in to the Dodgeball website, they could see a Google map of all the places they had checked in over the last 24 hours, week, month, six months or a year. In addition to maps of their own check-ins, the website also listed users' most recent check-ins on their profile webpages, as well as listing on the webpages of venues where Dodgeball members had recently checked in. Dodgeball also sent out a monthly email digest to users of their check-ins as well as the friends' check-ins. As discussed above, Dodgeball users could import RSS feeds of their check-ins to their blogs. Users could also import their check-ins into their calendar, such as Google Calendar or Outlook. Together, these mechanisms allowed Dodgeball users a way to record and catalogue their own behavior for themselves.

A number of Dodgeball users indicated that they found great enjoyment in looking at the maps of their Dodgeball check-ins. The aggregation of individual Dodgeball behavior on maps allowed people to see patterns in their behavior that they might not have been aware of otherwise. Indeed several participants reported enjoying seeing maps of where they and their friends had checked in on Dodgeball. For example, Irwin in Los Angeles said, "I like overlaying maps of where I've checked in over the last year versus all the other friends I have on Dodgeball. Things like that. But again you're making something that's usually invisible, visible." Dodgeball facilitated self-surveillance that allowed users like Irwin to see where he had been in ways that were previously much more difficult to do. Not only did Dodgeball keep an itemized list of his social outings, it also created a visual representation of outings on the Google map. By combining his map with the maps of his friends, he could visually compare and contrast social outings.

Other users felt like Dodgeball allowed them the power to link their behavior to databases in ways that were previously unavailable. For example, Leonard in Los Angeles suggested that Dodgeball allowed him to link information from online and offline sources; in particular, he liked "being the bridge between the network and the real world." As he linked his check-ins with his online activities, he also linked his offline world with his online world. Leonard spent a lot of time thinking, reading and writing about the relationships between online and offline communities, and between databases and lived experiences. While Leonard was thoughtful and creative in his use and integration of Dodgeball, he is not representative of general Dodgeball users. Even among my informants, Leonard is atypically technologically sophisticated.

Other informants admitted that they liked using Dodgeball as a kind of social diary to record where they've been. By checking in at social outings, they had a log of their social calendar without having to plan everything out. For example, not only did Enid enjoy receiving the email digests from Dodgeball, she also suggested that this cataloguing feature was a part of why she used Dodgeball as often as she did. Enid felt like it could be used as a passive social diary that she could keep stored on the Google server. Journals and diaries are an important way for people to connect the present to the past in their everyday lives (Rosenzweig & Thelen, 1998). The designers of Dodgeball recognized the social diary capabilities of Dodgeball and integrated the RSS feed and Google Calendar importation functionalities to encourage such use (Dennis Crowley, personal communication, May 11, 2006).

Dodgeball itself helped users to create a record of their behavior, but if paired with other collaborative technology such as blogs or photo sharing sites, Dodgeball data could be richly linked to images and descriptions of social behavior. In some instances, Dodgeball members were so accustomed to socially cataloguing their behavior on these sites or through check-ins that they expected their friends would do so as well. Dierdre described a situation where differential use of these varying systems caused social friction among her friends. Dierdre and her friends check in so often that when they did not and another friend saw photos on Flickr, the other friend wondered if they purposefully chose not to do so because they were trying to avoid her. The various other collaborative technologies allowed her and her friends to catalogue their night out so that others friends who were not there could find out despite not being in her Dodgeball network of friends. One of the main differences between "old-fashioned" journals or diaries and these online or mobile social blogs is the publicness of the journals. Friends, family members, employers and even strangers could read or see the various social activities of Dodgeball members on the Dodgeball website or on blogs or community websites. As Dierdre demonstrates, there can be social repercussions even among friends from publicly sharing such information that reflect social surveillance practices (Marwick, 2012). Expectations of continual information disclosure may arise amongst groups of friends and social friction or sanctions may occur when such expectations are violated.

Discussion

Privacy concerns among Dodgeball informants were minimal. Consistent with privacy research (Gandy, 1989; Stone, Gueutal, Gardner, & McClure, 1983), as long as people felt like they were in control of their personal information, they were unconcerned about their privacy. This is not a surprising finding since my informants were among the most active Dodgeball users in the country. Anyone who signed up for Dodgeball and had stopped using it due to privacy concerns or those who never signed up for Dodgeball because of privacy concerns would not have entered into my study. Nevertheless, it is important to understand how highly active users conceptualize and understand privacy when using mobile social networks because they are the early adopters who will help to shape normative practices and use of mobile social networks in the future.

Despite the lack of concern for privacy, there was evidence that mobile social networks can contribute to three kinds of surveillance. Once user information is relayed through a central server, it allows for corporate surveillance in that it creates a one-way system of monitoring behavior. Because mobile social networks, like other interactive services, are of some benefit to users, they willingly participate in the surveillance of themselves by others. The voluntary or "participatory panopticon" (Whitaker, 1999) is so powerful because it is a consensual and decentered surveillance. People willingly allow entities to monitor their behavior because such services provide a convenience for them. It is important to note that when I asked informants about privacy issues, no one brought up concerns about corporate or bureaucratic surveillance. While some scholars have argued that corporate surveillance can lead to discrimination and social control (Andrejevic, 2007; Gandy, 1993), this was not a salient concern for the participants in this study. While I am hesitant about over-interpreting this finding, it may suggest that such corporate surveillance is not an active concern to mobile media users. This seems to go against research that shows the majority of people are in fact concerned about companies monitoring their online behavior (e.g., Fox et al., 2000; Hart Research Associates, 2012). That said, Pew found that when asked, most Americans expressed concern about corporate tracking of their behavior, but their online behavior did not necessarily reflect this concern. "Despite Americans' high anxiety about being monitored online, only 10% of Internet users have set their browsers to reject cookies" (Fox et al., 2000:3). The lack of saliency of corporate surveillance among the Dodgeball participants in this study may be related to this finding that behaviors do not reflect concerns about corporate surveillance. It may be that while some people are concerned about corporate surveillance, it is not a highly salient concern that influences their everyday online or mobile use.

Lateral and social surveillance is the monitoring of user behavior by other users and can also be achieved through mobile social networks like Dodgeball. Users can monitor the behavior of other users. In fact, these systems rely on the monitoring of users by other users. Even if informants suggested there was an asymmetrical monitoring of behavior among users, most informants were not generally concerned about lateral surveillance as it relates to stalking. Most felt they had control over their information and did not believe that other Dodgeball users would use their personal information against them.

Finally, social networks can also contribute to self-surveillance, where people record their own behavior to be reexamined at a later time. Some Dodgeball informants greatly enjoyed the self-surveillance that Dodgeball allowed through the visualization of check-in information on maps as well as the aggregation of socio-spatial network information presented on maps as friend check-ins. For some informants, such self-surveillance even motivated their use of the Dodgeball system. They checked in at many places because they wanted to be able to later see a map of their locations. They enjoyed the ability to record their behavior and see it later in a new way, which in turn changed their future behavior of checking in to more venues.

It is also important to note that while Dodgeball facilitates all three kinds of surveillance, it does not do so evenly. The amount of information that Dodgeball and its partners had access to was far greater than the amount of information users have access to. Not only did the Dodgeball company have access to a greater breadth of information (i.e., information from all users across cities and friend networks), it also had a greater depth of information (i.e., information that is not presented back to users such as who responds to whose check-ins). In addition, each of the three kinds of surveillance evidenced in the Dodgeball case study contributes to a "digital enclosure" (Andrejevic, 2007). Despite people using the service to communicate with their friends, such usage of an interactive service generates information about behaviors, motivations and desires that is valuable consumer data. Even if Dodgeball members used the service to better understand their own behaviors through a self-surveillance mechanism, the system itself could also be learning about their behaviors but on a much larger scale when aggregated with other types of consumer information.

Transferability of Findings

Several things have changed about mobile social networks since the time of Dodgeball, which are important to take into account when assessing how transferrable the findings of this study are to services like Foursquare. The most important difference is the commodification of personal information from mobile social networks. Whereas when I did the original fieldwork in 2007, it was not clear how Dodgeball or Google were using the data collected, Foursquare makes it very clear how businesses can use Foursquare data to "keep and retain customers" (foursquare.com/business/). Foursquare gives all "merchants" who have claimed a business with the service free access to data about their customers, including daily check-ins over time, most recent visitors, most frequent visitors, gender breakdown of customers, what time of day people checkin and portion of check-ins that are broadcast to Twitter and Facebook. This difference might suggest that users of Foursquare may be more concerned about corporate surveillance since this information is not necessarily presented back to users. However, the fundamental feeling that the mobile social network users in this study were in control of when and where they checked in would suggest that even if they knew a service were providing check-in data back to the merchant, users would still not be concerned about corporate surveillance; because they feel like they have control over when and where they check in, they are not concerned.

A second important difference that influences the transferability of findings relates to the gaming aspect of Foursquare. On one hand, the gaming aspects, such as unlocking badges or competing for mayorships, may encourage self-surveillance in that users are checking in on the mobile social network for purposes besides sharing their locations with their networks of friends. Competitive gaming elements on mobile social networks may encourage interactivity with the service in the same way that self-surveillance activities and features do. Just as Dodgeball users became more conscientious of checking in when competing for top user each month, Foursquare users may also be highly self-monitoring about their check-in behaviors when competing for mayorships or trying to earn badges.

Another important difference between Dodgeball and a service like Foursquare is the interconnectivity with other services. Social media are increasingly connected so that one's Foursquare check-ins can be linked to other services and networks, which can help to spread messages about one's check-ins. While this kind of database interconnectivity was speculated about Dodgeball when it was purchased by Google, Dodgeball was never really integrated into Google's product and service offerings, nor did Dodgeball facilitate any connectivity with Facebook or Twitter. Foursquare allows users the opportunity to link their profiles on several social media sites. It even promotes it as one of the metrics Foursquare can report on to businesses. While this level of data interconnectivity was possible in 2007, we seem to see it increasingly becoming the norm for media companies and social media to encourage interconnectivity with other social media services.

This kind of interconnectivity, however, does occasionally bring about surveillance concerns, as demonstrated by the example of the public outcry against Girls Around Me in April 2012. Girls Around Me was a free app that combined Foursquare and Facebook data to identify the location of young women with public Facebook profiles who had recently checked in and the overall number of females who had also checked into a location. After concerns about stalking surfaced, Foursquare revoked the app's access to their API (Application Program Interface) and the creators of the app pulled it from the iTunes store (Hill, 2012). The concerns about this app, like those surrounding Dodgeball, were primarily centered on issues of lateral surveillance.

Conclusion

New mediaspaces (Couldry & McCarthy, 2004) created by mobile and online social network services are not only spaces for communication, coordination and interaction, but also monitored spaces of consumption and production. As people use these technologies to meet up, whether it be through an event organized through Facebook, an e-vite online or a mobile social network that shares real-time locations, users are not only telling their friends where they are or where they will be, they are increasingly telling this to marketers. This means that mobile and online social mediaspaces also become spaces of production.

> The de-differentiation of spaces of consumption and production achieved by new media serves as a form of spatial enclosure: a technology for enfolding previously unmonitored activities within the monitoring gaze of marketers. Spaces associated with leisure and domestic activities do become increasingly productive from a commercial point of view precisely because they can be more thoroughly monitored (Andrejevic, 2004:195).

Mobile social networks allow for the monitoring of behavior in ways that were previously unavailable to marketers. These spaces of sociality become sites of productivity. As people spend more time using these services, more of their personal information enters into the commercial gaze. Emerging interactive technologies are important sites through which to explore how information is collected and used, and the role of privacy and surveillance in this process.

The collection of personal information through mobile social networks is very much part of the surveillance society in which we live, but it is not inherently good or bad. To quote Meyrowitz (2007:20):

> To say that the surveillance society we live in is neither clearly good nor bad, however, is not to say that it is neutral or has no impact on our lives. And the impact does not have to be in our constant awareness to be significant. Surveillance technologies are now so pervasive, yet so subtle—many occurring automatically as we engage in purchasing, driving, or walking down a street—that they may transform the texture of everyday life without most of us being aware of the change.

In this chapter, I have tried to identify and discuss how the collection and aggregation of socio-spatial information of mobile social network users works in everyday practice. I have explored both micro and macro ways that such monitoring and surveillance manifests. I have also tried to ground a discussion of interactive technologies and surveillance in the everyday experience of Dodgeball users who overwhelmingly are not concerned about privacy and surveillance. This echoes others' findings that social surveillance (Marwick, 2012) is enacted in the everyday practices of engaging with social media. While mobile social networks like Dodgeball or Foursquare broadcast locational information, which may seem particularly sensitive or private, it was not experienced as such by participants. Nevertheless, the social and self-surveillance practices suggest new possibilities for watching and being watched through locational information, which in turn suggest new possibilities for ways to see others and ourselves.

Notes

1. This understanding of self-surveillance is similar to Vas and Bruno's (2003) discussion of self-surveillance, as "individuals' attention to their actions and thoughts when constituting themselves as subjects of their conduct" (p. 273). In both situations, the ability to observe one's own behavior beyond one's personal experience of it, calls attention to particular aspects of the behavior that one may not even be aware of. Both definitions are extensions understanding self-surveillances as the self-monitoring that results from the real or potential observation by another who is in a position of control (Foucault, 1977).
2. All Dodgeball informants are identified by pseudonym only.
3. This quote was originally taken from Dodgeball's Privacy Statement. www.dodgeball.com/privacy, but the website is no longer available.
4. In 2012, Google's privacy policies were dramatically changed and unified under one privacy policy for all Google products and services, whereas previously different products and services had specialized privacy policies. This discussion draws on Google's previous mobile privacy policy found at http://m.google.com/static/en/privacy.html and updated June 15, 2009, which is no longer available.

References

Albrechtslund, A. (2012). Socializing the city: Location sharing and online social networking. In C. Fuchs, K. Boersma, A. Albrechtslund, & M. Sandoval (Eds.), *Internet and surveillance: The challenges of Web 2.0 and social media* (pp. 187–197). New York: Routledge.

Albrechtslund, A. (2008). Online social networking as participatory surveillance. *First Monday, 13*(3), article 6. http://firstmonday.org/article/view/2142/1949/

Anderson, J. Q., & Rainie, L. (2008). *The future of the internet III.* Washington, DC: Pew Internet & American Life Project.

Andrejevic, M. (2007). *iSpy: Surveillance and power in the interactive era.* Lawrence: University Press of Kansas.

Andrejevic, M. (2006). The discipline of watching: Detection, risk, and lateral surveillance. *Critical Studies in Media Communication, 23,* 391–407.

Andrejevic, M. (2004). The webcam subculture and the digital enclosure. In N. Couldry & A. McCarthy (Eds.), *MediaSpace: Place, scale and culture in a media age* (pp. 193–208). London: Routledge.

Couldry, N., & McCarthy, A. (Eds.). (2004). *MediaSpace: Place, scale and culture in a media age.* London: Routledge.

Crowley, D. (2007). Me & Alex quit Google. (Dodgeball forever). http://www.flickr.com/photos/dpstyles/460987802/

Elmer, G. (2003). A diagram of panoptic surveillance. *New Media & Society, 5,* 231–247.

Elmer, G. (1997). Spaces of surveillance: Indexicality and solicitation on the internet. *Critical Studies in Mass Communication, 14,* 182–191.

Foucault, M. (1977). *Discipline and punish: The birth of the prison* (A. Sheridan, Trans.). New York: Pantheon Books.

Fox, S., Rainie, L., Horrigan, J., Lenhart, A., Spooner, T., & Carter, C. (2000). *Trust and privacy online: Why Americans want to rewrite the rules.* Washington, DC: Pew Internet & American

Life Project.

Gandy Jr., O. H. (1993). *The panoptic sort: A political economy of personal information.* Boulder, CO: Westview.

Gandy Jr., O. H. (1989). The surveillance society: Information technology and bureaucratic social control. *Journal of Communication, 39*(3), 61–76.

Hart Research Associates. (2012). *The online generation gap: Contrasting attitudes and behaviors of parents and teens.* Washington, D.C.: Family Online Safety Institute. http://www.fosi.org/images/stories/research/hartreport-onlinegap-final.pdf

Hill, K. (2012, April 2). *The reaction to "Girls Around Me" was far more disturbing than the "creepy" app itself.* http://www.forbes.com/sites/kashmirhill/2012/04/02/the-reaction-to-girls-around-me-was-far-more-disturbing-than-the-creepy-app-itself/

Humphreys, L. (2007). Mobile social networks and social practice: A case study of Dodgeball. *Journal of Computer-Mediated Communication, 12*(1), article 17.

Kay, P. (1978). Policy issues in interactive cable television. *Journal of Communication, 28*(2), 202–208.

Lyon, D. (2001). *Surveillance society: Monitoring in everyday life.* Buckingham: Open University Press.

Marwick, A. E. (2012). The public domain: Social surveillance in everyday life. *Surveillance and Society, 9*(4), 378–393.

McFarlane, L., & Bocij, P. (2003). An exploration of predatory behaviour in cyberspace: Towards a typology of cyberstalkers. *First Monday, 8*(9), article 5.

McLuhan, M., & Powers, B. (1980). Electronic banking and the death of privacy. *Journal of Communication, 31*(1), 164–169.

Meyrowitz, J. (2007 February 17–18). Watching us being watched: State, corporate, and citizen surveillance. Paper presented at symposium, The End of Television? Its Impact on the World (So Far), Annenberg School for Communication, University of Pennnsylvania, Philadelphia, PA.

Poster, M. (1990). *The mode of information: Poststructuralism and social construct.* Chicago, IL: University of Chicago Press.

Rosenzweig, R., & Thelen, D. (1998). *The presence of the past: Popular uses of history in American life.* New York: Columbia University Press.

Shirky, C. (2005, May 11). Google acquires Dodgeball. http://many.corante.com/archives/2005/05/11/google_acquires_dodgeball.php

Stone, E., Gueutal, H. G., Gardner, D. G., & McClure, S. (1983). A field experiment comparing information-privacy values, beliefs, and attitudes across several types of organizations. *Journal of Applied Psychology, 68*, 459–468.

Vas, P., & Bruno, F. (2003). Types of self-surveillance: From abnormality to individuals "at risk." *Surveillance and Society, 1*, 272–291.

Vidmar, N., & Flaherty, D. H. (1985). Concern for personal privacy in an electronic age. *Journal of Communication, 35*(2), 91–93.

Westin, A. F. (2003). Social and political dimensions of privacy. *Journal of Social Issues, 59*, 431–453.

Whitaker, R. (1999). *The end of privacy: How total surveillance is becoming a reality.* New York: The New Press.

7

Collaborative Surveillance and Technologies of Trust

Online Reputation Systems in the "New" Sharing Economy

Jennie Germann Molz

Through my living room window, I see my overnight guest pulling into the driveway in a sudden downpour. I grab an umbrella and run out to meet her. Bonnie[1] and I have found each other through Couchsurfing.org, a free online hospitality exchange website. She needed a place to stay on her drive back to Maine and my spare bedroom happened to be en route. Our only interactions so far have included a few emails via the Couchsurfing website to nail down arrival times and directions. I have also read her Couchsurfing profile and the references other members have posted for her. She admits later that she Googled my name before requesting to stay with me. Having used these online systems to establish a degree of trust, we greet each other offline standing in the driveway under my umbrella. I welcome her into my home where she spends the night before continuing on the next morning. The day after she leaves, an email message arrives from Couchsurfing reminding me to go online and review my experience with my "surfer." Bonnie must have gotten a similar email, because she logs on the same day to leave a reference for me.

Introduction

This chapter focuses on two interrelated trends that shape my interactions with Bonnie: the emergence of the "new" sharing economy and the spread of online social surveillance. Couchsurfing, a free online hospitality exchange network, and its for-profit counterpart, Airbnb, are emblematic of a new sharing economy that marshals the connecting power and global scale of the internet to facilitate social and economic exchanges among strangers. In the sharing economy, people use social networking sites to share their bikes, lend out their cars and offer up their spare bedrooms to complete strangers. But what makes people willing to share their tools with a stranger or let a traveler they've never met before sleep on their couch? The simple answer is trust. Beyond just putting strangers in touch with one another, these social networking sites must also help people establish a sense of trust, which is where social surveillance technologies enter the picture.

In many ways, Couchsurfing, Airbnb and the other sites that make up the sharing economy are emerging into a social environment where online surveillance among peers has become almost completely normalized. For example, on social media sites like Facebook and Twitter, people socialize by following, watching and updating one another. The sharing economy translates these tracking technologies into new opportunities for trading with one another by making surveillance the basis for trust. On sharing websites like Couchsurfing and Airbnb, for example, increasingly sophisticated online reputation systems encourage users to rate, review and report on one another in order to build up trustworthy reputations. As we will see, trust and reputation—the glue that holds the sharing economy together—is a function of social surveillance.

In this chapter, I describe the new sharing economy and the technologies of trust that make sharing among strangers possible. I examine the way these technologies draw on and further embed a logic of interpersonal surveillance via online reputation systems that encourage users to monitor and report on themselves and others. Finally, in keeping with the terminology of "collaborative consumption" and "collaborative lifestyles" that peppers the discourse on the sharing economy, I introduce the concept of "collaborative surveillance" to illustrate the way technology, trust, reputation and surveillance intersect to shape exchanges and experiences of togetherness between strangers in this new economic regime. Along the way, I raise questions about the way these systems resist and reinforce power hierarchies. In some ways, the new sharing economy appears to reconfigure top-down hierarchies of surveillance into more dispersed and potentially more democratic forms of interpersonal monitoring. However, I call for a more careful critique of the rhetoric of "empowerment" that valorizes trust and reputation—and, by extension, online social surveillance—within the sharing economy. Along these lines, I conclude by exploring several paradoxical characteristics of "collaborative surveillance," namely the dispersal and recentralization of power, the "responsibilization" of users and self-moderating communities, and the normalization of surveillance as a way of relating with strangers.

The "New" Sharing Economy

The term "sharing economy" refers to the social and economic phenomenon of technologically mediated peer-to-peer exchanges. It includes a long and growing list of websites and mobile applications that allow friends and strangers to barter, lend, rent or swap one another's bikes, books, cars, handbags, household goods or spare bedrooms. According to Rachel Botsman and Roo Rogers, who chronicle the rise of the sharing economy in their book *What's Mine Is Yours: The Rise of Collaborative Consumption*, instead of perpetuating the unsustainable level of hyperconsumption that has marked the last few decades, the sharing economy revolves around forms of "collaborative consumption" that emphasize access and experiences rather than ownership. They are quick to point out, however, that the "new" sharing economy is not really all that new. If anything, collaborative consumption reinvigorates age-old principles of neighborly exchange. What is new, however, is the scope and scale of these exchanges. This is not just about neighbors sharing with neighbors, but complete strangers sharing their possessions, their time, and even, in the case of Couchsurfing and Airbnb, their homes with one another—whether they are next door or on the other side of the planet.

Sharing with strangers relies on innovative technological solutions for establishing trust, something that has been notoriously difficult to do in online environments. One journalist, expressing her scepticism about sharing with strangers she meets online, remarked: "As anyone who has corresponded with a Nigerian prince knows, there are serious trust issues" (Kamenetz, 2011). In the new sharing economy, technological platforms replace or supplement the old mechanisms for establishing trust. Members report back to the community through ratings and review systems that make users accountable to one another and become the basis for an individual member's reputation within sharing networks. This is not unlike the way word-of-mouth, references and reputation established trustworthiness in traditional communities, but now extended to a much wider community that may never meet face-to-face. As Andrejevic (2005:481) notes:

> Surely, there is nothing particularly new and earth-shattering about the fact that peers develop strategies for keeping track of one another, and those who write about new media might even go so far as to suggest that contemporary strategies for mutual monitoring merely rehabilitate, in technological form, the everyone-knows-everyone-else's-business world of traditional village life, undoing the anonymity of urbanized modernity.

Reputation systems alleviate a sense of anonymity by encouraging users to disclose information about themselves and to report on the actions of others. This, in turn, provides reliable information that members can use to decide whether to trust and trade with one another.

The sharing economy thus emerges out of an already existing social framework in which trust and reputation are a function of surveillance. Instead of dismantling this framework, the internet shores it up, extends it and further normalizes peer-to-peer surveillance as a basis for economic exchange. In the next section, I explore the relationship between surveillance and technologies of trust in order to better understand how reputation systems produce and police trust in the sharing economy.

Surveillance and Reputation in the Sharing Economy

Once the domain of powerful entities such as governments or large corporations, surveillance has now become an everyday aspect of social and economic life. With their social networks on the move and at a distance, and with the new tools of surveillance at their fingertips, individuals are increasingly likely to socialize with friends, family members, acquaintances and strangers through online practices of watching, tracking, monitoring and following. Scholars have offered several concepts to describe this phenomenon: "lateral surveillance" (Andrejevic, 2005), "participatory surveillance" (Albrechtslund, 2008), "social listening" (Crawford, 2009) and "social surveillance" (Tokunaga, 2011). In her discussion of social networking sites such as Facebook, Foursquare and Twitter, Marwick emphasizes the sense of reciprocity entailed in social surveillance: "broadcasting information to be looked at by others and looking at information broadcast by others" (2012:379). It is this reciprocity that distinguishes social surveillance from typical top-down or state-sponsored surveillance regimes associated with Orwell's "Big Brother" or Foucault's "panopticon" (see Haggerty & Ericson, 2000). This is not a case of the state watching and disciplining its populace, but rather a case of willing participants using online networking technologies to watch themselves and each other in a decentralized, non-hierarchical system of surveillance.

That said, neither social surveillance nor online reputation systems do away entirely with top-down arrangements of social control. In fact, the social, political and economic implications of networking technologies have been the source of much debate among critical surveillance scholars. On the one hand, scholars highlight the pleasurable, playful and empowering effects of watching and being watched by others. Albrechtslund (2008), for example, points toward the "mutual, empowering and subjectivity building" potential of social surveillance, arguing that online social networking "facilitates new ways of constructing identity, meeting friends and colleagues as well as socializing with strangers." From this perspective, individuals are not victims of surveillance, but rather active participants who can use surveillance to their own benefit. For example, the ability to rank, rate and review retailers online is seen as democratizing the public sphere and empowering consumers (see Draper, 2012; Hearn, 2010). According to some scholars, by giving users control over what they make visible online—that is, what aspects of their identities and lives they make available for social surveillance—these technologies enable individuals to participate in "empowering exhibitionism" and thereby reclaim "the copyright of their own lives" (Koskela, 2004). For others, the positive effects of social surveillance are evident in the new forms of togetherness and intimacy that it affords (Germann Molz, 2006, 2012). Crawford (2009) notes that following people on Twitter involves mutual practices of disclosure, listening and paying attention that can produce a strong sense of connection, affinity and intimacy in social media settings. In this sense, the decentralized and "fundamentally social" (Albrechstlund, 2008) nature of social surveillance offers new resources for self-expression, for empowerment, and for intimacy and connection among friends and strangers.

On the other hand, many scholars argue that surveillance is always embedded in and productive of asymmetrical relations of power (see Allmer, 2011). Despite the potentially positive effects of social surveillance, critics remain skeptical about the extent to which it empowers individuals in comparison to government or corporate surveillance regimes. For example, Andrejevic's concept of lateral surveillance gestures not only toward the sociable aspects of peer-to-peer surveillance, but also to the ways in which these practices foster "the internalization of government strategies and their deployment in the private sphere" (2005:479). And Allmer (2011:582) draws our attention to the "the vast collection, analysis, and sale of personal data by commercial web platforms such as Google, Facebook, Twitter, YouTube, and Blogger." From this angle, social surveillance is not distinct from, but rather embedded in, the forms of economic surveillance that discipline production, circulation and consumption in the marketplace (ibid.).

Ellerbrok (2010) synthesizes these perspectives by pointing out that online social networks involve multiple levels of social and economic visibility. It is really only at the first level, where people can watch and be watched by friends and strangers on social networking sites, that sociable, intimate and empowering interaction occurs. However, Ellerbrok explains, social surveillance is then situated within broader governmental and economic regimes that expose users to other powerful entities, including regulatory and law-enforcement bodies and marketing interests that collect and aggregate consumer data. Under the guise of sociability and empowerment, "the intimate disclosures of citizens [are] repackaged as profitable data" (Ellerbrok, 2010:217). In other words, forms of surveillance that appear to be empowering at a social level are co-opted by government or corporate interests.

Social surveillance is thus intertwined with economic surveillance in the shape of online feedback and reputation systems, a point that is especially salient as we turn to the "new" sharing economy. Indeed, as we will see, surveillance in the sharing economy resists the binary distinctions that have tended to shape critical debates about surveillance technologies like Facebook and Twitter. Just as these technologies can have both empowering and disempowering effects (Ellerbrok, 2010), so too can they be both social and economic, as well as both hierarchical and decentralized. Interrogating the complex power dynamics of surveillance in the new sharing economy requires us to pay attention to these intersecting dimensions, and a good place to start is with the concept of reputation.

Reputation

According to proponents of the new sharing economy, online exchanges between strangers will increasingly revolve around reputation capital rather than monetary capital. Eventually, they argue, it will be our online reputations rather than cash or credit scores that grant us access to the goods, services and collaborative lifestyles of the sharing economy (Botsman & Rogers, 2010). But what exactly is meant by "reputation" in this context? How are the personal and social aspects of reputation translated into economic value? And how is reputation capital accumulated and circulated through social surveillance?

The term "reputation" is a slippery one with many connotations in various contexts. It can be used to describe not only individuals, but also groups and communities, places, brands, corporations and so on. Here, I focus primarily on individual online reputations, which constitute trustworthiness through a complex amalgam of personal attributes, social networks and attention. Reputation is seen as a reflection of personal qualities such as character, integrity, skills, talent or accomplishments, and of the way such attributes are perceived by others. This means that reputation is also a function of attention.

While reputation has always relied on the aggregation of attention, "the mechanisms for its generation have changed and intensified in recent years," resulting in what Hearn refers to as a "digital reputation" (Hearn, 2010:434). According to Hearn, a digital reputation reflects the depth and intensity of an individual's online social relationships: "the number of times a name comes up in a Google search, an eBay rating as a buyer or seller, the number of friends on Facebook or followers on Twitter" (ibid.:422). In addition to personal attributes and the attention they garner, then, reputation also refers to the extent of one's social network online and the value it can generate both online and offline.

Digital reputation thus has both intrinsic and exchange value. In one sense, the attention an individual attracts on the basis of his or her skills or accomplishments may result in a sense of personal pride. Likewise, having an extensive social network may be an end in itself, providing a sense of belonging or emotional support. However, when an individual is able to channel and validate attention in particular ways, his or her reputation may also produce tangible economic rewards such as job offers, business opportunities or word-of-mouth information about inexpensive housing, childcare or other products and services (Ellison, Steinfield, & Lampe, 2007; Ellerbrok, 2010; Hearn, 2010). In fact, digital reputation is often described in explicitly economic terms as a form of "property" (Blocher, 2009), as something that can be "banked" (Kahn, 2010) or as a type of "capital" or "currency" to "build trust between strangers" (Botsman & Rogers, 2010:224; Ashby & Doctorow, 2011; Cañigueral, 2011). As Kahn (2010:184) puts it, "attention is a scarce resource, and whoever captures it can gain in the reputation economy."

What is significant for establishing trust in the sharing economy, and particularly in the context of collaborative lifestyle sites like Couchsurfing and Airbnb, is the notion that an individual's digital reputation provides a "shadow of the future" (Resnick, Zeckhauser, Friedman, & Kuwabara, 2000). In the absence of personally verified information about an individual's past behaviors, users can look to an individual's online reputation to predict their future trustworthiness (ibid.). Perhaps more important, reputation is not only an indicator of future behavior based on past behavior, but a way of disciplining present behavior in otherwise risky marketplaces (Hearn, 2010; Dellarocas, 2003). Social surveillance in online networking environments encourages people to not only watch, rate or report on others, but also to monitor themselves and their own online reputations. Because each interaction with a friend or stranger online bears the specter of a future review, users engage in self-surveillance as they internalize community norms (Germann Molz, 2006; Marwick, 2012). Indeed, one columnist writing about the sharing economy asks whether the transparency of the internet is making us more honest, suggesting that the best way to be trusted in the sharing economy is to *be* trustworthy (Myers, 2012).

By putting reputation and trust at the center of the sharing economy in this way, collaborative lifestyle sites like Couchsurfing and Airbnb reveal the extent to which online exchanges are shaped in terms of mutual surveillance between participants and a generalized surveillance across the sharing community. In the next section, I explore in more detail the way the Couchsurfing and Airbnb websites and their online reputation systems frame trust and security against an implicit backdrop of surveillance.

Collaborative Surveillance in Hospitality Exchange Sites[2]

In order to understand how Couchsurfing and Airbnb mobilize and normalize a logic of surveillance among their members, it is important to understand the "technologies of trust" each site makes available to its members. The objective behind Couchsurfing and Airbnb is to connect travelers with people willing to host them in various locations (see Germann Molz, 2011). Couchsurfing members offer hospitality to travelers for free, whereas Airbnb guests pay a nominal fee to rent space from their hosts. Both sites boast members in the millions living in nearly 200 countries around the world, and both sites are based on an extensive searchable online network of user profiles where members describe themselves and the type of accommodation they are able to offer in words and photographs. User profiles also display the references members leave for one another after they have met in person. These references and the record of a member's participation in the network comprise an individual's reputation, which serves as the basis for accessing free or cheap accommodation as well as for establishing trust and safety within the community.

Descriptions of these online reputation systems appear on both websites and serve to socialize new users into the proper functioning of the network. These detailed descriptions may also serve as a hedge against some highly publicized breaches of trust. In 2009, a 29-year-old female Couchsurfer from Hong Kong was allegedly raped by her host in the U.K., and in 2011, an Airbnb host in California reported that her home had been robbed and ransacked by a guest booked through the website. In light of these incidents, Couchsurfing and Airbnb emphasize the importance of using the online reputation system carefully to make "good" decisions about whom to host or stay with.

Couchsurfing's reputation system is based on four primary mechanisms. The first is a security feature that simply verifies a user's true name and physical address by processing a small credit card charge. The second feature is a somewhat higher level of verification called vouching. A member can only be vouched for by other members who have already reached this level and whom they have met in person. Once a member receives at least three "vouches," he or she can begin to vouch for other members. Third is a reference system that allows hosts and guests to leave a message describing their experiences with each other. These references indicate how this person has interacted with other Couchsurfers, and members can rate their encounters as "positive," "neutral" or "negative." The fourth feature is the profile, which displays icons confirming whether the member has been verified or vouched for, all of the references left by or for other members, links to the members' friends in the network, and a narrative about their personalities, interests, lifestyles and life philosophies. The template used to produce these profiles prompts members to describe themselves clearly and honestly. After all, according to the website, "honest profiles lead to positive experiences." The information posted on a user's profile helps other members decide whether or not they want to meet this person, so the website urges users to: "Be yourself, and you'll have a better chance of meeting people you'll like." Together, these features establish an individual's reputation within the network.

Airbnb employs a similar set of mechanisms, including detailed profiles with members' full names and verified photos, reviews and references from previous hosts and guests, an online messaging system that also enables voice communication, content moderation, and a trust and safety team that is, according to the Airbnb website, "continuously developing new features and services that make our community safer." Because Airbnb is a for-profit enterprise that allows hosts to rent out their space to paying guests, the site also includes mechanisms for securing financial transactions, such as secure payments, 24/7 customer service, and security deposits as well as a $1 million host guarantee that insures against loss or theft. Like Couchsurfing, Airbnb emphasizes the importance of its reference and reputation system for members' safety: "Trusted reviews are a cornerstone of the Airbnb marketplace."

In the discussion below, I draw primarily on extracts from these safety documents posted on Couchsurfing and Airbnb. These documents are published by site administrators, and thus represent each site's official take on their safety systems. As such, they should be read as idealized depictions of the way technical mechanisms and reputations systems work to establish trust and security within these communities. In the case of Couchsurfing, I also include comments from Couchsurfing members I interviewed during an eight-month ethnographic study of Couchsurfing conducted in 2009. Interview extracts are more reflective of users' lived experiences of negotiating trust and security using these mechanisms. Drawing on these empirical materials, I argue that these hospitality exchange sites reflect an emerging form of "collaborative surveillance" that underpins the sharing economy more broadly. In this context, collaborative surveillance refers to the collective production of online reputations through shared practices of monitoring and reporting (on oneself and others), often in the name of securitizing the community as a whole. In the sections that follow, I detail three important characteristics of collaborative surveillance: (1) it is rhizomatic and amplified, (2) it "responsibilizes" users as members of self-moderating communities and (3) it normalizes surveillance as the basis of encounters and exchanges between strangers.

Rhizomatic and Amplified

As I noted earlier, one of the questions that animates debates about surveillance and new social technologies is whether these technologies have a decentralizing effect.

In contrast to top-down systems of surveillance, new technologies put the tools of surveillance in the hands of the people, allowing them not only to "gaze back" at powerful governmental or corporate entities, but also to watch one another (Mann, Nolan & Wellman, 2003; Leistert, 2012). Instead of thinking about surveillance as centralized or decentralized, however, it might be more accurate to think of collaborative surveillance as rhizomatic and amplified.

In many ways, collaborative surveillance is diffuse. It is not the founders or administrators of Couchsurfing or Airbnb who are watching members, but rather the members themselves—scattered around the world and meeting each other in brief, isolated encounters—who are casting a surveilling gaze upon one another. As each user is tasked with monitoring and reporting on every other user they interact with in the community, these atomized interactions disperse the practice of surveillance throughout the network. Rather than a top-down gaze, reputation systems entail multiple perspectives drawn from across the membership, as the Couchsurfing website's statement on safety emphasizes:

> **A single perspective can't compete with multiple points of view.**
> The Couchsurfing organization is one, but not the only, source of relevant safety information for our community. The announcements, tips, and alerts that we share are a complement to the member-to-member communications that we support through our systems.

Drawing on Deleuze and Guattari's concepts of "assemblages" and "rhizomes," we can understand this multiplicity of perspectives as a kind of "rhizomatic leveling of the hierarchy of surveillance" (Haggerty & Ericson, 2000:607). In contrast to arborescent systems characterized by deep root structures and vertical trunks, rhizomes are plant structures that spread out along the surface, held together by interconnected horizontal root systems. For Haggerty and Ericson, the concept of "rhizomatic surveillance" captures new technological possibilities for the populace to watch and monitor the powerful, however, it also resonates with the emerging forms of mutual social surveillance in online reputation systems.

In addition to spreading out, online reputation systems also re-aggregate, centralize and amplify the information produced through surveillance. Lampe points out that it is difficult to personally evaluate the trustworthiness of each individual in an online community, but "reputation systems leverage the collective work of other users to reduce the costs of evaluation" (2011:78). In this sense, Couchsurfing and Airbnb are as much clearinghouses for surveillance-generated information as they are platforms for connecting hosts and guests. Leveraging the work of individuals, as Lampe put it, these systems aggregate and order information into visible and searchable formats; that is, into individuals' reputations.

At the same time, unlike a spoken rumor that passes from one person to the next, reputation information is amplified as it is broadcast to the entire network. In an interview for Botsman and Rogers's book on collaborative consumption, Couchsurfing founder Casey Fenton explains that disagreements in everyday life are unlikely to tarnish one's reputation because the disagreement is confined to the individuals involved. "But in Couchsurfing somebody cannot just tell one person, but tell everybody about it. So the consequences are vastly different. It means you really have to go the extra mile in the way you interact with people" (cited in Botsman & Rogers, 2010:218). Fenton's comment about going "the extra mile" implies that the specter of the reference shapes one-on-one encounters in specific, ideally positive, ways. Reputation systems thus exercise a disciplining effect on individuals, which leads to a second characteristic of collaborative surveillance: "responsibilization."

Responsibilizing Hosts and Guests

In the context of hospitality exchange networks and reputation systems, the disciplining nature of surveillance takes on a specific tone of "responsibilization" (Andrejevic, 2005). Hospitality exchange networks, and the sharing economy more generally, reflect a climate of risk and responsibility in which individuals are required to take matters of security into their own hands. Instead of *caveat emptor* (buyer beware), the motto for the sharing economy might be *caveat socius* (sharer beware). The message is that dealing with strangers is risky, but the new technologies of trust at our disposal, if used properly, will mitigate that risk (Germann Molz, 2007). This message aligns with broader strategies for shifting duties of surveillance and security onto individuals, strategies that Andrejevic argues are associated with neoliberal forms of governance that address risk in both public and intimate realms. According to Andrejevic, what we end up with is "the need to enlist monitoring strategies as a means of taking responsibility for one's own security in networked communications environments in which people are not always what they seem" (2005:481). In Couchsurfing and Airbnb, individuals are made responsible for their own behavior as a host or guest in the hospitality encounter, of course, but also for using online information to make "good" decisions about whom to host or stay with and for actively contributing to the site's surveillance systems to make the community a safer place for everyone.

The refrain of empowering individual decision making is common on both sites, where reputation systems are framed as decision machines. Under a headline stating that "Your safety is our most important feature," the Airbnb website explains that: "We're committed to building a trusted, collaborative marketplace. That's why we've built best-in-class tools and services to help you make the right decisions."

Among the features listed are a set of "Reputation and Research Tools" that enable users to see a guest's full name, to view verified photos of the space being rented and to search references left by and about other members. The tagline that accompanies these features reads: "Know before you go. These tools are designed to help you make safe, informed decisions on Airbnb." Airbnb lays responsibility squarely on the individual's ability to read and interpret online reputational information.

The Couchsurfing website similarly positions users as decision makers, suggesting obliquely that surveillance produces the necessary information for making those decisions. Couchsurfing claims that:

> **We empower people to make the most informed decisions possible.**
> Couchsurfing members are active participants in the safety of our community. By sharing information through our systems, educating themselves about trust and safety, and making careful decisions about who to meet, Couchsurfers keep themselves and everyone else safer.

Sharing information, both in terms of self-disclosure on one's profile and through references about other members, is presented as a crucial decision-making resource.

Like Airbnb, the Couchsurfing website conflates reputation and decision making under the explicit rubric of safety, but also under an implicit logic of surveillance. Both sites define themselves as self-moderating communities in which members are also responsible for securing the safety of the community as a whole, which is achieved through surveillance between members. According to Lampe, reputation systems "can provide the feedback necessary to assist in the governance of online communities" by "socializing new members and sanctioning normative behavior" (2011:77, 85). Although guidelines for use and safety are posted on the Couchsurfing and Airbnb websites, members themselves are tasked with the responsibility of socializing and sanctioning one another via reputation systems. For example, after hosting or staying with another member, Couchsurfers are strongly encouraged to:

> **Leave a reference to help strengthen our community**
> The safety of our community depends on every member contributing to our trust systems. After spending time with your Couchsurfer, be sure to leave a reference describing your experience. Your perspective will help other members make informed decisions and have positive interactions with each other.

In this statement and throughout the website, there is an emphasis on the self-governing and self-policing nature of the community: "We're a self moderating community, which means we work like a neighborhood watch program: we keep each other safe." Here, reputation systems are analogous to neighborhood watch programs, where a sense of safety emerges through a regime of interpersonal surveillance.

In my interviews with Couchsurfers, I found that this responsibility to keep each other safe is often internalized by users. This was evident in an interview with Therese, a Couchsurfer in her twenties from Canada. She explained that although her Couchsurfing encounters have been almost entirely positive, she experienced an uncomfortable incident in which one of her hosts, a single man, made sexual innuendoes during her stay. Initially, because her host had made no physical advances, Therese left a positive reference for him. Later, after seeing a discussion on the Couchsurfing website about a Couchsurfer being raped, she decided to revise her reference for the sake of the community's overall safety:

> That [report of the rape] was kind of an occasion to start to remind people of the need to be honest in their references....And I realized that...I avoided being honest. It was an uncomfortable situation, but this individual didn't ever harm me or even touch me, but because he kept choosing to focus on sexual topics...I was very uncomfortable that night....I chose [to leave a] positive [reference]....I wanted to acknowledge that he put me up last minute and made me a nice breakfast. Yet it was nagging me....I don't think it was appropriate the way he acted and I wouldn't want another girl to stay with him alone like I did....So I went back and I left neutral...[and] I explained in detail why it was neutral.

Therese's comments underscore her sense of obligation to accurately reflect her experience with this host, but also her sense of responsibility to other female Couchsurfers and to the Couchsurfing community. In other words, what Therese describes here is her sense of obligation to be both an object and an agent of surveillance, which brings us to the third characteristic of collaborative surveillance: normalization.

Normalizing Surveillance

Reputation systems can certainly be used to sanction normative behavior and govern online communities, as Lampe (2011) suggests. As we see above, members use the reference system to police the limits of sexual behavior, and throughout the site a range of normative codes of host-guest behavior are policed through references. For example, did the guest bring a small gift, help with the dishes or smoke in the house? Did the host make the guest feel welcome, set rigid schedules, keep the dog under control? These norms may be fluid and contested, but feedback left in references lets members know what these community norms are and how well they have adhered to them. Beyond governing normative behavior, however, these reputation systems also normalize and sanction the act of surveillance itself. The expectation that members will not only self-disclose, but also monitor and report on one another is a premise of the trust and security of the community. In other words, a self-governing community of "responsibilized" individuals presumes a more generalized norm of social and self-surveillance.

This normalization of surveillance is evident in a question posted to Couchsurfing's safety and disputes team. A Couchsurfer writes to ask for advice about whether to leave a neutral rating for an experience that wasn't necessarily good (e.g., the guests didn't pick up after themselves), because she is worried that the other member will retaliate by posting something negative about her in return. The Couchsurfing administrator replies:

> References are really important. Leaving one could help someone else make a more informed decision—and this is true even when the experience wasn't a total disaster....I understand that you're concerned about maybe getting a neutral or negative reference back....However, if you do get one, it's important not to let yourself feel like it's the worst thing in the world....If members see that you have a negative reference, they'll read it to see what it says. And that means they see both what you and the other member wrote....A reference says as much about you as it does the person you leave the reference for, so just keep it classy.[3]

The member's concern and the administrator's response both valorize the practice of surveillance: "References are really important." Moreover, the very act of surveillance (reporting on the bad behavior of another member) becomes normalized as an *object* of surveillance. In other words, the reference itself becomes a basis for judging the person who writes it. In order to participate properly in the network, the concerned Couchsurfer is not only required to surveil and report on others, she is also required to monitor her own skills of (self-)surveillance by submitting an honest and "classy" report.

It is striking that this member's concerns focus primarily on doing social surveillance "correctly" rather than on any negative implications of self-surveillance and interpersonal monitoring. Part of the normalizing effect we see here may be attributed to the encapsulating consequences of online networks more generally, where people tend to interact with like-minded individuals who reinforce rather than challenge accepted views of the group. Many of the Couchsurfers I interviewed described Couchsurfing as a community of like-minded strangers who were similarly flexible, open-minded, trusting and trustworthy. Because of these shared values, they saw the community itself as generally trustworthy. In this sense, sharing economy websites like Couchsurfing are not really connecting members to "complete strangers," but to "kindred spirits" who share their interests, viewpoints and life philosophies. In fact, online communities are often described as "echo chambers," where similar values are mirrored back to members. In this case, the value of surveillance and its conflation with trust and the securitization of the community as a whole is taken almost entirely for granted.

Although the word "surveillance" never appears in the safety documentation on Couchsurfing or Airbnb, exhortations to leave "authentic" references, follow-up emails that prompt members to report on one another and statements linking safety directly to the sharing of information about oneself and other members all extend a logic of surveillance into hospitality encounters between strangers. Couchsurfers often internalize this logic, willingly offering up photographs and detailed information about themselves, monitoring and reporting on other members, and using the reputation system to provide data and make informed decisions. In this sense, collaborative surveillance is part of a more general "surveillancization" of social relations.

We see this trend in social networking sites like Facebook and Twitter where friends are encouraged to update, follow and monitor one another as a way of being together online (Germann Molz, 2012). As Marwick notes, in social media contexts:

> Individuals strategically reveal, disclose and conceal personal information to create connections with others and tend social boundaries. These processes are normal parts of day-to-day life in communities that are highly connected through social media. (Marwick, 2012:391)

We also see this trend in the ranking and rating systems that online marketplaces like Amazon and eBay have now made commonplace. Through reputation systems, where individuals monitor and report on one another and on themselves, the sharing economy combines these social and economic dimensions of interpersonal surveillance, rationalizing surveillance through a discourse of trust and togetherness.

Conclusion

Through the new sharing economy and online reputation systems, we see how interpersonal surveillance becomes woven into the fabric of social and economic relations, underpinning new ways of being, exchanging and interacting with friends, neighbors and strangers. Reputation systems capitalize, quite literally, on this conflation between surveillance and sociality by translating social interactions into exchange value that provides access to shared goods, experiences and lifestyles. Embedded in a rhetoric of trust and reputation, surveillance among peers becomes an ever more normal and valuable aspect of the sharing economy. Trust is held up as a "good thing" that lubricates the gears of sharing and trading; as conduits of trust, surveillance and reputation systems enjoy a kind of transitive valorization.

In many ways, collaborative surveillance may be seen as part of a wider resistance against the top-down surveillance regimes of state and corporate power or against the isolating consequences of corporate capitalism and hyperconsumption.

Its democratizing effects are evident in its rhizomatic structure. Collaborative surveillance disperses the responsibilities, but also the rewards of participating in a self-moderating community of social and economic exchange. In the case of Couchsurfing and Airbnb, for example, interpersonal monitoring is the basis for convivial encounters among strangers that many members describe as deeply meaningful and fulfilling (Germann Molz, 2012). However, critical surveillance scholars might remind us to weigh the transgressive potential of the sharing economy against the power asymmetries embedded in systems of surveillance. Although the sharing economy is often touted as an alternative to corporate consumerism or as an empowering resistance, its reliance on surveillance (however implicit) should alert us to questions of power. To what extent do these social surveillance regimes empower people to share on more equal terms in a new marketplace? And who is excluded or marginalized from these collaborative marketplaces? When participants in the sharing economy are "responsibilized" and tasked with the safety of the community as a whole, who is relieved of responsibility? Finally, we might also ask what other forms of visibility or exposure reputation systems entail. In this sense, Ellerbrok's (2010) argument that new technologies of surveillance entail multiple forms of visibility brings our attention to the possibility that what we *can* see online—strangers meeting and sharing with one another based on references, ratings, reviews and reputations—belies what we *can't* see—the various ways in which data is aggregated, ordered, packaged and mined and for whose purposes and whose profit. These are the questions that a critical approach to surveillance and new media will help us address as the sharing economy transforms social and economic interactions among strangers.

Notes

1. The names of Couchsurfing members have been changed.
2. Extracts from Couchsurfing.org and Airbnb.com were collected in July 2012 from www.couchsurfing.org/safety and from www.airbnb.com/safety, respectively. Since then, the content of both websites has undergone revision, however the underlying themes described here remain apparent.
3. Cited from http://beta.couchsurfing.org/news/safety/taken-advantage-of/, site accessed 12 July 2012.

References

Albrechtslund, A. (2008). Online social networking as participatory surveillance. *First Monday*, *13*(3). http://firstmonday.org/article/view/2142/1949

Allmer, T. (2011). Critical surveillance studies in the information society. *tripleC: Communication, Capitalism & Critique. Open Access Journal for a Global Sustainable Information Society*, *9*, 566–592.

Andrejevic, M. (2005). The work of watching one another: Lateral surveillance, risk, and governance. *Surveillance & Society, 2*, 479–497.

Ashby, M., & Doctorow, C. (2011). "I hope you know this is going on your permanent record." In H. Masum & M. Tovey (Eds.), *The reputation society: How online opinions are reshaping the offline world* (pp. 195–204). Cambridge, MA: MIT Press.

Blocher, J. (2009, January). Reputation as property in virtual economies. *Yale Law Journal Pocket Part 120*. http://yalelawjournal.org/the-yale-law-journal-pocket-part/property-law/reputation-as-property-in-virtual-economies/

Botsman, R., & Rogers, R. (2010). *What's mine is yours: The rise of collaborative consumption.* New York: HarperCollins.

Cañigueral, A. (2011). Can I trust you really?: The reputation currency. Blog entry posted on Shareable.net. http://www.shareable.net/blog/can-i-trust-you-really-the-reputation-currency-0

Crawford, K. (2009). Following you: Disciplines of listening in social media. *Journal of Media & Cultural Studies, 23*, 525–535.

Dellarocas, C. (2003). The digitization of word of mouth: Promise and challenges of online feedback mechanisms. *Management Science, 49*, 1407–1424.

Draper, N. (2012). Group power: Discourses of consumer power and surveillance in group buying websites. *Surveillance & Society, 9,* 394–407.

Ellerbrok, A. (2010). Empowerment: Analysing technologies of multiple variable visibility. *Surveillance & Society, 8*, 200–220.

Ellison, N. B., Steinfield, C., & Lampe, C. (2007). The benefits of Facebook "friends": Social capital and college students' use of online social network sites. *Journal of Computer-Mediated Communication, 12*(4). http://jcmc.indiana.edu/vol12/issue4/ellison.html

Germann Molz, J. (2012). *Travel connections: Tourism, technology and togetherness in a mobile world.* New York & London: Routledge.

Germann Molz, J. (2011). Editorial. Couchsurfing and network hospitality: "It's not just about the furniture." *Hospitality & Society, 1*, 215–225.

Germann Molz, J. (2007). Cosmopolitans on the couch: Mobile hospitality and the internet. In J. Germann Molz & S. Gibson (Eds.), *Mobilizing hospitality: The ethics of social relations in a mobile world* (pp. 65–80). Aldershot: Ashgate.

Germann Molz, J. (2006). "Watch us wander": Mobile surveillance and the surveillance of mobility. *Environment and Planning A, 38,* 377–393.

Haggerty, K. D., & Ericson, R. V. (2000). The surveillant assemblage. *British Journal of Sociology, 51*(4), 605–622.

Hearn, A. (2010). Structuring feeling: Web 2.0, online ranking and rating, and the digital "reputation" economy. *ephemera: theory & politics in organization, 10*, 421–438.

Kahn, D. H. (2010). Social intermediaries: Creating a more responsible web through portable identity, cross-web reputation, and code-backed norms. *Columbia Science and Technology Law Review, XII*, 176–242. http://www.stlr.org/cite.cgi?volume=11&article=7

Kamenetz, A. (2011, March). The case for generosity. *Fast Company, 153*, 52–54.

Koskela, H. (2004). Webcams, TV shows and mobile phones: Empowering exhibitionism. *Surveillance & Society, 2*, 199–215.

Lampe, C. (2011). The role of reputation systems in managing online communities. In H. Masum & M. Tovey (Eds.), *The reputation society: How online opinions are reshaping the offline world* (pp. 77–88). Cambridge, MA: MIT Press.

Leistert, O. (2012). Resistance against cyber-surveillance within social movements and how surveillance adapts. *Surveillance & Society, 9,* 441–456.

Mann, S., Nolan, J., & Wellman, B. (2003). Sousveillance: Inventing and using wearable computing devices for data collection in surveillance environments. *Surveillance & Society, 1,* 331–355.

Marwick, A. (2012). The public domain: Surveillance in everyday life. *Surveillance & Society, 9,* 378–393.

Myers, C. (2012, April). Living in the sharing economy: Is the internet making us more honest? Blog entry posted on thenextweb.com. http://thenextweb.com/insider/2012/04/14/living-in-the-sharing-economy-is-the-internet-making-us-more-honest/

Resnick, P., Zeckhauser, R., Friedman, E., & Kuwabara, K. (2000). Reputation systems. *Communications of the ACM, 43,* 45–48.

Sacks, D. (2011, May). The sharing economy. *Fast Company, 155,* 88–93.

Tokunaga, R. (2011). Social networking site or social surveillance site? Understanding the use of interpersonal electronic surveillance in romantic relationships. *Computers in Human Behavior, 27,* 705–713.

8

Textures of Interveillance

A Socio-Material Approach to the Appropriation of Transmedia Technologies in Domestic Life

André Jansson

Introduction: "What Are All Others Doing Right Now?"

The opening question is taken from an advertising campaign in early 2012 for the new Nokia Lumia 800 smartphone. The blue phone presented in the advert displays small photographic icons of young people in social situations: smiling faces, posing in front of the camera. A young man is captured when thrown into a swimming pool. The selling point is the mobile's function as a technology for social coordination and monitoring; speaking to the core of what David Riesman (1950/2001) once termed the "other-directed self." Allegedly, what is most important to the target group is to keep track of the activities and appearances of friends and acquaintances via embedded tools such as text/image messaging and Facebook.

The Nokia advertisement not only resonates with general sociological diagnoses of an increasingly narcissistic and socially anxious society. It also resonates with the results of recent studies on what contemporary networked ("social") media are most frequently used for, namely for entertaining social trust and close ties within pre-existing peer groups, and for maintaining one's position within such constellations (e.g., Ellison, Steinfield, & Lampe, 2010; Humphreys, 2011; Germann Molz, 2012). In short, people's intensified need to know what others are doing and thinking is paired with a willingness, or a felt need, to share information about themselves and having their lifestyles socially confirmed. These expectations on mutual social disclosure within, and sometimes beyond, peer groups, generate a para-doxical state of monitoring, where social sharing (and caring) becomes more or less inseparable from narcissistic behavior, and also bound up with commercial forces of interactive surveillance (Andrejevic, 2007).

This is what I refer to as an expanding culture of "interveillance" (Jansson, 2012)—a cultural condition where identity creation, expressivity and mediated peer-to-peer monitoring come together. In late modern societies, interveillance, and the media applied, have become a routinized means (amongst others) for maintaining a sense of ontological security (Giddens, 1991).

This development can be analyzed and understood at different levels, and in relation to various types of structural change. Besides the transitional processes related to new technological affordances as such, one must also take into account changes in the institutional logics of modern surveillance, associated with decentered, increasingly ambiguous structures of data gathering and observation (Haggerty & Ericson, 2000), as well as broader meta-processes such as individualization (Giddens, 1991; Beck & Beck-Gernsheim, 2002) and commercialization (particularly of information) (Gandy, 1993; Fuchs, 2012). Interactive platforms such as Facebook epitomize the prevalence of interveillance, both through their social pervasiveness, and through their mode of profit making (van Dijck, 2012). The focus of this chapter is on the former aspect. My ambition is to provide a deeper understanding of how interveillance plays into the social construction of new media platforms as indispensable technologies. I am particularly interested in the moral structures through which these technologies, including their expanding affordances as social monitoring tools, are legitimized, and what type of textures those technological appropriations sustain. Texture, which stands at the center of my socio-material approach, refers to the "communicative fabric" of space (Jansson, 2007), that is, the meaningful and felt structure of communicative resources and processes in everyday life. In addition, my analysis brings together two key concepts. First, through the concept of "moral economy" (Silverstone, Hirsch, & Morley, 1992), I explore the ways in which interveillance, seen as a socially negotiated need, drives the appropriation of new technologies in ordinary households. Second, through the concept of "moral geography" (Cresswell, 2006), I further assess how spatial values, notably attitudes to geographical mobility, saturate the shaping of textures of interveillance.

Studies of mediated networking, surveillance and community making have often attained a focus on certain media platforms and/or particularly active users, thus failing to grasp how broader movements of social transformation are produced. Therefore, my empirical focus here is on the "average consumer": the majority of "not-so-early" adopters. More specifically, my analysis is based on qualitative interviews carried out in Swedish small-town settings among a diversified sample of middle-class households. The life trajectories of my interviewees are marked by an enduring (intergenerational) tendency for upward socio-economic mobility, paired with relatively low levels of geographical mobility and strong attachments to the home region.

The results actualize a strong resonance between sedentarist values and extensive media appropriation. In the context of this study, networked media platforms—most significantly, the mobile (smart) phone—operate by and large as a social stabilizer, a means of fixity. This means that interveillance—and thus, the general complicity with systemic structures of surveillance (see Christensen, Chapter 1 of this volume)—becomes socially integrated and legitimized, foremost through community building processes in the local context (the family project, engagement in various organizations, and so on). The chapter contains two analytical parts. In the first part, I discuss the general significance of interveillance as a socio-material regime, saturating everyday life through mediated practices. In the second part, I narrow down the focus, analyzing the mediating role of moral economies and moral geographies in texturation processes, that is, in the (re)production of textures through communicative and spatial practices. Before turning to the analytical parts, however, I will briefly outline the study.

The Study

The forthcoming analyses and discussions are grounded in empirical fieldwork conducted within the research project "Secure Spaces: Media, Consumption and Social Surveillance" (Karlstad University, Sweden).[1] An important aim of the project was to provide deeper knowledge of how various media forms are socially integrated as private means of surveillance and social control, and how such patterns are related to structural conditions (notably in terms of socio-economic factors), as well as cultural mechanisms at the level of everyday life. Empirically, the project gathered data from both a national survey and qualitative interviews conducted in different social settings. In the survey we asked questions about people's perceptions of privacy threats related to different media (see Jansson, 2012), as well as the social functions of various media. The qualitative interviews dealt with a similar problem area, but covered a much broader social terrain, giving more nuanced understandings of social backgrounds, lifestyles and the environments of everyday life. A total of 40 interviews were carried out in three social settings, representing different positionalities, trajectories and mobilities in social as well as geographical space: (1) young Turkish migrants in the greater Stockholm area, (2) globally mobile people in the inner city of Stockholm and (3) locally rooted individuals in Swedish small-town settings.

As already mentioned, this chapter applies material from the third category of informants, in order to capture the social role of new media and surveillance/interveillance in relatively stable, and presumably more sedentarist, social environments. The sample consists of 12 interviews, carried out in the towns of Mariestad (ten interviews) and Karlstad (two interviews) from November 2010 to February 2011.[2] There are an equal number of male and female informants in the sample, ages 26 to 63 years. They also represent different household circumstances, meaning that five of the informants had children living at home, and two informants lived in single households. The rest were cohabiting couples without children, or grown-up children. Most informants lived in privately owned houses, except for the two informants in Karlstad, who rented apartments.

Socio-economically, the sample was constructed to represent typically middle-class conditions, which means that the majority of the interviewees had white-collar jobs (banking, sales administration, teaching, social work, etc.), but was not in any leading or executive positions (with one exception). The level of education can best be described as intermediary, with limited representation of university studies or completed degrees. This is also reflected in the interviewees' overall lifestyle patterns, which were oriented towards family life, home improvement, gardening, sports, media entertainment and social events in the local context, rather than more intellectual or artistic interests. What is also striking about the sample is that all informants were born and raised in the town where they lived and worked at the time of the interview (or in its vicinities). None of them had any concrete intention of moving somewhere else. As we will see, the latter circumstances, which unite the individuals of the sample, provide an important backdrop to our analysis of mediated interveillance.

Interveillance as a Socio-Material Regime

I will begin this analysis by clarifying what interveillance means, and how it is both different from, and thoroughly integrated with more systemic forces of surveillance, especially commercially driven online surveillance. My key point is that interveillance is to be understood as an expanding "socio-material regime" through which human needs for social recognition and control are at once re-articulated and subsumed within technologized conditions of "complicit surveillance" (Christensen, Chapter 1 of this volume, 2012, 2011; Christensen & Jansson, forthcoming).[3] It is a "regime" in the sense that it provides a certain normalized framework of opportunities and limitations as to what forms of human association and identity making are socially and materially sanctioned. As such, at the practical level, interveillance not only involves the peer-to-peer monitoring associated with mobile communication (text messaging, etc.), online sharing and exchange of information via various platforms, but also processes of self-monitoring and expressivity, notably via the management of individual profiles online, and associated engagement with various kinds of social simulacra ("personalized" publicity offers, recommended "friends" and events, etc.) based on interactively generated data (e.g., Andrejevic, 2007; van Dijck, 2012).

Interveillance is thus a concept that provides a more complex understanding of the everyday socio-material embeddedness of mediated monitoring than more technologically and institutionally defined concepts such as "lateral surveillance" (referring to the structural spreading of panoptic forces in social life) (Andrejevic, 2005) and "participatory surveillance" (referring to the playful, potentially empowering aspects of surveillance practices through social media) (Albrechtslund, 2008). My definition of interveillance has much in common with Marwick's (2012) notion of "social surveillance," highlighting the reciprocity between social actors in general, and users of social media sites in particular. Speaking of interveillance, as opposed to surveillance, however, underscores that we are dealing with a phenomenon based on, in principle, non-hierarchical and non-systematic forms of data collation and observation. This is not to deny that power flows through all social relationships (ibid.:382), nor that interveillance is bound up with structural (notably commercial) dynamics of surveillance. Taking interveillance as the analytical starting point, however, is to critically consider the open-ended character of contemporary media circulation, as well as the multilayeredness of identity, implying that every subject is positioned in relation to a number of intertwined power structures.

Identity, Reflexivity and Morality

A number of international studies have concluded that people commonly handle mediated surveillance in a pragmatic manner, sometimes even with indifference. Three positions are often instanced. First, people tend to accept a certain level of surveillance, as a "price worth paying," as long as certain benefits can be expected (e.g., Kim, 2004). A typical example is commercial surveillance via smartcards, loyalty cards, and so forth, which is understood as a means for receiving more personalized offers and better deals as a consumer (see also Zurawski, Chapter 2 of this volume). Second, it is a widespread opinion that surveillance, for example CCTV-systems in public spaces, or geographical tracking of mobile phones, is important for public security reasons. Thus, if one has "nothing to hide," one should not worry (e.g., Best, 2010). Third, surveillance, notably in online contexts, is often understood as being too complicated and abstract to grasp, and thus one should worry as little as possible (e.g., Taddicken, 2012). Altogether, these positions reflect a general mode of complicit surveillance (Christensen, 2011)—which means that surveillance is not merely accepted as an external force, but also understood and legitimized as an integral part of social life. In some contexts, it is even perceived as a means of empowerment and pleasure (e.g., Albrechtslund, 2008).

In the present study there are many similar examples. Surveillance is rarely seen as problematic at the systemic level, but rather as a means to certain ends; improved security, customer services, personalized information and so forth. What is perceived as a greater threat to privacy, however, is the circulation of private information among social actors themselves, notably via digital media. This brings us directly into the realm of interveillance, where media technologies and their affordances are typically thought of in a matter-of-fact way, leaving a great deal of responsibility to the individual for managing his/her privacy:

> All of us have places where we want to be in peace and quiet without being monitored, to which we can withdraw and put on our headphones and listen to music without thinking about anything else. It's the same thing with the internet. But there I think it's up to each and every one....I mean the media *do exist*. You can do anything today, but you have to protect yourself and share only what you think you can share. So privacy is important. But there are many, especially younger people, who don't understand that. But then if I'm in town, being surveilled by a camera, which doesn't bother me. If you have nothing to hide, you don't have to think about it. But you should still have some kind of shelter if you want to be in private. (42-year-old salesman and family father)

> *Q:* What do you think about the development of private information on the internet?

> *R:* I don't know....There will always be exhibitionists, I guess. [laughter] Hopefully one can teach one's children good manners and common sense. But I believe that each generation to come will have a better knowledge of how things work out there. But people love to expose themselves, so it will at least be on the level we see today, that's what I think. (26-year-old factory worker, union representative, and father)

These attitudes resonate with results from our survey, suggesting that online circulation opens up, and necessitates, a new mode of everyday reflexivity. This is particularly obvious among the younger population using social media on a day-to-day basis. The survey also shows that persons with left-wing political orientation, especially women working in the cultural or social sectors, are relatively more concerned with privacy risks associated with social media and online circulation (Jansson, 2012; see also Fuchs, 2010). Our small-town interviews (which did not include young people) provide a nuanced picture, showing that most concerns refer to "others," especially children, young people and "exhibitionists" rather than to themselves. Furthermore, there is little inclination to associate interveillance with structural forces, or to discuss systemic responsibility. Rather, the current development of the media landscape is taken as an unstoppable force, and the solution to its potential harmfulness to privacy becomes a matter of individual responsibility, learning and "common sense" (see Barnard-Wills, Chapter 9 of this volume).

Altogether, these empirical observations illuminate the socio-material nature of interveillance. They also point to something of a paradox. On the one hand, the expansion and convergence of various digital platforms, which today (in broadly modernized, "connected" societies) leave more or less nobody unaffected, call for everyday reflexivity and refined management of information, which sometimes collapse into anxiety. On the other hand, such reflexivities are bound up with the very processes of identity (re)creation that mediated communication and sharing are ultimately all about, and thus increasingly turned into a routinized part of social life. This is to say that interveillance is a double-edged sword: an ongoing process of mediation, grounded in the social need for ontological security (at the intersection of subjective autonomy and social integration), always involving the risk of generating opposite consequences.

Most of our informants—even those who were not themselves especially involved in online circulation—could relate to the dual implications of interveillance in one way or another. Among the most frequent users of Facebook we could identify high levels of "literacy," reflected in more advanced forms of management (through adjusted privacy settings, blockings, etc.) for keeping appropriate information within their peer groups. In most cases, however, Facebook attained the status of a routinized, low-level-involvement channel used simply for keeping an eye on what family and friends were doing:

> I don't use the internet very much. Mostly it's for checking Facebook and a little bit of Aftonbladet [news service] and checking email. So it's not very much time....When it comes to Facebook I use it mainly to see if somebody has written something funny, so it takes just two minutes before I log out if nobody has written anything to me....It's been nice to find old friends and classmates and so on there [on Facebook]. That's the best function; that it's possible to check out what they are doing. It might mean that one has a chat at some point, but then probably not much more. (28-year-old male shop assistant)

In several interviews, there was also evidence of how the routinized "checking" of others is bound up with self-monitoring and social discipline. One example is the monitoring of whether/how one is exposed by friends, for example, through tags and images. Under certain conditions, "bad exposure" might even become a reminder of the moral premises of social integration:

> When I was drunk the very last time....Then I went on Facebook the day after and discovered that "no, hell, now I'm up there." I was standing there with my girlfriend's sister,

and it was nothing bad really about the picture, but at that point it was like . . . "that's how it was . . ." Like a reminder. But I've kept that picture on Facebook, so now I can look at it there and see "that's how stupid I am when I'm drunk, and I will never be that again" [laughter]. (26-year-old factory worker, union representative, and father)

This leads us back to the core ambiguity of interveillance. When integrated as a routinized part of the lifestyle, interveillance contributes to the stability of everyday life and the confirmation of pre-established social constellations and moral frameworks. In our interviews, this was expressed foremost as a desire to preserve those social and moral constellations that defined the individuals' bonds to the local setting, such as family relations and childhood friends. Similarly, other scholars have pointed out that much communication occurring in the realm of social media is akin to phatic communication (Miller, 2008), whose function is primarily to keep social and normative structures in place. Blending with phatic communication, then, interveillance most often appears as "common practice," not causing any deeper moral considerations. One woman explicitly stated, in relation to the circulation of private images, that she actively tried "to see to the positive sides of it, rather than the negative," keeping in mind that "people are basically good." At the same time, however, precisely because of its moral underpinning (which is relative to socio-cultural context), there are certain, most often mutual, understandings of when the boundaries of privacy, comfort and security are broken. Risk can thus not be totally eliminated.

Interveillance and the Texturation of Households

As indicated above, our understanding of interveillance must take into account material as well as social forces. The concept of texture provides exactly this bridge between the material and the social. On the one hand, it points to how various, regularly appearing symbolic and spatial processes materialize into more or less solid, structuring patterns of everyday life, and on the other, to how material resources and their spatial organization are given symbolic, communicative qualities through social practice. Texture can be understood as a weave, or a fabric, with a particular pattern and a particular material feel. Patterns and qualities can be altered, as we will see, but only successively, since there are certain social and material logics as to how textures are composed and what "goes with what."

The evolving status of interveillance as a regime for moral communion, associated with mediated recognition, coincides with the social construction of digital media technologies as "indispensable possessions." In our sample, even though many informants held that they were not particularly interested in new technology, the basic level of media possession was high. In households with more than one person, it was common to have several television sets, computers and mobile phones—even though these digital technologies often pass through a descending trajectory of functionality and eventually reach a state of total obsolescence (Löfgren, 2009). When asked about which media possession they considered most indispensable, most informants singled out their mobile (smart)phone because of its mobility and diverse affordances. These conditions highlight an ongoing "textural transformation" of contemporary households—seen as a shift from "mass-media textures" (with the television set placed at the social and spatial center) to "transmedia textures" (with smartphones and laptops taking center stage as communicative nodes) (Jansson, forthcoming). This shift both modifies pre-existing modes of social interaction and implies the naturalization of new, more assemblage-like (Haggerty & Ericson, 2000), technological architectures, which inevitably link media users to the systemic level of surveillance (Andrejevic, 2007; Trottier & Lyon, 2012).

Interveillance is not a direct function of transmedia textures, however. In a longer historical perspective, (mediated) interveillance emerges as a socially motivated response to life conditions marked by individualization, "other-directedness" (Riesman, 1950/2001) and the "pluralization of lifeworlds" (Berger, Berger, & Kellner, 1973). It (re)articulates and (re)mediates human desires for social integration, control and security. Indeed, many new media technologies, when socially appropriated and positioned between the "I" and the "world" (see Ihde, 1990: Chapter 5), have played a significant role for sustaining the continuity of basic community forms, such as family and kinship. For example, the social role of television as a "gathering place" (Adams, 1992), a coordination tool and a mediator of family relations and values has been well documented in media and cultural studies over the years (e.g., Lull, 1990; Morley, 1992). Similarly, scholars such as Ling (2008) have more recently pointed out that mobile telephones contribute to the maintenance of social cohesion and close bonds, especially within households. Interveillance is thus not a singular phenomenon operating through just a few channels such as the social networking sites referred to in the previous section. Rather, there are various media technologies involved, as well as various modes of expressivity and control, altogether creating different textural formations.

Furthermore, the textures that tie individual subjects together (symbolically and materially) are culturally and morally molded. Studies from different parts of the world show, for example, that notions of privacy as well as direct everyday expressions of mediated monitoring between spouses may look very different in different cultural settings (see, for example, studies from Ethiopia [Kenaw, 2012] and Germany [Linke, 2011]). Moral variations are also to be found at more fine-grained levels of analysis—and such variations, one might expect, become more accentuated in the era of transmedia textures, due to the broadened scope of technological affordances.

This is to say that media technologies attain a dual relationship to morality. First, as with all private technologies, their appropriation and incorporation in everyday life are regulated through the moral economy of the household (Silverstone et al., 1992). This means that both materialities and modes of use are saturated with economic processes of transaction and value transformation, which, in turn depend on, and express, the moral underpinnings of the domestic community. Second, in contrast to other technologies, the media (through communicative practice) hold a key function in the (re)production and negotiation of moral structures themselves. These negotiations occur through both mediated interpersonal communication and engagement with mass distributed and shared media content. However, as Silverstone and colleagues (1992) point out, the social dynamics between household spaces and media spaces are far from frictionless:

> Information and communication technologies make the project of creating ontological security particularly problematic, for media disengage the location of action and meaning from experience, and at the same time (and through the same displaced spaces) claim action and meaning for the modern world system of capitalist social and economic (and moral) relations. Indeed, the media poses a whole set of control problems for the household, problems of regulation and of boundary maintenance. (Silverstone et al., 1992:20)

This volatility, related to the potential intrusion of "strangers" and antagonistic worldviews within the household, has been broadly discussed in relation to broadcasting (e.g., Morley, 2000). Under conditions of mobile, individualized transmedia technologies, which may cause further disintegration of previously closely knit communities, these challenges of moral boundary maintenance and control are bound to become even more critical. However, as already mentioned, empirical evidence tells us a more complex story, suggesting that contemporary transmedia textures, notably by means of their fluid nature, also reinforce social cohesion and control.

Accordingly, the moral economy of the household must to a greater extent account for the potential conflict between fluidity and fixity, between mobile life conditions and the stability of (home) place. Such concerns, the morality of spatial relations, are not new, as Cresswell (2006) argues, but are enmeshed within more foundational "moral geographies" of modernity. In Cresswell's view, spatial values are generally structured around either the metaphysics of flow (nomadism), celebrating spatial flexibility, openness and mobile life forms, or the metaphysics of fixity (sedentarism), seeing rootedness and spatial durability as key to social sustainability. I argue that these foundational value orientations have become increasingly significant to our understanding of people's appropriations and uses of new media forms in general and interveillance affordances in particular. First, moral geographies saturate, as one of several dimensions, the moral economy of households at a general level, and thus have an impact on the everyday processes of texturation. Second, they hold a more particular impetus with regards to the socio-material management of interveillance, which is directly linked to the question of ephemeral flows of information and culture versus boundary maintenance and moral containment. In the forthcoming sections, these two points are analyzed in turn, based on the case study from Sweden.

Materialities and Boundaries of the Comfort Zone

As to the first point, from a general perspective it can be argued that many households today are marked by the overabundance of media technologies, involving more or less obsolete objects, as well as new objects with a surplus of functions. In the present study, many informants spoke of telephones they could not fully master, and old television sets and computers that were still around in the household, occupying more restricted areas of use (such as children's gaming). Such "devalued" technologies also tended to occupy more marginal spaces in the home, whereas the main television sets (flat-screens) were centrally placed, and mobile phones were described as more or less indispensable. What these "key media" have in common and what obviously makes them more indispensable than others is that they contribute to the reproduction of the household (regardless of its composition) as a social comfort zone. The comfort zone does not only involve the "home-place" as a physical entity, but also its extensions via mobility patterns and communicative bonds with close friends and family.

Whereas the formation of transmedia textures through smartphones, laptops and so on enables geographical dispersal, or centrifugality, of the comfort zone, our empirical data more significantly speak of centripetality. Among our informants, the appropriation of new media technologies was mainly motivated on grounds of security: the need for coordinating household activities in time and space, as well as for taking safety measures when on the move. Furthermore, most of the informants stated that they did not have any great interest in the technology as such, but were mainly concerned with getting access to those basic functions that could strengthen the ties within the family and peer group(s). Appropriation processes—which were often mediated through significant "others" (colleagues, children, etc.), typically referred to as persons with greater technological skills—were thus predominantly described in a sedentarist language, especially among middle-aged and older informants:

My children made me get a cellphone [laughter]. That's how it is. When "mother" was in Örebro [Swedish city] in the middle of the night and got a flat tire, they asked me if I understood why they wanted me to have a cellphone. And then I had to accept that....I had to get one of my own. (63-year-old female pedagogue)

I don't know much about phone models. My daughter has one of those iPhones. But I don't know which one is the best....It's about a year [since getting the smartphone]. Yes, less than a year. We have some "techno-freaks" here at work. But what do *I* actually use it for? Well, we added a few things, so now I have email too. I use my calendar, make calls now and then, and send text messages. But I could easily do with a simpler mobile. (52-year-old male executive manager of small company)

Morally, our interviewees gave expression to the social durability of work ethics and traditional family values, sustaining a certain "communicative pragmatism." The emergence of materially abundant media textures (which also characterized the households of the above two informants) could thus be seen as the outcome of social cohesion rather than consumerist desires for "the new" (Campbell, 1992). In general, there was a prevailing inward dynamic that steered the flows of information towards the hearth of the household, constituting it as a site of ontological security. This especially marked the function of mobile media. In accentuated cases, the domestic sphere was constructed as a more or less self-contained unit with a sophisticated spatial structure for sustaining various communication needs among its members.

The before-mentioned celebration of mobile media must thus not be mistaken for a nomadic moral geography—quite the opposite. Whereas mobile media, as well as certain online platforms such as Facebook, were certainly a key to the geographical expansion of the social comfort zone, this type of boundary work is different from the nomadic, or cosmopolitan, orientation towards cultural difference, boundary transgression and risk-taking. Among our informants, global mobility and longer stays abroad were by and large seen as exceptional episodes of the life-biography, associated either with a bygone adventurous period in their youth or with the potential comforts of future retirement. New media were sometimes mentioned as important means for staying in touch with people who had left the region, such as relatives living in Australia or retired parents residing on the Canary Islands. They were also thought of as an essential safety measure, if one should travel abroad.

Our case study thus contributes to an understanding of interveillance as a socio-material regime that cuts across socio-cultural and moral lines of division, albeit in different ways. A comparable case study (Jansson, 2011; Christensen & Jansson, 2012) among members of a globally mobile class fraction—Swedish expatriates working within the international development sector in Latin America—highlighted a condition in which interveillance largely operated as a means for entertaining and negotiating the boundaries of the (transnational) social field

(Bourdieu, 1980/1990), rather than those more organic community forms foregrounded in the present study. Similar patterns have been reported from other studies among transnationally mobile professionals (e.g., Beaverstock, 2002). This is not to say that household monitoring is unimportant in expatriate contexts. But the appropriation and incorporation of new media seems to follow a more distinctively shaped pattern, signifying nomadic lifestyles and "liquid life paths" (Mas Giralt & Bailey, 2010). What binds these diverging cases together is, again, the quest for ontological security, meaning that interveillance reproduces, above all, those textures that connect the individual subject to the social epicenters of the Self.

Interveillance, Doubt and Moral Durability

Besides its material and textural implications, boundary work is also about morality. As pointed out in a number of previous studies, media use in general, and online media practices in particular, tend to rearticulate those orientations and nodes of identification that govern (offline) everyday practices at large (e.g., Jansson & Andersson, 2012; Hepp, 2009; Andersson, 2008). In the current case, as we have seen, media practices were generally biased towards the metaphysics of fixity; they even contributed to an extension of local "small-town life." Whereas this type of setting, as several informants noted, implies that one is constantly recognized in town, and thus rarely finds a public space that may sustain anonymous forms of expressivity, it is a social shelter that alleviates any tendencies to moral doubt. The strength of these social and moral ties is most clearly spelled out when threatened. In a striking example, one of the interviewees described how he and his colleagues had redirected a surveillance camera placed at the heart of their workplace:

> In the new factory there are mounted cameras, about ten cameras, which overlook the whole production in the new hall. And those who built the new factory can watch it, in Slovenia....Right at the steering unit there was a camera pointing straight down on us, and we never understood why it had to be there, so we poked it upwards a little, just so it couldn't see us. Because it felt like nobody trusted us. (26-year-old factory worker and father)

In this case, community-based morality was experienced as actively called in doubt by an external, monitoring force—thus spurring oppositional tactics on the part of the workers. This is an exceptional case, however, in the sense that the informants in general expressed great compliance with most systemic forms of surveillance (commercial online monitoring, public camera surveillance, etc.), as long as these were not directed towards themselves specifically. Under collective conditions surveillance was not associated with moral doubt, but rather seen as a moral amplifier.

It was not only when discussing issues of top-down monitoring that our informants mentioned the importance of moral integration and togetherness. It was a key theme also when discussing such forms of communication that more directly pertained to interveillance and horizontal integration. One informant, a 41-year-old single social worker who lives alone, revealed that she was hesitant to participate in discussions about societal issues, being afraid of "having the wrong opinion" when "everything becomes so big." She sometimes felt she even wanted to move somewhere else, where she could "start all over," not being recognized by anyone. However, the importance of rootedness and having old friends and family nearby had still kept her "in place." In her case, as among other regular online media users in the sample, Facebook had become a ritualized means, sometimes even an epicenter, for reproducing such closely knit circles of old friends and relatives with whom communication was experienced as consensual and morally unproblematic.

> Facebook is the page I always return to. When I start up I immediately go to Facebook and read until the end of the first page. And then I go somewhere else and do something else, to Aftonbladet or Expressen [newspapers], for example....But then I spin back to Facebook, and see "hmm, two new updates," and then one has to check them out. (41-year-old female social worker, single)

However, crossing the social and moral boundaries, that is, exposing oneself beyond the comfort zone, or losing control over information, was generally associated with considerable unease. Similarly, inappropriate self-disclosure among others was discussed in a critical, even morally condemning manner:

> I think it's rather sick that people put everything out there. Writing about everything one does. Then I think it's a matter of getting attention somehow; confirmation that what you do is really good, or whatever the purpose is....To some people nothing is private, it seems, like ultrasound pictures, that's the level! Such things...and there is the boundary I think. Anyone can go in there, and have a look....No, I would never do that. (28-year-old female teacher)

> I don't write very much myself, but mostly look at what others have done, that's funny sometimes. There is no particular function to it really, but more out of curiosity. That's what I use it for....But sometimes I share pictures and stuff. It's fun to show the kids and what we've been doing. Mostly for showing things that I'm proud of, perhaps. I don't mind if people take a look at it, it's just fun. And it can also be fun, even though I don't have any contact with my classmates from 25 years ago, to have them as friends on the internet and see how they live, and see some pictures from their lives....Mostly to know that they are still there. (35-year-old shop assistant and father)

The management of interveillance is thus associated with the elimination of moral doubt and ambiguity, that is, a mode of mutual social legitimation. To the extent that our informants spoke about violations of moral boundaries and proper forms of expressivity and sharing, such occasions referred to a diffuse crowd of "people" or "others," and thus not (at least not explicitly) to their closest peer group. Thus, clear lines of division between the morally sound "inside" and the more dubious and uncontrollable "outside" were invoked. As indicated in the above quotes, the "inside" was constructed in terms of a sedentarist moral geography, emphasizing social durability and fixity.

Conclusion

Whereas this study, of course, cannot be taken as *the* account of sedentarist moral geographies, it contains enough empirical data for clarifying how the emergence of (online) transmedia textures imposes a new realm for the (re)mediation of such moral orientations. As demonstrated in this chapter, the moral appraisal of fixity and social durability rarely operates as a counterforce to extensive technological appropriation and accentuated flows as such. Quite the opposite, the mobile nature of new media makes them suitable for peer-to-peer monitoring at the local level, and contributes to the geographical extension of household textures. This is one reason why mobile telephones and computers, along with the television set, come to serve an indispensable function in everyday life, beyond the celebratory settings of early adopters. This does not mean that the household and other local communities lose their meaning as moral enclosures, however. As shown throughout this case study, transmedia textures even contribute to the strengthening of the moral and social boundaries that separate the household and its associated communities from their "outsides."

These observations raise a number of critical issues related to the broader socio-cultural implications of transmedia textures of interveillance. First, they reveal the social-material regime through which everyday life gets intertwined with systemic forms of surveillance, also in settings where people maintain a rather strict view on the disclosure of private information. Within the realm of interveillance, privacy management is normalized as a matter of individual responsibility and common sense, thus having a neutralizing impact on more structural concerns. Second, the technologically enhanced status of sedentarism, ultimately constructing the "networked household" as a more or less self-contained moral unit, highlights the ongoing competition between cosmopolitan and capsular forces in society (Christensen & Jansson, forthcoming). As Silverstone (2007) points out, cosmopolitanism is essentially a matter of hospitality, which in its true shape necessitates social and cultural risk taking. The current study, however, reveals the stronghold of moral economies and moral geographies that by and large mold media textures in the opposite direction.

Notes

1. The "Secure Spaces" project was funded through a grant from the independent research foundation Riksbankens Jubileumsfond during 2009–2012 (project number P2008–0667:1-E).
2. The author wants to thank research assistant David Kvicklund for conducting and transcribing all the interviews, as well as the informants for volunteering and participating in the study.
3. The concept of complicit surveillance was first introduced by Christensen (2011, 2012) and has subsequently, within the framework of this research project, been discussed in relation to interveillance (Christensen & Jansson, forthcoming). Interveillance is also elaborated in Jansson (2012).

References

Adams, P. C. (1992). Television as gathering place. *Annals of the Association of American Geographers, 82*(1), 117–135.

Albrechtslund, A. (2008). Online social networking as participatory surveillance. *First Monday, 13*(3).

Andersson, M. (2008). The matter of media in transnational everyday life. In I. Rydin & U. Sjöberg (Eds.), *Mediated crossroads: Theoretical and methodological challenges.* Göteborg: Nordicom.

Andrejevic, M. (2007). *iSpy: Surveillance and power in the interactive era.* Lawrence: University Press of Kansas.

Andrejevic, M. (2005). The work of watching one another: Lateral surveillance, risk, and governance. *Surveillance and Society, 2*(4), 479–497.

Beaverstock, J. V. (2002). Transnational elites in global cities: British expatriates in Singapore's financial district. *Geoforum, 33,* 525–538.

Beck, U., & Beck-Gernsheim, E. (2002). *Individualization: Institutionalized individualism and its social and political consequences.* London: Sage.

Berger, P. L., Berger, B., & Kellner, H. (1973). *The homeless mind: Modernization and consciousness.* New York: Random House.

Best, K. (2010). Living in the control society: Surveillance, users and digital screen technologies. *International Journal of Cultural Studies, 13*(1), 5–24.

Bourdieu, P. (1980/1990). *The logic of practice.* Cambridge: Polity.

Campbell, C. (1992). The desire for the new: Its nature and social location as presented in theories of fashion and modern consumerism. In R. Silverstone & E. Hirsch (Eds.), *Consuming technologies: Media and information in domestic spaces.* London: Routledge.

Christensen, C. (2011). Online social media, communicative practice and complicit surveillance in transnational contexts. In M. Christensen, A. Jansson, & C. Christensen (Eds.), *Online territories: Globalization, mediated practice and social space.* (pp. 222–238). New York: Peter Lang.

Christensen, M. (2012). Online mediations of sociality in transnational spaces: Cosmopolitan re/formations of belonging and identity in the Turkish diaspora. *Journal of Ethnic and Racial Studies, 35*(5): 888–905.

Christensen, M., & Jansson, A. (Forthcoming). *Cosmopolitanism and the media: Cartographies of change*. Basingstoke: Palgrave Macmillan.

Christensen, M., & Jansson, A. (2012). Fields, territories, and bridges: Networked communities and mediated surveillance in transnational social space. In C. Fuchs, K. Boersma, A. Albrechtslund, & M. Sandoval (Eds.), *Internet and surveillance: The challenges of Web 2.0 and social media*. London: Routledge.

Cresswell, T. (2006). *On the move: Mobility in the modern Western world*. London: Routledge.

Ellison, N. B., Steinfield, C., & Lampe, C. (2010). Connection strategies: Social capital implications of Facebook-enabled communication practices. *New Media and Society, 13*(6), 873–892.

Fuchs, C. (2012). Critique of the political economy of Web 2.0 surveillance. In C. Fuchs, K. Boersma, A. Albrechtslund, & M. Sandoval (Eds.), *Internet and surveillance: The challenges of Web 2.0 and social media*. London: Routledge.

Fuchs, C. (2010). StudiVZ: Social networking in the surveillance society. *Ethics and Information Technology, 12*(2), 171–185.

Gandy, O. (1993). *The panoptic sort: A political economy of personal information*. Boulder, CO: Westview.

Germann Molz, J. (2012). *Travel connections: Tourism, technology and togetherness in a mobile world*. London: Routledge.

Giddens, A. (1991). *Modernity and self-identity: Self and society in the late modern age*. Cambridge: Polity.

Haggerty, K. D., & Ericson, R. V. (2000). The surveillant assemblage. *British Journal of Sociology, 51*, 605–622.

Hepp, A. (2009). Localities of diasporic communicative spaces: Material aspects of translocal mediated networking. *Communication Review, 12*(4), 327–348.

Humphreys, L. (2011). Who's watching whom? A study of interactive technology and surveillance. *Journal of Communication, 61*(4), 575–595.

Ihde, D. (1990). *Technology and the lifeworld: From garden to earth*. Bloomington: Indiana University Press.

Jansson, A. (Forthcoming). Mediatization and social space: Reconstructing mediatization for the transmedia age. *Communication Theory*.

Jansson, A. (2012). Perceptions of surveillance: Reflexivity and trust in a mediatized world (the case of Sweden). *European Journal of Communication, 27*(4): 410–427.

Jansson, A. (2011). Cosmopolitan capsules: Mediated networking and social control in expatriate spaces. In M. Christensen, A. Jansson, & C. Christensen (Eds.), *Online territories: Globalization, mediated practice and social space*. New York: Peter Lang.

Jansson, A. (2007). Texture: A key concept for communication geography. *European Journal of Cultural Studies, 10*(2), 185–202.

Jansson, A., & Andersson, M. (2012). Mediatization at the margins: Cosmopolitanism, network capital and spatial transformation in rural Sweden. *Communications, 37*(2), 173–194.

Kenaw, S. (2012). Cultural translation of mobile telephones: Mediation of strained communication among Ethiopian married couples. *Journal of Modern African Studies, 50*(1), 131–155.

Kim, M. (2004). Surveillance technology, privacy and social control: With reference to the case of the electronic national identification card in South Korea. *International Sociology, 19*(2), 193–213.

Ling, R. (2008). *New tech, new ties: How mobile communication is reshaping social cohesion.* Cambridge, MA: MIT Press.

Linke, C. (2011). Being a couple in a media world: The mediatization of everyday communication in couple relationships. *Communications, 36*(1), 91–111.

Löfgren, O. (2009). Domesticated media: Hiding, dying or haunting. In A. Jansson & A. Lagerkvist (Eds.), *Strange spaces: Explorations into mediated obscurity.* Farnham: Ashgate.

Lull, J. (1990). *Inside family viewing: Ethnographic research on television's audiences.* London: Routledge.

Marwick, A. E. (2012). The public domain: Social surveillance in everyday life. *Surveillance & Society, 9*(4), 378–393.

Mas Giralt, R., & Bailey, A. J. (2010). Transnational familyhood and the liquid life paths of South Americans in the U.K. *Global Networks, 10*(3), 383–400.

Miller, V. (2008). New media, networking and phatic culture. *Convergence: The International Journal of Research into New Media Technologies, 14*(4), 387–400.

Morley, D. (2000). *Home territories: Media, mobility and identity.* London: Routledge.

Morley, D. (1992). *Television, audiences and cultural studies.* London: Routledge.

Riesman, D. (1950/2001). *The lonely crowd.* New Haven, CT: Yale University Press.

Silverstone, R. (2007). *Media and morality: On the rise of mediapolis.* Cambridge: Polity.

Silverstone, R., Hirsch, E., & Morley, D. (1992). Information and communication technologies and the moral economy of the household. In R. Silverstone & E. Hirsch (Eds.), *Consuming technologies: Media and information in domestic spaces.* London: Routledge.

Taddicken, M. (2012). Privacy, surveillance, and self-disclosure in the social web: Exploring the user's perspective via focus groups. In C. Fuchs, K. Boersma, A. Albrechtslund, & M. Sandoval (Eds.), *Internet and surveillance: The challenges of Web 2.0 and social media.* London: Routledge.

Trottier, D., & Lyon, D. (2012). Key features of social media surveillance. In C. Fuchs, K. Boersma, A. Albrechtslund, & M. Sandoval (Eds.), *Internet and surveillance: The challenges of Web 2.0 and social media.* London: Routledge.

van Dijck, J. (2012). Facebook as a tool for producing sociality and connectivity. *Television and New Media, 13*(2), 160–176.

PART III

Politics

9

The Non-Consensual Hallucination

The Politics of Online Privacy

David Barnard-Wills

Introduction

Online privacy is a political issue, with impacts upon freedom, life chances, distribution of resources, political communication, identity creation and performance, deliberation and knowledge. It is an issue with contested norms and active legislative debates tied into broader conflicts around the way that the online environment is politically constructed. Online privacy is also implicated in access, internet freedom and surveillance debates.

The politics of privacy online is a complex socio-technical politics that must incorporate multiple technologies, social institutions, social practices, actors and individuals. It operates across institutional, economic and national boundaries. A single social theory is unlikely to explain the extent of phenomena experienced online. Using the de facto terminology of "online" or "digital" is itself reductive of this incredibly complex mediation of a vast range of social practices. Our existing theories (and empirical approaches) may give us some purchase, but some will have to be reworked with attention and care.

This chapter will relate the politics of online privacy to surveillance and through an engagement with the discourse theory of Chantal Mouffe, Ernesto Laclau, David Howarth and Jason Glynos. The political philosophy and social science analytic framework developed by these theorists allows us to examine the politics of online privacy from two related directions—those of hegemony and identity.

The chapter makes the argument that privacy and surveillance enter into and mediate the language games through which individual subjects both make sense of the world and apprehend their own identity, and demonstrates that this is a political and contested process. I have written elsewhere about the importance of discourse to understanding the politics of surveillance and identity (Barnard-Wills, 2012a) and wish to expand some of these arguments in relation to the specific example of the more global online environment and in direct relation to the politics of privacy. I hope to suggest that (1) the way that privacy is constructed is significant, and (2) understanding the politics of privacy rapidly takes us into areas of identity creation and contestation. This suggests a type of political contestation that is not often well captured in privacy debates, which often assume "realist" ontology and an individualistic relationship between an individual and "their" personal data.

The chapter is divided into two parts, both of which are applications of theory to the particular issue of online privacy. The first part examines the concept of hegemony in discourse theory and applies this to a wide range of political positions. The intent here is to demonstrate how there is far from consensus over the way the internet operates, is governed and how it should develop in future. It will demonstrate the discursive dimension opens up a number of ways of thinking about online privacy. This includes a way to resolve the apparent "privacy paradox": the contradiction between avowed privacy beliefs and apparent privacy behaviour. The second part applies the concept of identity from discourse theory to the question of online privacy. This allows us to address the way that contemporary digital identities are composite, multiple, constructed, often attributed and contested. Digital identities are a composite of self-generated and revealed information, biographical information, information generated by transactions and behaviour and data associated with categories to which the individual is assigned. All of this is shared, combined and mined in databases both known and unknown to the individual. These attributions often interact oddly with our own sense of self or group identity. The conclusion draws together these two sets of theoretical insights, and looks for potential ways to move forward from there. This will include thinking about the way that we can collectively respond to the impacts upon privacy and the role of contingency in online politics.

Discourse Theory

This section sets out the origin and profile of discourse theory and its theoretical commitments and presumptions. This will support our later thinking about privacy and identity in discourse theory terms.

Ernesto Laclau and Chantal Mouffe's *Hegemony and Socialist Strategy* (2001, originally published in 1985) was both an attempt to conduct a genealogical mapping of the concept of hegemony within Marxist political theory (Andersen, 2003:49) and an attempt to set out a new approach to understanding politics. The book draws upon both Gramscian and Foucauldian theory to set out discourse as a key category of political analysis. The "Essex School" of discourse theory was pivotal in developing empirical studies drawing upon discourse theory (Howarth & Stavrakakis, 2000). The most recent move to expand discourse theory into a fully applicable theory of social research is Jason Glynos and David Howarth's *Logics of Critical Explanation in Social and Political Theory* (2007). Their intention is to negotiate the distinction between "value-free" positivism and non-generalisable hermeneutic approaches reliant upon self-interpretation, with the goal of allowing social research that is explanatory, critical and incorporates an appropriately political dimension. They aim to:

> Develop an ontological stance and a grammar of concepts, together with a particular research ethos which make it possible to construct and furnish answers to empirical problems that can withstand the charges of methodological arbitrariness, historical particularism, and idealism. (Glynos & Howarth, 2007:7)

The version of discourse theory as set out by Glynos and Howarth has two fundamental ontological principles. The first premise is that all practices and regimes are discursive entities. This makes understanding meaning central to political analysis. It also means that objects (including people) have their identities conferred upon them by particular systems of meaning (discourses), and that constellations of social practices are pulled together (into "regimes") by a shared discourse.

This allows us to think about privacy practices (and indeed any personal information practice) as a discursive practice, which is to draw attention to the fact that it has meaning for social agents. This political perspective on meaning would, for example, suggest that a dictionary definition of a term is not objective fact, but rather an active attempt to set the meaning of a concept in the face of other alternate meanings. Discourse is material; it is not just ideas but is embodied in institutions, rituals and practices. The implication here is the impact of discourse upon both the representation of the online environment and the way that such representations are embodied as thought made practical (Dean, 2010:42).

The second premise is that any field of discursive social relations is marked by radical contingency. Radical contingency suggests that society could have been otherwise, and that its structure and identity are not logically necessary. It rejects the concept of a fully formed constitutive essence of any practice, regime or object (Glynos & Howarth, 2007:110). For our purposes in regard to the politics of online privacy, this has two key implications. The impossibility of final fixation of meaning relates to the concept of hegemony developed by Laclau and Mouffe, and can inform our understanding of the ways that discourses attempt to construct impossible objects, a fixed understanding of how the online environment functions, and how privacy functions within this. Second, this means that online identities are also inherently unstable, and that a full, stable identity is an impossibility. This is contrary to a prevailing attitude that information technology allows either a more powerful expression of some essential identity, or allows the identity and characteristics of individuals and collectives to be more accurately mined and either commodified or securitized. It also provides a way of opening up the ethical dimension of identity and privacy-related practices. With these presuppositions and implications in hand, we can now turn to the first of our two analytic concepts, hegemony, via cyberpunk literature.

(Non-)Consensual Hallucinations

In William Gibson's 1984 classic cyberpunk novel *Neuromancer*, the protagonist, Case, describes a vision of cyberspace in the following terms:

> A consensual hallucination experienced daily by billions of legitimate operators, in every nation, by children being taught mathematical concepts...a graphic representation of data abstracted from banks of every computer in the human system. Unthinkable complexity. Lines of light ranged in the nonspace of the mind, clusters and constellations of data. Like city lights, receding...(Gibson, 1984/1995:51)

Case is referring in this instance to the fictional "Matrix," the virtual reality to which he connects to pursue an artificial intelligence. Whilst the Matrix diverges from the internet in several ways, the description provides us with a way of approaching the politics of online perception, information and interaction, and in particular the politics of online privacy.

"Consensual hallucination" is a powerful, evocative phrase. It carries a sense of social interaction resulting in some form of negotiated shared understanding, but that this shared understanding is illusory, contingent and vulnerable. Like all hallucinations, it borders on intangibility and is prone to collapse like gossamer on the wind. The phrase captures the constructed, social nature of the online environment. The internet and associated technology can be thought of as constructed in two layers. First, there is the material construction of servers and computers, fibre optic cable, modems and so on. This is the most obviously constructed layer, and it is easy to reflect upon its construction even if this infrastructure has a tendency to fade into the background. This hardware and software infrastructure is designed and built. Code is written (Lessig, 1999). The second layer of construction is the social and linguistic construction of the online environment. This is construction through politics and processes that includes norms and values as well as future-oriented goals and ambitions. It includes visions of how the internet should be organised, governed or left free to develop under its own logic.

However, whilst "consensus" captures the idea that our understanding of the internet is collective, it presents too harmonious and homogeneous an image. Consensus is agreement, and therefore fails to identify contestation and conflict. Chantal Mouffe's engagement with Carl Schmitt is particularly telling on this, seeing the assumption that there can be an end to, or absence of political antagonism as an evasion of politics (Mouffe, 2005). This is where hegemony becomes relevant. The next section examines the concept of hegemony, demonstrates how this is useful to understanding the contemporary politics of online privacy, before the following section sets out a number of particularly hegemonic discourses.

Hegemony

The concept of hegemony developed by Laclau and Mouffe is a development of Antonio Gramsci's version of the concept. Gramsci was attempting to understand the role of particular classes in bringing about revolutionary change and the features of the social world that worked against this. Hegemony was a way of expressing how a particular class was able to make its vision of the world applicable across all other social classes. Laclau and Mouffe's critical move was to decouple the concept of hegemony from class-based politics and make it a general model of articulatory and discursive politics (Glynos & Howarth, 2007:179), making hegemony a way of thinking about the whole of the social sphere (Laclau & Mouffe, 2001:96).

Hegemony then refers to the way that particular discourses dominate articulatory practice, becoming powerful ways of speaking and understanding the world. The concept of hegemony is therefore really a way of speaking about fixity and discursive power within a context of radical contingency. The way the social world is represented and understood now is not a necessary arrangement. It could have been otherwise, and could change. However in the here and now, a particular representation is dominant and difficult to challenge. Because of radical contingency, hegemony is never complete. Rather than a model of total consensus, we have one of conflicting world views, with different discourses competing to make sense of the same social space.

It should be fairly apparent how this notion of conflicting discourses starts to be useful in understanding the politics of online privacy. Statements about the internet attempt to fix it and provide particular representations that fit in with a particular world view. Discourse theory would think of these clusters of ways of thinking, representing and understanding the online environment as different *discourses*. Hegemony allows us to avoid technological determinism, recognise discursive features and the importance of representation as a political practice. Importantly it allows us to move beyond continual attempts to define what is "public" or "private" as if those had pre-existing ontological status. The continual attempts to define privacy should be a clue to its contested nature (Solove, 2008).

Hegemonic and Counter-Hegemonic Discourses of the Internet

We should first take a step back and account for the range of political perspectives relating to technologically mediated communication networks. Discourses of online privacy do not emerge sui generis but connect to other existing discourses, in this case, discourses on the online environment itself. Providing some concrete examples of these different perspectives will be illustrative. It will demonstrate the divergent perceptions of the same object associated with different political perspectives, and the different policy prescriptions that flow from these perceptions. We'll engage with Californian neoliberalism, internet utopianism, security discourses and radical left discourses. These discourses exist in tension with each other, and they are operating in the same world, oriented towards the same substrate. By speaking about it, they reflect the political importance of internet technology and that it is worth representing and contesting. They each provide a perspective on the online environment, provide guides to action in that environment, as well as a set of goals for the future direction of that environment.

Richard Barbrook and Andy Cameron have written about what they call the "Californian Ideology" (1996). They see this as a combination of the "free-wheeling spirit of the hippies and entrepreneurial zeal of the yuppies" (44), and as "a bizarre mish-mash of hippie anarchism and economic liberalism beefed up with lots of technological determinism" (53). The theorists of the Californian Ideology include Marshall McLuhan, Alvin Toffler, Howard Rheingold and John Perry Barlow, with *Wired* magazine as its "house journal."

Californian Ideology emerged from a group of people living within a specific country with a particular mix of socio-economic and technological factors, but has become incredibly influential in the development of the contemporary internet. Barbrook and Cameron identify well-paid "digital artisans" with considerable autonomy over their own work and employment but no guarantee of continued employment (1996:48). Hackers, like Case in *Neuromancer*, embody this self-sufficient technologically capable individual. The Californian Ideology resolves conflict between its influential intellectual traditions through a shared anti-statism. The New Left attacked the state as a military-industrial complex, whilst the New Right attacks it for interfering in economic activity. Both converged on a form of Jeffersonian democracy. Big government should stay off the backs of entrepreneurs, as interference with emergent properties will rebound. The internet is emancipatory in that free expression within cyberspace and technological development inevitably creates an electronic agora (Barbrook & Cameron, 1996:47), whilst existing power structures wither away replaced by unfettered interactions between autonomous individuals and their software (50). The liberty it will encourage is the liberty of individuals within the marketplace. This ideology has been criticised for wilful blindness towards racism, poverty and environmental degradation (45), as well as ignoring state involvement and subsidies, particularly from defence, in the actual history of technological media, and over-favouring the role of private enterprise (51).

Closely related to the Californian Ideology, but characterised by its application to international politics, Evgeny Morozov's *The Net Delusion* (2011) provides an account of what he terms "cyber utopianism." This is the idea that the internet inherently favours democratic and open political systems over authoritarian and closed systems. In this school of thought "large doses of information technology are lethal to the most repressive of regimes" (xiii) and the internet favours the oppressed over the oppressor. Morozov is highly critical of this way of thinking, believing it naïve, offering examples of how authoritarian regimes make use of the internet to track and crack down upon opposition movements. Policy that emerges from this area includes what Morozov labels "The Google Doctrine"—"the enthusiastic belief in the liberating power of technology accompanied by the irresistible urge to enlist Silicon Valley start-ups in the global fight for freedom" (2011:xiii), and fund social media companies in authoritarian regimes (see Clinton, 2010)

The Californian Ideology is pivotal for the development of the politics of online privacy that we are enmeshed in today. It is arguable that contemporary social media, Google and Facebook emerge from this tradition. Statements by Google CEO Eric Schmidt that "If you have something that you don't want anyone to know, maybe you shouldn't be doing it in the first place" (as quoted in Dvorak, 2009), and by Scott McNealy that "You have zero privacy anymore. Get over it" (Sprenger, 1999) are both examples of the ideological function of this discourse. It can also be seen clearly in Facebook founder Mark Zuckerberg's statement that privacy is really no longer a social norm.

> People have really gotten comfortable not only sharing more information and different kinds, but more openly and with more people. That social norm is just something that has evolved over time…But we viewed that as a really important thing, to always

keep a beginner's mind and what would we do if we were starting the company now and we decided that these would be the social norms now and we just went for it. (O'Brien, 2010)

These statements are performing an ideological discursive function. In a shift away from a notion of false consciousness or the popular conceptions of being aligned with a particular political program, for discourse theory, ideology is an ontological category. It is any type of discursive act that denies the fundamental contingency of the social or of particular elements of it. These speakers are presenting an understanding of privacy that is supportive of their business interests as if it were objective social reality. They are denying the political nature of privacy and the online environment. In this construction, privacy is individual, archaic and attempts to exercise it run counter to the entrepreneurial active spirit of the age. Within cyber utopianism, privacy is to be protected for democratic dissidents elsewhere, and is less necessary in societies that have achieved the status of democracy.

Another perspective on the online environment might be termed "realist-securitocratic." In this perspective, embodied by thinkers such as Joseph Nye, author of *Cyber Power* (2010), the internet is a source of threat and a subject of strategic international activity, potentially in a militarised form. Features of this particular discourse include attention to vulnerability and exposure to threat, and the need to secure the potential battlespace of cyberspace (Barnard-Wills & Ashenden, 2012:2). Policy responses in this environment include bringing internet-related policy within the sphere of influence of security institutions, increasing the surveillance of cyberspace, issuing various cyber security strategies and even preparing for cyber war (see Rid, 2012 for a strong challenge to this). Privacy here is threatening, a shield for terrorism and crime. State and commercial information, on the other hand, is not "private" but rather is secured.

Proponents of policies such as the U.K.'s Communications Data Bill (Secretary of State for the Home Department, 2012) suggest that technology has left the state behind somewhat, to the extent that its policing and intelligence agencies are no longer able to exercise powers they had with centralised telecommunications. In this light, a set of new powers for these agencies is simply a response to changed conditions. For the opponents, it is a much more politically charged move, in which the policing and intelligence agencies make a grab for greater powers of surveillance, with potentially damaging impacts upon communicative life.

Some more minoritarian perspectives explicitly recognise the internet's political nature (rather than downplaying it, being actively hostile to political perspectives or using a privileged security politics position to determine which claims about the online environment have validity). These include non-hierarchical perspectives informed by anarchism and critical Marxist perspectives. Both attempt to explicitly create types of technology and use patterns to support their political values. The explicitly political social network N-1 (https://n-1.cc/) attempts to embody and make functional political values and precepts in supporting the Occupy and M15 movements. These activist movements are engaged in a social network because they are interlinked across geographically separate territories, with a need to create and share social and cultural capital. Existing commercial social networks do not offer sufficient privacy, reliability, flexibility or control over data, and are based upon business models that the activist groups cannot support. The response is to establish usable social network systems that allow control over data and privacy, whilst seeking horizontal consensus and avoiding power relations (N-1, 2012). The name N-1 comes from Giles Deleuze and Felix Guattari's discussion of the concept of the rhizome in *A Thousand Plateaus* (2004:7). Here a political understanding of the world is explicitly used to construct communications network infrastructure that supports that political dimension. Privacy is politically necessary, and under threat from both technology and hostile forms of politics. Dmytri Kleiner's *Telekommunist Manifesto* (2010) lays out another perspective on digital politics arising from the free software community and adopting a lens of class conflict. In this perspective, various forms of power attempt to prevent the circulation of information outside of their control. The technology of the internet could allow non-hierarchical networks, and is in contradiction to the enclosure and control upon which capitalism is predicated. The political challenge here is the commercialisation of the internet. Policy proposals arising from the manifesto include the concepts of copyfarleft and venture communism. Technology as a whole is not seen as inherently emancipatory, but particular network topologies are the product of certain forms of socio-economic organisation and can also reinforce those forms.

> The Internet started as a network that embodied the relation of peer-to-peer communism; however, it has been reshaped by capitalist finance into an inefficient and un-free client server topology. (Kleiner, 2010:8)

In this sense then, the internet and other forms of online networking are a site of contestation between different models of economic and political organisation, and a model for a nascent form of organisation.

The contrast and difference (as well as some interesting similarities) between these different discourses on what the internet is (and should be) should be fairly apparent, even from these thumbnail sketches. These few perspectives far from exhaust the universe of political discourses relating to the online environment. We might also include the motivating philosophies behind WikiLeaks or Anonymous. These discourses do have differing levels of permeation. The Californian Ideology appears dominant, especially with technologists and technology commentators. It has policy influence and can potentially coexist with cyber security discourse in the Google Doctrine.

This is far from a consensus. Different understandings support and motivate different policies. See, for example, the debate around communications data retention in the U.K., or around the Stop Online Privacy Act (SOPA) and Cyber Intelligence Sharing and Protection Act (CISPA) in the U.S. Contrast, for example, a governmental cyber security strategy with the declaration of internet freedom (http://www.internetdeclaration.org/) or the social media "Bill of Rights" (Swift, 2010). These policies can and will have substantial effects upon the material conditions of the online environment, as well as upon dominant representations in the future as further layers of discourse sediment meanings and understandings.

Privacy Paradox

The privacy paradox is an example of contested discourses involved in the politics of online privacy, and also how a discursive approach can cut through some persistent debates in this field. We should understand this paradox against the background discourses discussed previously.

The idea of a privacy paradox fundamentally revolves around an apparent contradiction between beliefs and behaviours in relation to privacy (Acquisti & Grossklags, 2003; Coopamootoo & Ashenden, 2011). The idea is that individuals or groups express a concern for privacy, and might even work for or advocate privacy, or criticise privacy-invasive technologies or policies. Yet the paradox emerges when these same individuals or groups engage in privacy-reducing behaviour, such as freely and voluntarily giving up personal information, joining a social network with poor privacy controls or accepting a free service in exchange for targeted advertising. The privacy paradox has been written about fairly extensively, and in social reality often hangs upon issues of young people's supposedly problematic attitudes towards privacy, some kind of generational shift in attitudes and the use of social networking sites (Utz & Krämer, 2009; Nissenbaum, 2010; boyd & Hargittai, 2010).

The apparent contradiction is broken down in two main ways. The privacy rejecting position resolves the inconsistency by favouring behaviour over statements and concern. If people give up their privacy, then their statements must be inauthentic, not reflect true priorities or be self-serving in some other way. Perhaps they wish to have their cake and eat it too. If the concern over privacy is inauthentic or self-serving, then it can be discounted politically (no need for privacy-protecting legislation) or commercially (there is unlikely to be any economic damage to a company's reputation for infringing privacy, and there is unlikely to be any competitive advantage to be gained from adopting privacy-protecting measures). This discounting can also be applied across sectors—colloquially, if people are willing to give personal data to a social network or supermarket, then how can they complain if a government collects that data? We are back to Zuckerberg's belief that privacy is no longer a social norm and the Californian Ideology's entrepreneurial view of privacy.

Alternately, if we privilege intentions and desires, expressed through speech, over behaviour, then the inconsistency is resolved in a different direction. In this case, behaviour appears more contingent, affected by context or, importantly, open to manipulation—exactly the reason why N-1 has to reject existing social networks. The debate bogs down within the positivist paradigm. The answer is, of course, both. For the most part, people care about privacy in some contexts and not in others. A more accurate picture could be provided through contextualised self-interpretations articulated with political discourses of privacy, personal decision making, governmental responsibilisation and capitalist information economies. Individual privacy activity online must be contextualised against a range of much broader political, social and economic environments, including the personal information economy (Lace, 2005) in which individuals are made visible to corporate and governmental entities through a huge and growing market for personal information. Research into consumer surveillance has also identified discrimination based upon data profiles (Turow, 2006). Similarly, sociologists have discussed the concept of the "surveillance society" (Lyon, 1994; Murakami Wood, 2006) in which social sorting—discrimination on the basis of personal information—frequently has substantial impacts upon the lives of individuals and communities (Gandy, 2009).

Privacy is hard to achieve online, even for the informed and committed. This is due to a number of interlinked factors. Reducing costs of storage, combined with more powerful computer processors have facilitated the storage of large volumes of data, mined for additional information. This generates an interest in the acquisition of personal data, at the same time as data can be assumed to persist. This has been described as the death of forgetting (Mayer-Schönberger, 2009). James Bridle takes this further, describing the internet as essentially "machine-augmented memory, with all the strange ripple-effects that this produces" (Bridle, 2012). Second, many of the business models built around the provision of free content online are dependent upon advertising revenue. Combined with the nature of digital media, and also attempts by various governments to monitor internet traffic for security purposes, this creates an environment where several prominent actors have interests in reducing individual privacy. This is compounded by the theoretical multiplicity and contested nature of the concept of privacy, across academic disciplines and broader social life. Privacy is described as multidimensional, multifaceted (Solove, 2008), contextual and situated (Nissenbaum, 2010). We need to be cautious about any attempt to fix privacy in one particular form across context and for all time. Solove's account of privacy as not a state, but a response to a certain class of political problem is close to this (and you can see the influence of Wittgenstein on both Solove's concept of privacy and on discourse theory). One side effect of this is to problematise privacy-rights language, which might be unacceptable to privacy advocates. Rejecting an absolute definition of privacy is not a retreat to relativism, but rather an awareness of context, community norms and political contestation. Thinking about rights in discursive terms does not undermine them, but rather highlights their political fragility, and the way they can be undermined by other political discourses that articulate them in different ways.

Identity in Discourse Theory

Having examined hegemony's relation to privacy, we move now to the second contribution from discourse theory to online privacy, the concept of identity. Like many contemporary social theories, discourse theory has a subjectivist understanding of identity. Radical contingency rejects the idea that identity is fixed and essential. Identity is not simply the product of a socio-economic position and because every subject position is discursive, identities must be radically contingent rather than fixed (Glynos & Howarth, 2007:115). Identity is at the same time a fiction and a principle of social organisation. Identity is fundamentally political, and a process rather than an object. This is not, however, identity politics in the sense of the political activity of pre-formed groups with a shared identity, nor the realisation of shared identities through political struggle. Whilst these are certainly manifestations of politics that can flow from a subjective sense of identity, there is a core ontological politics to identity construction, the politics-in-identity apart from these particular manifestations of identity-in-politics.

If identities are not fundamentally given but rather socially constructed, then this draws attention to the process of their construction. For the discourse theorists, the core element of the construction of identity is the role of discourse. Identities are made up through discursive processes. For Laclau and Mouffe, drawing upon Louis Althusser, this was a function of the available subject positions within a given discourse (Laclau & Mouffe, 2001). Subject positions were the positions within a discourse from which it was possible to speak, and with which it was possible to identify. Jason Glynos and David Howarth (2007) expanded this account of identification, focussing on the process of subjectification, and the way that subjects identified with particular discourses and reacted to the radical contingency of identity. If every symbolic order is essentially lacking and never closed, if every subject is discursively constructed and if every identity is relational, positioned vis-à-vis other identities—subjectivity is not the passive effect of structures, nor active self-determination. Rather subjectivity is the result of the incomplete closure of the system of meaning. Identity can never be completely provided by any given discourse, and subjectivity is therefore the gaps that need to be filled through identification. It is, at least in part, how we respond to radical contingency.

Why Is This Important for Privacy?

Privacy is often conceptualised in a liberal individualist framing. This is often noticeable in personal data protection policy and language, where information about an individual is constructed as a form of property, which they can choose to alienate to other people or organisations. Similarly, privacy advocates often operate with a liberal human-rights frame of reference that attempts to protect this individual from threats to their privacy. In this model of privacy, the private sphere comes first, and creates a safe space within which to develop a personality, opinions, beliefs and characteristics. These aspects can then be exposed to the world or retained in private. However, this picture of possessive information individualism (Barnard-Wills, 2012a:135) fails to capture the social and relational nature of many contemporary information flows. Information about me is often information about my relationships, or groups to which I may belong, and is therefore information about others (see Wills & Reeves, 2009, for an example of this). Privacy is as much about control over the information applied to us as it is about the protection of some secret core. Labelling, attribution and categorisation are all central to identity construction (see Clarke, 1994; Lyon, 1994; Haggerty & Ericson, 2000). Second, our exposure or isolation from particular flows of information is part of our identity formation. It has direct effects upon our interpretive reservoirs and the discourses to which we are exposed (Pariser, 2011). As an example, what we read, watch or listen to, and how we relate this to other types of information that we have not been exposed to, matters for our development, learning and citizenship. This is not to say that healthy, ethical identity formation must be an entirely open pathway, but rather that identity creation is an intrinsically social activity, and that the idea of the pre-social identity is something of a phantom.

Unthinkable Complexity of Identity

Contemporary practices of personal information are substantial and increasing in both the public and private sectors. The information-gathering capacity of even an individual actor is substantial, and individuals become "legible" not just to states, but to a range of other actors. Surveillance and social media leads to a proliferation of sites of identification, whilst widespread surveillance and dataveillance can threaten subjects with what we might term "interpellative collapse" as multiple identities are pulled together, fixed and found contradictory.

Interpellation is a concept that Laclau and Mouffe acquired from the structuralist Marxism of Louis Althusser and then stripped of its class connotations. It is the process through which discourses address people in ways that construct them as particular subjectivities (Torfing, 1999:302), for example as a mother, a foreigner, a good sales prospect and so on. Given that discourse is material, interpellation is not just "hailing," but also includes categorisation and social sorting. Mark Poster described databases as forms of interpellation, but that instead produce "objectified, rather than subjectified" subjects through processes we were generally not aware of (Poster, 1999:177). This is close, but not quite right. The impacts and implications of having particular identities ascribed through social media and through surveillance practices are becoming more of a part of general debates about the online environment. Ian Hacking (1986) has written about how even arbitrary institutional categorisations can become significant parts of subjective identities.

At a social level these interpellative collapses occur when sufficiently different articulations of identity are brought into the presence of each other. An example might be a parent seeing his or her child's behaviour as a young adult on a social network and feeling the disconnect between their expectations and the information they are presented with (see Turkle, 2011, for several examples of this). Another might be a police officer reading a transcript of the braggadocio of teenage males, and being directed by a lack of appropriate context, alongside an institutional process that is abstracted to the point of being unable to accommodate ambiguity, into an interventionist response that escalates the situation. Do we have sufficient social and political mechanisms for navigating these interpellative collapses, and does the dominance of objective conceptions of identity work against this?

Merging Hegemony and Identity in the Politics of Online Privacy

Privacy and surveillance enter into and mediate the language games through which individual subjects both make sense of the world and apprehend their own identity. This chapter has hopefully demonstrated the ways that concepts and approaches drawn from discourse theory can shed light upon how we are drawn into the structures and logics of surveillance, both as a particular type of subject, constructed in multiple ways with differing illocutionary force, and as a political subjectivity finding positions within available discourses. Discourses of online politics and privacy are multiple and in conflict with one another. They offer particular ways of understanding the online world and frame politics occurring in relation to that environment. Attempts to define privacy and identity are political.

As identities are discursively constructed, they are also subject to hegemonic effects. Particular understandings of identity can have greater or lesser grip and purchase upon individuals and upon society. Glynos and Howarth draw upon distinction between ontical and ontological categories. For our purposes, this would translate into hegemonic forms of identity (loyalty cards, passports, single sign-on, a user account on a social network) and hegemonic qualities, characteristics of individual identities (such as a credit card number or balance, a username, age or Klout score). These interrelate because a form of identity that becomes socially hegemonic will carry with it associated ways of providing, validating, authenticating, measuring, naming and changing that identity. This will mean that counter-hegemonic means of filling in individual identities face conflict and contestation.

The concepts of politics and hegemony allow us to understand the multiple, conflicting representations of the online environment, and the way that privacy, surveillance and identity are articulated by different discourses. Rather than consensus over the way that personal information should be used online, or how digital identities should be incorporated into offline identities, there is conflict between a wide range of interested actors. The dominant, near hegemonic model of individual control and responsibility for managing one's own privacy in a market economic context, carries with it a number of negative consequences.

The idea that identity could be fixed or fully captured by some particular data system is fully ideological in the discourse-theory sense of the term. It is an impossible object. Impossible objects to be achieved through technological means are not rare in the field of surveillance. The diagram of the panopticon is perhaps the chief among these. A perfected prison which would remove resistance and allow the processing of docile bodies, it is perhaps most useful as an example of the way that discourses of power and security were dreamt and imagined during its period of writing, than as a universal diagram of how disciplinary power actually functions in societies. The all-seeing identity management database is the contemporary manifestation of this dreaming.

Moving Forward

One of the most important political questions of a shared online environment is how we are to collectively deal with the impacts upon identity and privacy of a technologically mediated, intrinsically surveillant environment. This would include how we are to deal with interpellative collapse, power asymmetries in the attribution and reading of identities, as well as the other negative impacts of surveillance. Individual "dealing" would not be political. Rather it would be a form of management or pragmatic consumerism. There are many existing discourses such as e-safety (Barnard-Wills, 2012b), or individual identity management (Barnard-Wills & Ashenden, 2010) that demonstrate the problems with this individual direction.

The sheer scale of the potential collectives ("billions of legitimate operators" to borrow Gibson's phrasing) involved is daunting. We might, however, consider some potential ways of leveraging the communicative nature of the online environment to support this sort of collective response to surveillance potential and online identity attribution. Might we find ways to express and negotiate our information preferences? Not in the same way as opaque, other-directed "personalisation," but in a collectively aware sense. In a practical form, this might include ways of articulating "I would rather you didn't share that" in a way that is understood. Returning to Bridle's concept of the internet as memory, "memory, socially and culturally constructed, is not only what we, as individuals, have experienced; it is what we, all of us, have experienced: collectively, forever" (Bridle, 2012).

Radical contingency should draw our analytical attention to the systemic capacity for the tolerance of ambiguity. Tolerating ambiguity is not something we appear to be culturally or psychologically well suited for, or that we build information systems for. But what are the structures and processes for resolving contradictions in different accounts of identity? To borrow from computer science, what is the protocol when one social actor makes an identity claim, and another social actor attributes a different identity? If identity is understood as non-political, then these decisions appear administrative. Only by bringing those decisions and processes back into the sphere of political deliberation can we hope to avoid reconstructing and supporting existing power structures and asymmetries. This suggests that we should promote the dislocation of the ideology of contained, attributed, known identity arising from surveillance practice. We should attempt to reveal the radical contingency and lack in the construction of identity and identities. We should encourage a proliferation of ways of thinking about identity. This is part of a broader discursive politics of foregrounding the ethical dimension of social reality, of identity and privacy practices. It might include looking at surveillance and identity technologies and their claims to knowledge, and point out that this is a gossamer hallucination, hopefully receding.

References

Acquisti, A., & Grossklags, J. (2003, May). *Losses, gains, hyperbolic discounting: An experimental approach to information security attitudes and behaviour.* Paper presesented at the 2nd Annual Workshop on Economic and Information Security—WEIS 2003. University of Maryland.

Andersen, N. Å. (2003). *Discursive analytical strategies: Understanding Foucault, Koselleck, Laclau, Luhmann.* Bristol: Policy.

Barbrook, R., & Cameron, A. (1996). The Californian Ideology. *Science as Culture, 6*(1), 44–72.

Barnard-Wills, D. (2012a) *Surveillance and identity: Discourse, subjectivity and the state.* Farnham & Burlington: Ashgate.

Barnard-Wills, D. (2012b). E-safety education: Young people, surveillance and responsibility. *Criminology and Criminal Justice, 12*(3), 239–255.

Barnard-Wills, D. & Ashenden, D. (2012). Securing virtual space: Cyber war, cyber terror and risk. *Space and Culture, 15*(2).

Barnard-Wills, D. & Ashenden, D. (2010). Public sector engagement with online identity management. *Identity in the Information Society, 3*(3), 657–674.

boyd, d., & Hargittai, E. (2010). Facebook privacy settings: Who cares? *First Monday, 15*(8).

Bridle, J. (2012, July 24). *The internet considered as fifth dimension, that of memory.* Booktwo.org. http://booktwo.org/notebook/internet-fifth-dimension-memory/

Clark, R. (1994). The digital persona and its implication to data surveillance. *The Information Society, 10*(2), 77–92.

Clinton, H. (2010, January 21). *Remarks on internet freedom.* http://www.state.gov/secretary/rm/2010/01/135519.htm

Coopamootoo, P. L., & Ashenden, D. (2011). Designing usable online privacy mechanisms: What can we learn from real-world behaviour? In S. Fischer-Hübner, P. Duquenoy, M. Hansen, R. Leenes, & G. Zhang (Eds.), *Privacy and identity* (pp. 311–324). IFIP AICT 352. Heidelberg: Springer.

Dean, M. (2010). *Governmentality: Power and rules in modern society* (2nd ed.). London: Sage.

Deleuze, G., & Guattari, F. (2004). *A thousand plateaus.* London: Continuum.

Dvorak, J. (2009, December 11). Eric Schmidt, Google and privacy. *Wall Street Journal: Market Watch.* http://articles.marketwatch.com/2009–12–11/commentary/30712576_1_privacy-advocates-chief-executive-eric-schmidt-cnet-article

Gandy, O. H., Jr. (2009). *Coming to terms with chance: Engaging rational discrimination and cumulative disadvantage.* Farnham: Ashgate.

Gibson, W. (1984). *Neuroromancer.* New York: Ace.

Glynos, J., & Howarth, D. (2007). *Logics of critical explanation in social and political theory.* London: Routledge.

Hacking, I. (1986). Making people up. In T. Heller & C. Brooke-Rose (Eds.), *Reconstructing individualism.* Stanford, CA: Stanford University Press.

Haggerty, K., & Ericson, R. V. (2000). The surveillant assemblage. *British Journal of Sociology, 51*(4), 605–622.

Howarth, D., & Stavrakakis, Y. (2000). *Discourse theory and political analysis: Identities, hegemonies and social change.* Manchester: Manchester University Press.

Kleiner, D. (2010). *The telekommunist manifesto.* Amsterdam: Network Notebooks. http://telekommunisten.net/the-telekommunist-manifesto/

Lace, S. (2005). Introduction. In S. Lace (Ed.), *The glass consumer: Life in a surveillance society.* Bristol: Policy/National Consumer Council.

Laclau, E., & Mouffe, C. (2001). *Hegemony and socialist strategy: Towards a radical democratic politics* (2nd ed.). London: Verso.

Lessig, L. (1999). *Code and other laws of cyberspace.* New York: Basic Books.

Lyon, D. (1994). *The electronic eye: The rise of surveillance society.* Minneapolis: University of Minnesota Press.

Mayer-Schönberger, V. (2009). *Delete: The virtue of forgetting in the digital age.* Princeton, NJ: Princeton University Press.

Morozov, E. (2011). *The Net delusion: How not to liberate the world.* London: Penguin.

Mouffe, C. (2005). *The return of the political.* London: Verso.

Murakami Wood, D. (Ed.). (2006). *A report on the Surveillance Society for the Information Commissioner by the Surveillance Studies Network: Full report*. Information Commissioner's Office, http://www.ico.org.uk/~/media/documents/library/Data_Protection/Practical_application/SURVEILLANCE_SOCIETY_FULL_REPORT_2006.ashx

N-1. (2012). *About*. N-1.cc. https://n-1.cc/about (translated from Spanish to English using Google Translate).

Nissenbaum, H. (2010). *Privacy in context: Technology, policy and the integrity of social life*. Stanford: Stanford Law Books.

Nye, J. S., Jr. (2010). *Cyber power*. Cambridge, MA: Harvard Kennedy School, Belfer Center for Science and International Affairs. http://belfercenter.ksg.harvard.edu/files/cyber-power.pdf

O'Brien, T. (2010, January 11). Facebook's Mark Zuckerberg claims privacy is dead. *Switched.com*. http://www.switched.com/2010/01/11/facebooks-mark-zuckerberg-claims-privacy-is-dead/

Pariser, E. (2011). *The filter bubble: What the internet is hiding from you*. London: Viking.

Poster, M. (1999). Databases as discourse, or electronic interpellation. In K. Racevskis (Ed.), *Critical essays on Michel Foucault*. New York: G.K. Hall.

Rid, T. (2012). Cyber war will not take place. *Journal of Strategic Studies, 35*(1), 5–32.

Secretary of State for the Home Department (U.K.). (2012, June). *Draft communications data bill*. Cm8359. http://www.official-documents.gov.uk/document/cm83/8359/8359.pdf

Solove, D. (2008). *Understanding privacy*. Cambridge, MA. Harvard University Press.

Sprenger, P. (1999, January 26). Sun on privacy: "Get over it." *Wired*. http://www.wired.com/politics/law/news/1999/01/17538

Stalder, F. (2002). Privacy is not the antidote to surveillance. *Surveillance and Society, 1*, 120–124.

Swift, M. (2010, June 22). Privacy advocates craft social media "bill of rights." *Phys.org*. http://phys.org/news196445607.html

Torfing, J. (1999). *New theories of discourse: Laclau, Mouffe and Zizek*. Oxford: Blackwell.

Turkle, S. (2011). *Alone together: Why we expect more from technology and less from each other*. New York: Basic Books.

Turow, J. (2006). *Niche envy: Marketing discrimination in the digital age*. Cambridge, MA: MIT Press.

Utz, S., & Krämer, N. C. (2009). The privacy paradox on social network sites revisited: The role of individual characteristics and group norms. *Cyberpscyhology: Journal of Psychosocial Research on Cyberspace, 3*(2) article 1. http://cyberpsychology.eu.

Wills, D., & Reeves, S. (2009). Facebook as a political weapon: Information in social networks. *British Politics, 4*(2), 265–281.

10

Surveillance as a Reality Game

Liisa A. Mäkinen & Hille Koskela

What a wonder, he thinks, that the long, bitter, heart-wrenching history of the planet should allow curious breathing spaces for the likes of mere toys and riddles; he sees them everywhere. Games, glyphs, symbols, allegories, puns and anagrams, masquerades, the magician's sleight-of-hand, the clown's wink, the comic shrug, the somersault, the cryptogram in its all forms, and especially, at least to Lawrence J. Weller's mind, the teasing elegance and circularity of the labyrinth structure, a snail, a scribble, a doodle on the earth's skin with no other directed purpose but to wind its sinuous way around itself.
—CAROL SHIELDS, *LARRY'S PARTY* (1997)

In the past decade or so, the understanding of surveillance in the academic research has shifted from viewing it as a top-down control mechanism to understanding it as a habit in which almost anyone can contribute (e.g., Ball & Webster, 2003; McGrath, 2004; Haggerty, 2006; Koskela, 2009). The distributed communications networks, such as the internet, have increased the possibilities for not only the state and corporations, but also individuals, to access surveillance (Andrejevic, 2007:212; Bruno, 2012:343). The equipment enabling surveillance is not necessarily used for only one purpose, but people use this technology for purposes beyond its original meanings. The usages are constantly changing and negotiated by different groups in different times (Albrechtslund & Nørgaard Glud, 2010:243). Hence, the public is no longer simply targeted by surveillance, but they can resist, play with or conduct surveillance themselves. Even though this chapter focuses more on individual participation, it is worth noting that there often is a "counter hegemonic engagement within surveillance practice" (McGrath, 2004:218). While people participate in surveillance in various ways, it is also possible to identify "a wide-spread pattern of unconventional politics through which ordinary people can express and mobilize their opposition to surveillance policies" (Gilliom, 2006:113; see also Wilson & Serisier, 2010).

In the past several years, the notion of surveillance containing performative practices and incidental monitoring in which the authorities play no role has been emphasized, and the idea of play in the context of surveillance has been discussed increasingly (e.g., McGrath, 2004; Albrechtslund & Dubbeld, 2005; Andrejevic, 2007; Albrechtslund, 2008). Besides the motive to control or to influence those whose data has been garnered (Lyon, 2001:2), surveillance techniques are "able to perform entertainment functions" and they are more and more used for entertainment (Albrechtslund & Dubbeld, 2005:217). Hence, it has been argued that they should also be "considered as toys or playthings" themselves (Ellerbrok, 2011:538). Surveillance can be "a playful experience for the users" (Monahan, 2011:500). On the one hand, this playfulness might come from using equipment meant for surveillance in a playful manner—in other words, not for surveillance but for purposes of enjoyment, fun or practical use—for example, playing with facial recognition systems in social media environments (e.g., Ellerbrok, 2011). This "toys and riddles" element of surveillance equipment and the playful experience of contributing in surveillance have created a remarkable change in subject positions. People can perceive and exercise identities that are far from the old-fashioned surveillance experience of being "under control." In brief, they turn from targets to agents. On the other hand, this playfulness might mean that surveillance itself is turned into—or disguised as—a game, where the purpose of the game itself is to surveil others: the monitoring process is set out as a game.

In this chapter, we explore the latter of these two possibilities: the game-like nature of surveillance practices. We consider situations where people conduct monitoring themselves by using surveillance equipment, but in a game-like setting, situations that are forming into a sort of surveillance reality game. To concretize this idea, we analyze the Internet Eyes site (the IE site; www.internet eyes.co.uk/) operated from the United Kingdom. The IE site is a privately operated online notification system that allows registered viewers to watch live feed from video surveillance cameras installed in shops and other businesses. If the viewer sees or suspects to see something illegal going on, (s)he can send out an alert to the owner of the camera. The most vigilant viewers receive monetary compensation as a reward.

The idea of harnessing private citizens to act as the eyes and ears of the police is not a new one. The intensity of encouraging informing has varied across times and cultures, being notoriously famous in, for example, the former East European countries. In the current West, new forms of requests to give information on others have come along with the neoliberal ideology emphasizing citizens' and communities' responsibilities. Individuals are increasingly induced to take positions previously held solely by the authorities as non-state mechanisms are enrolled in official forms of control and the state seeks to use "citizens as adjuncts to law enforcement by watching others" (Marx, 2006:40; see also e.g., Rose & Miller, 1992; Rose, 2000; Garland, 2001). TV programmes with "hotlines" have long been one feature in this development, now followed by using the internet and online cameras. In 2008 in the U.S., the state of Texas launched a website called the Texas Virtual Border Watch Program (in detail, see Koskela, 2011), which has given the citizens the possibility to participate in monitoring the border between U.S. and Mexico via webcams placed in strategic locations on the border. Participants who notice suspicious activity on the border can use a hotline to alert the Texas sheriff who will then decide how to react to the situation. These responsibilization policies are characterized by an emphasis on risk, insecurity and individual preparedness (Monahan, 2010; see also Marx, 2006). The nature of these policies is not labeled by "the carrot of participation," but by "the stick of generalized risk" (Andrejevic, 2005:482), and in them individuals are seen and produced as "entrepreneurs and consumers, whose moral autonomy is measured by their capacity for 'self-care'" (Brown, 2006:694). One of the consequences of responsibilization is that the seemingly obvious change from targets to agents is distorted. The pressures for individual preparedness and moral autonomy make it less clear who is in charge and for what. The individual's subject position as someone who can play with surveillance and enjoy it is muddled up. Free agents start to remind one of marionettes.

This chapter begins with an introduction to the IE site followed by an analysis of responsibilized surveillance in the context of the site. The two sections following are framed by the idea of surveillance as a reality game. We identify five different game metaphors revealing varying aspects of surveillance more generally, and then consider briefly one of those metaphors parallel to the IE site and especially the context of reality where that particular game is played.

Internet Eyes: An Overview

The Internet Eyes site is a privately operated website allowing registered viewers to watch a 24/7 live feed from surveillance cameras installed in IE client businesses. The site was launched in October 2010 (Farrier, 2010), after a rocky start. Initially the site was intended to launch in late 2009 (BBC News, 2009), but due to a complaint[1] made by non-governmental privacy organizations Privacy International and No CCTV sent to the Information Commissioner (ICO), the launch was postponed whilst the ICO investigated the plans. At that point, by December 2009, the site had over 14,000 people registered as potential viewers, but they could not yet watch the feed because of the site being reviewed (BBC News, 2010a).[2] After investigating the case, the ICO decided to allow the launch, presuming some modifications were made. These included allowing only subscribers ages 18 and over to access the site and making it obligatory for them to pay for the use, so that their personal details could be checked and "any voyeurism and misuse of the system" could be prevented (BBC News, 2010b). The site was opened on October 4, 2010, and it has been running since.

The IE company offers its service to shop owners and business customers who are in need of additional surveillance in their premises. The IE service receives live feed from their cameras and that stream is routed online to the webpage where registered viewers can watch the feed. Anyone living inside the EU, EEA (European Economic Area) or in selected other countries can register as a viewer. The viewers cannot choose themselves which feeds they would like to view, but a four camera feed set-up is randomly chosen for them as they log in. Also, the viewers are not informed about the locations of the premises where the feed is coming from, and the feed of a camera is not routed to a person who has stated to have the same postal code area as where the feed is coming from. The feed seen by the viewer is equipped with an alert function that can be clicked on. When clicked, the image freezes and enlarges. If, after viewing the situation more carefully, the viewer decides to send an alert, the system automatically sends a text message (SMS) and an email containing the frozen image to the business customer. That customer can then view if something wrong is going on or not, and take appropriate action. Each alert is rated by the business customer according to three types. A positive rating and ten points is given when the viewer witnessed a theft or "other unlawful or anti-social behavior." A neutral rating and one point is given when no theft or such occurred but nevertheless the business customer thinks the viewer acted in good faith. And finally, an incorrect rating is given and two points are lost when the viewer had no reason to give the alert or (s)he is suspected to having acted maliciously. Rewards are then issued according to the points: the most vigilant viewers will receive a reward fund of "no less than £1,000 per month."[3] The site also rewards the watching itself, with £0.50 given for watching the feed over 30 hours per month, £1 for over 45 hours per month and £1.50 for over 60 hours per month. As the annual registration fee is £12.99, it is possible to cover that fee by watching the feed excessively.

Currently, the site has more than 8,000 registered viewers. Almost half of them are from the United Kingdom (approximately 48%), about one-fourth (approximately 27%) are from France and roughly 6% are from Italy. There are also viewers from Switzerland, Belgium, Germany, Spain and Poland, to mention a few. The majority of the viewers are male, sex ratio being 60:40. When divided into age segments, 23% of the viewers are 18–30 years old, 24% are 31–40 years old, 33% are 41–50 years old, 11% are 51–60 years old and 9% are over 61 years old. The most common viewer is a male between ages 35 and 55.[4]

Internet Eyes and Responsibilized Surveillance

Before moving on to the analysis of surveillance as a game, we will consider the special characteristics the kind of responsibilized surveillance enabled by the Internet Eyes site has in comparison to other forms of surveillance, specifically those labeled as "peer-to-peer," "lateral" or "participatory" (Lyon, 2001; Andrejevic, 2005; Albrechtslund, 2008), and how surveillance done via the IE site differs from surveillance done via more traditional video surveillance cameras. We will also consider the nature of discipline in the framework of responsibilized surveillance and the possible challenges this type of surveillance entails.

As the responsibilized surveillance executed through the IE site targets random customers in selected businesses and the watching is made remotely via cameras, it differs both from participatory surveillance, which emphasizes the sharing practices and the reciprocality of the information gathering (Albrechtslund, 2008), and from lateral surveillance, which focuses more on keeping track of spouses, friends and relatives (Andrejevic, 2005). The mutuality of participatory surveillance has mostly been studied in the context of social networking sites (e.g., Ellerbrok, 2010; Trottier & Lyon, 2012), but unlike in those, in the IE case there is no "mutual gaze." The information moves only in a single direction: the direction allowed by the operators of the camera. In addition, the IE site is meant exclusively for surveillance, whereas social networking sites also have (or at least argue to have) other purposes. But social networking sites and the IE site do share the playful manner in which the technology enabling surveillance is used (see also Ellerbrok, 2011). When compared to "lateral surveillance," the difference is that the aim of the watching in the IE site is not to surveil specific people who are, for instance, known by the watcher. On the contrary, the possible viewing and recognition of someone familiar is attempted to be prevented by blocking feeds from the postal code area where the viewer lives. Hence, the watching is supposed to target the actions taken by the people seen; the identity of those watched is strived to fade away into the background.

At first glance, the site seems to take us back to the hierarchical conception of surveillance and the traditional dichotomy of the watcher and the watched. The power is put "into the hands of the watcher while the watched is a more or less passive subject of control" (Albrechtslund, 2008:par. 4). This view is somewhat disturbed by the fact that the roles of the watcher and the watched might change at any given moment as any of the watchers might become watched when entering a premise with this system in place, and vice versa. Additionally, it is worth noting that the roles of the watcher and watched in the IE context are different than what they were and still are with traditional video surveillance cameras. Traditionally, the feed of a surveillance camera was routed to a monitor in a control room, where, it was possible—even though it might have been difficult—to find out who (if anyone) was watching and where the feed was routed to. But with the IE system in operation, the watcher might be anyone, and the feed could be routed to almost anywhere (even anywhere in the world). Furthermore, the watchers (of the IE) are no longer in a position that the watchers (of a CCTV systems) previously held. IE watchers do not get to choose which feed to watch, know whether or not someone else is watching too, or even know where the feed they are watching is coming from. When they give an alert, they are routed away from the feed so that they cannot see the consequences of the alert they have given. Hence, as those watched are not given any information on the watchers, and those watching are not even given the location of the places watched, the surveillance seems in fact to have become "impossible to trace" (Mathiesen, 2012:xix), at least to anyone except the professionals working for the IE.

It has been argued in a societal level that in the name of our own good, we are all invited to become spies in a disciplinary society (Andrejevic, 2007:239–240; Albrechtslund, 2008:par. 4). The broadcasting of surveillance footage advances the "rising culture of informing" (Doyle, 2006:202). The disciplining effect of responsibilized surveillance works on two levels: relying on the internalized discipline of both the watched and the watchers (Andrejevic, 2005:239). The invitation to participate in the shared monitoring is inciting individuals to construe their lives according to the very norms they themselves are enforcing, and by participating the individual is also participating in the creation of her/himself as a subject of the governing power (Rose & Miller, 1992:187). In the IE site, surveillance becomes distributed, and moves not only from the public sector to the private sector, but also towards a private individual. Surveillance undergoes a "re-privatization" (Koskela, 2009:148) process, the responsibility to surveil is extended to "anyone" and that anyone—meaning the user—is framed as a surveillant (Bruno, 2012:347). When earlier the media was labeled as the disciplining authority (Frohne, 2002:255), now there is no single authority; rather, discipline is crowd-sourced, and the online media seem to be the prime technology aiding this.[5]

The challenges of the responsibilized participation lie in three basic questions: Participation of whom? Participation for whom? Participation in what? In participatory politics, there is a seeming promise of an equal opportunity of participation for everyone. In reality, not everyone has the same possibilities (due to, for instance, the lack of access to required technology) to truly engage in these activities. Moreover, the effects of broadcasting surveillance material "tend to work to the advantage of dominant institutions and groups, and against the less powerful" (Doyle, 2006:206). So these politics might not actually increase the possibilities and life chances of those in weaker positions in the society. Furthermore, "cybernetic participation enlists the labor of those who submit to monitored forms of interaction, but it stops short at the point of allowing shared control over shaping goals and designating desired ends" (Andrejevic, 2007:44). This critique is especially concrete in the IE case, where the participants are allowed and encouraged to monitor the feed and report incidents, but not to choose which feed they see, or to monitor the consequences after sending out the alert. It appears that the citizens' role is merely to verify and to gather evidence (Koskela, 2009:153).

Surveillance as a Game

Understanding surveillance in a cultural context means that "playing, gaming and leisure activities" are emphasized (Albrechtslund & Nørgaard Glud, 2010:238). Instead of being perceived as a threat or punishment, surveillance is increasingly understood in terms of hedonism, pleasure and amusement where "observation is not a menace; observation is entertaining" (Weibel, 2002:215; see also Haggerty, 2006; Koskela, 2009). As Luis A. Fernandez and Laura Huey (2009:198) argue, "not only does the public experience surveillance in their daily lives, but they also consume it as entertainment." The idea of consuming surveillance as entertainment might, in its simplest form, mean watching TV programmes exploiting surveillance-enabling techniques, or TV programmes that are based on constant surveillance (such as the TV show *Big Brother*, which locks people in an apartment for a certain period of time and makes them conduct irrelevant tasks under constant surveillance), or playing online games in which surveillance is an instrumental element. The popularization of the internet created new avenues for games that use surveillance as a feature (Albrechtslund & Dubbeld, 2005), but in these surveillance games, surveillance itself is not the purpose of the game as such. Surveillance is used to catch someone in the game: the catching is the purpose, not the surveillance with the help of which it is accomplished. However, the relationship between surveillance and game is two-sided as in addition to the entertainment value the surveillance function may provide, real surveillance also has many different game-like functions. By exploring and categorizing the game elements and game metaphors that surveillance entails, we aim to offer a different view on surveillance than what is captured when looking at it, for example, from the viewpoint of power structures, discipline or various actors engaged in it. We analyze surveillance and its contradictory nature through five game metaphors.

To begin with, surveillance can be understood as a cat-and-mouse game. "Catching of someone in the act" has been a traditional motive for the monitoring of places and people. For example, video surveillance conducted in urban space aims at a real-time quick chase of those who have committed crime or behaved in an "anti-social" manner. Furthermore, surveillance is conducted in order to try to prevent crimes and mishap, and cameras have been treated no different than people who just happened to be on the scene: as eyewitnesses able to tell something afterwards (Koskela, 2009:147). But as surveillance has become increasingly dispersed and the techniques enabling it are more widely available, the "old story about the 'good police officers' chasing 'evil criminals' has begun to sound like a naive fairy tale" (Koskela, 2009:151). Countersurveillance has also reached the cat-and-mouse point, since official controllers and activists have ended up in a situation where "my video" is evaluated against "your video" (Wilson & Serisier, 2010).

The basic nature of surveillance also relates to the metaphor of hide-and-seek: monitoring is used in order to find someone or something hidden. In urban space, this might include helicopters with search lights (Pinck, 2000). Crime displacement is one of the classic failures of surveillance: the hiding element "wins." However, unlike a cat-and-mouse game, which is characterized by speed, hide-and-seek is often slow by nature. Furthermore, it can highlight elements other than urban environment. Traces are left (and sought) also in electronic environments. This brings a more complex nuance to the game as the nature of surveillance is not merely about finding and extracting information, but it can also be about creating information (Marx, 2002).

The third type of game to be revealed is the labyrinth formed by surveillance. This metaphor helps to describe how people navigate through, and sometimes try to avoid, surveillance. Perhaps the most telling example is the labyrinth of an urban environment. The Institute for Applied Autonomy (AA) has been one of the pioneers for organising "surveillance-free zones" (Schienke & IAA, 2002). Their project, iSee, provides the public interactive online maps in which they can indicate points of origin and destination and then those maps display a "path of least surveillance." The project is designed to allow people "to play a more active role in choosing when and how they are recorded" (Schienke & IAA, 2002:106). The online map with the routes drawn to it resembles a labyrinth that has to be solved in order to get from one place to another without being seen. Commensurate navigation also happens in other less visible surveillance environments where people try to cope with different levels of surveillance. For instance, Facebook could be categorized as a labyrinth: people navigate through "multiple variable visibility" (Ellerbrok, 2010), revealing only what they choose to reveal and being able to see only what is shown to them.

The sleight-of-hand metaphor bears close resemblance to one of the archetypal surveillance-related images: a bank robbery, where the perpetrators have covered their faces so as not to be identified. These kind of "magic tricks" are extremely easy when facing traditional video surveillance. Caps, hoods and masks are used to cover faces in protests and other such activities. In an online environment, fake identities are an example of this sleight-of-hand: "fake or anonymous online identities make surveillance more difficult; but also allow the intensification of surveillance based on the argument that anonymity is dangerous, might foster antisocial behavior, and therefore needs to be controlled" (Fuchs, Boersma, Albrechtslund, & Sandoval, 2012:19). On the other hand, playing with one's identity can also be the main point of a website[6] where the idea is to create a fake identity in a form of an avatar. In a way, these sites give a promise of something different: a chance to be someone else, to escape one's own identity. As has been argued, in the developing surveillance culture, just as there have been "multiple, often contradictory systems observing us," there have also been "multiple, contradictory selves produced by this surveillance" (McGrath, 2012:89).

The fifth metaphor of a game introduced here is poker. Arguably, a part of the appeal of a poker game—one hook of the game—is never knowing what the opponent is hiding. As some cards are visible to the player and others are not, the final truth is not to be known (until it is too late), and one has to make a decision based on the information available at any given moment in the game by calculating probabilities of what might be hidden. This type of calculation, estimation or even guessing, happens also in social media sites where people form images of each other based on the information posted online. As a more sinister example, this metaphor comes to resemble a counterterrorist scheme, where observations on actions and background of people are cross-referenced with pre-calculated probabilities on certain factors being connected to terrorism. Decisions (for instance on questioning the suspect, denying access, etc.) are made based on these connections. At worst this might mean racial profiling.

These five metaphors are overlapping and they do not provide an exhaustive description of the game-like nature of surveillance—one could find other metaphors to add to these already mentioned. However, each of them reveals a vital aspect of surveillance, and helps to understand that in fact the game-like nature of the IE case is not so different from the game elements of surveillance more generally. Thus surveillance and games are more intertwined than might have previously been recognized.

Internet Eyes as a Reality Game

In the public statements of the Internet Eyes site representatives, and especially its managing director Tony Morgan, it has repeatedly been stated that IE is not a game. According to the company statements: "Internet Eyes is not a game…It's a crime prevention tool that has been developed to let the public catch criminals . . ."[7] and continuing elsewhere: "We are just rewarding people for their vigilance" (BBC News, 2010a). Opposing arguments have also been presented in the media. On a BBC interview, Charles Farrier from No CCTV stated that the IE "is encouraging a growing trend of citizen spies. If people are so concerned about crime, they should contact the police. They are hiding behind computer screens and willing crime to happen so they get a prize. It is a game" (BBC News, 2010b). In this section, we consider the game-like elements of the IE site: we analyze how surveillance is turned into a game with points and prizes, and how it takes advantage of peoples' various reasons to participate. We will also briefly discuss the site in the context of the poker metaphor introduced in the previous section. In our view, the metaphor of a poker game has the most to offer to our analysis of the site, although we could also investigate it through the others. For instance, in order to understand the site in the framework of a cat-and-mouse metaphor or hide-and-seek metaphor would mean to emphasize the "catching of someone in the act" side of the site, or the attempt one makes when trying to hide one's deeds from the watching eye— this also comes close to the sleight-of-hand metaphor. The metaphor of a labyrinth in the context of the IE site could be approached either from the viewpoint of those occupying the surveilled space, perceiving it as a labyrinth through which they are navigating, or it could be understood from the perspective of the viewer, who might perceive the view (s)he is seeing as a maze with places hidden and places visible, and which should be seen in its entirety for the desired outcome for the game. However, for the purposes of this chapter, we will focus more on the fifth metaphor and especially the framework of reality where this game is played.

When the IE site is characterized as a game, perhaps the most intriguing question forms around its connection to reality. The IE programme is characterized by its existence in the borderline of both virtual and material places. It is a "surveillance-enabling technology which operates in…spaces that combine the online and offline worlds" (Albrechtslund & Nørgaard Glud, 2010:236). It is mainly the presentation of material spaces in the virtual online space that creates a "space in-between": through the visual representations, the virtual becomes embedded with the real. It becomes less clear "where space lies," or where the viewers and their objects exactly are. As Miyase Christensen and André Jansson (2012) note, the online environment opens up new possibilities for creating alternative spatialities. Additionally, this type of surveillance comes to resemble that of reality TV: in both of them, the viewer is offered the possibility of conducting constant scrutiny and an opportunity to act on what is seen (for example "voting someone out" in *Big Brother* or informing about a suspected crime in the IE). Arguably, people behind a computer screen are not that different from people behind a TV screen. When surveillance material is broadcasted, the watcher can be described as follows:

> The gaze of the TV spectator watching reality TV becomes an inspecting gaze of power. The TV viewer is like the warden in a panoptic prison. The people in reality TV shows become images, spectacles, observed, and controlled. The spectator in front of the picture screen has the pleasure on the controlling gaze. (Weibel, 2002:218)

But there seems to be a difference in the level of what is real when comparing reality TV to this type of surveillance. While reality TV sets out the promise of filming real people and unscripted events, and the shows might even be based on reality, they seldom actually are real (see e.g., Dubrofsky, 2009). It has been argued, that the format of reality TV "offers not an escape from reality but an escape *into* reality" (Andrejevic, 2004:8, emphasis in original). However, this argument seems even more accurate when considering the IE setting; there the "reality" the viewer is "escaping into" is actually real and is actually happening at the very moment it is seen. Hence, we argue that alongside reality TV we should increasingly speak of reality games. However, at the same time, we acknowledge that the concept "reality game" is controversial; at first glance it in fact seems to be an oxymoron. Games in a traditional sense are not about reality: they are a way to bend the reality or even escape reality. As a matter of fact, combining a game with reality makes it an atypical game.[8] Therefore, when the reality of the site is examined parallel to the game-like nature of the site, the combination becomes increasingly interesting.

Games and shows provide entertainment for the public, and the entertainment surveillance provides reaches one of its culminations in the spectacle of reality TV. In reality TV shows, the viewer is "presented with the spectacle of how fun surveillance can be" (Andrejevic, 2004:8; see also McGrath, 2004). If a spectacle is understood in the traditional sense, it means a theater-like event where the viewers are passive. However, Mark Andrejevic (2004:2) notes that the "promise deployed by reality TV is that submission to comprehensive surveillance is not merely a character-building challenge and a 'growth' experience, but a way to participate in a medium that has long relegated audience members to the role of passive spectators." It seems that the addictive appeal of reality TV is similar to that of the reality game: the viewer is given an opportunity to participate, to become an active agent. So in a sense, the IE site is also more than a spectacle: it is a truly participatory experience. But at the same time, the IE site seems to be labeled by the failure of the spectacle. The viewer is in constant anticipation of a crime about to happen, but if and when it finally happens, and (s)he reports it, (s)he cannot see the outcome. The spectacle has no high point. The site retains an impression of "[t]he constant *potential* for breaking news" (Pinck, 2000:65, emphasis in original), but at the same time it demonstrates for the viewer "the addictive appeal of never quite seeing enough" (McGrath, 2012:86). In a sense, by hiding the outcome of the spectacle from the viewer and not showing the consequence of the player's actions, the site distorts reality. The only consequence for the player comes in the form of the points. This brings us back to the poker metaphor from the previous section. In contrast to a poker game, where a part of the appeal of the game might come from the fact that some things are hidden from the player and the game climaxes on the revealing of the cards, the IE site never reaches this point. The cards are never revealed. The site distorts reality insofar that the reality in the IE is the reality of a game—the reality of points and rewards—not the reality of the actual events, which are merely objects of the game.

So why do people participate in the game? In our view, the possibility to win money, that is, the monetary reward, is one of the reasons for participation. As the site rewards not only the most vigilant but also the most forbearing watchers, one could simply argue that money is one of the attractions of the site. On the other hand, participation can also be connected to the before mentioned "culture of informing" (Doyle, 2006:202) and the increasing everydayness and access to new technologies. The internet is facilitating "a globally networked form of surveillance" operating in real time, thus enabling "surveillance at a distance" (Fuchs et al., 2012:3, 15; see also Rose & Miller, 1992:180). Hence, with the help of programmes such as the IE, it becomes possible to "create a widespread voluntary vigilante group—a kind of *global neighborhood watch*" (Koskela, 2011:53, emphasis in original). Participation can also be connected to the play and entertainment the site offers. Play has been defined elsewhere as "the lighthearted use of a technology or technological system for purposes of personal entertainment, amusement or fun" (Ellerbrok, 2011:538). Fun and entertainment might not necessarily be the only reasons for watching, but they can nevertheless play a part. People use surveillance equipment for their own purposes and with their own motivations. This does not necessarily form any critical or political statements, and most often there is no orga-nisational structure behind it: "[t]here is no agenda" (Koskela, 2009:163). The watching can merely be entertainment for the watcher. However, at the same time, the IE site aims to increase surveillance and control. It forms an intriguing hybrid of fun and entertainment on the one hand, but discipline and control on the other. As Rachel Hall (2009:55, emphasis in original), studying transnational security and war on terror, notes: "[f]or the privileged spectators of the war on terror, wartime surveillance provides discipline *and* entertainment or better yet, discipline-as-entertainment."

Retelling this for the privileged spectators of the IE site, broadcasted surveillance provides discipline-as-entertainment.

Among entertainment, this privileged spectator can feel pride and desire to help in societal tasks—which can also be separated as one reason for participation. According to Tony Morgan, managing director of Internet Eyes, the aim of the participation should be "to help society in the fight against crime."[9] This seems fitting with the spirit of the neoliberal agenda, where "it is essential to provide the anxious public with the impression that they are able to 'do something'" (Koskela, 2011:60). Similar to the Texas Virtual Border Watch Program mentioned above, where the viewer is given a status of a virtual sheriff, the IE site also appoints the viewer with a specific authoritative role. When agreeing to the IE terms and conditions,[10] the viewers will become data processors under the UK Data Protection Act 1998. The desire to aid in a societal task can be a positive feeling, creating pride and facilitating empowerment, but it can also stem from negative observations, such as annoyance that nothing is done about crime. It can also entail a more "punitive, vengeance-oriented approach to crime and control, parallel to past spectacles of punishment, but also new in key ways" (Doyle, 2006:201). In the Texas Virtual Border Watch Program, "the motivation for watching is, above all, patriotic," and can even be described as "patriotic voyeurism" (Koskela, 2011:61). This emphasizes the division the watcher makes between an "us" and a "them," and the creation of "collective subject positions of 'harmful others'" (Hier, 2008:174). This brings us back to the IE site. Fernanda Bruno (2012:347) warns that while the ideal behind "participatory transparency" is that the gaze of an average citizen will somehow allow the state of the world to be seen in a truer light, what actually happens is that "instead of creating alternative processes of visibility, the transparency demanded by participatory surveillance ends up reiterating the principles that reproduce the logic of suspicion, accusation and fear."

These different possible reasons for participating in the game bring out the controversial nature of the IE site: it is very likely that not all the participants think they are playing when entering the site. Besides the private reasons people might have—for example, entertainment and possible rewards—participation can also be justified with societal reasons, such as being annoyed about the state of the affairs. Bruno (2012:347) claims that in the IE site: "surveillance becomes a kind of game. Thus, Internet Eyes constitutes an 'open circuit television' [OCTV, see Koskela, 2004] monitored by different collaborative eyes, combining surveillance, entertainment and business in one product" (Bruno, 2012:347). When considering the business side of the IE site, it can be seen as a part of a wider development of "commercial deployment of interactivity as information-gathering strategy" (Andrejevic, 2007:213) where individual watching or presenting practices are tied into the process of consumption, and "surveillance is becoming primarily a citizen (or consumer) activity"

(McGrath, 2012:83). Internet Eyes Ltd. works as a mediator between a business in need of surveillance and a citizen willing to do the watching. The user participation is being "captured and capitalized on" (Bruno, 2012:344), but so is the need for additional surveillance expressed by those customers buying IE's services. One cannot deny the intriguing appeal of a marketing plan that argues to respond to the demand of the audience and the businesses when IE is actually creating business for itself by offering this kind of service.

Bringing Reality Back to Reality

John McGrath (2012:83) argues that:

> At the end of the decade…a universal system is more or less effectively in place—the product not of a government plan, but of the semi-chaotic interplay of Google's mapping ambitions and the widespread embrace of social networking—whereby an extraordinary amount of public and private activity is recorded, uploaded and shared online.

The Internet Eyes site brings its own nuance to this mess of techniques increasingly showing our everyday life online. The "system is in place" and it continues to expand, at least in the hopes of the IE representatives: "Without our viewers' continued support the system cannot continue to expand as we know it will over the coming months and years."[11]

What we aim to emphasise in this chapter is the embedment of virtual with reality in a new way. This new combination of virtual and reality is different from the mere spectacle of reality TV or broadcasting surveillance material online, and it might make people forget that it actually is real. When compared to other forms of broadcasting surveillance material online, it seems that the IE brings reality back to reality. Peter Weibel (2002:211) has argued, that "[i]n the media world, the world as event disappears and becomes a mere image, a spectacle and likewise a phantom." Similarly, it is possible that the people watched via the IE site are not regarded as mere people anymore, but as "objects of seeing" (Weibel, 2002:215) and "spectator in front of the picture screen has the pleasure of the controlling gaze" (Weibel, 2002:218). It makes no difference how the monitored people ended up where they are (being filmed) and it does not matter who they are: they are a part of the game. And the more IE is perceived as a game, the less the players think about the real context in which this game takes place. For the viewers, reality might become merely the reality of the game.

New individual identities are not necessarily formed within the pro-surveillance versus countersurveillance distinction. We can recognize three overlapping subjectivities here: the surveillance target self, the surveillance agent self, and the marionette self. Individuals are increasingly travelling between these identities without a clear direction. Furthermore, even though the notions of amusing, playful and game—when connected to surveillance—are mostly used in a positive way, pointing to empowerment, agency and such, they are not always positive. A game can also be brutal, where the strong benefit and the weak lose. The game-like nature of the IE site does not fade out the moral problems of it, on the contrary. As the fun and the excitement seem to fade out the reality context even further, a critical analysis of the site becomes of utmost importance.

The history of surveillance studies has largely been about reflecting metaphors. As the theoretical understanding increases, and the practice of surveillance expands and changes, new carefully reflected and justified metaphors are needed in order to help scholars to examine and explain their topic more deeply. During the past decades, it has become quite clear that the panopticon is not a sufficient metaphor: it positions subjects as mere passive objects of "the gaze," denying any other positions. Consequently, other more sophisticated metaphors have been taking over. To name but a few—all valid in each context—we can distinguish the following: performativity (McGrath, 2004), pleasure (Weibel, 2002), play, art, entertainment (Albrechtslund & Dubbeld, 2005; Ellerbrok, 2011), field, territory, bridge (Christensen & Jansson, 2012) and empowerment (Koskela, 2004; Ellerbrok, 2010). Nevertheless, we claim that since the practice of surveillance is becoming more complex, mutual and difficult to understand as (only) a control mechanism, the game metaphors presented in this chapter could provide fresh and fruitful ideas for conceptualizing present-day surveillance and its multiple agents and directions.

Notes

1. Complaint: Internet Eyes, October 27, 2009, http://www.no-cctv.org.uk/materials/docs/ICO_complaint_internet_eyes.pdf
2. The information on the number of viewers is from the Internet Eyes Facebook page on March 22, 2010, https://www.facebook.com/InternetEyeshttp://news.bbc.co.uk/2/hi/uk_news/8485056.stm
3. Starting from June 2012, the reward has been 2000£ (Internet Eyes newsletter, May 2012).
4. Information is based on email exchange between Liisa Mäkinen and Internet Eyes staff, October 12–24, 2012.
5. According to Information Commissioner's report to Parliament on the state of surveillance (2010:32): "Crowdsourcing describes the outsourcing of work to a wide group of people, usually via an open call or competition." See also Howe, 2006.
6. For example: Second Life (www.secondlife.com), Habbo Hotel (www.habbo.com)
7. Quoted from Internet Eyes Facebook page, status update October 5, 2009, www.facebook.com/interneteyes

8. We thank Maria Heiskanen for making this point.
9. Audiotape on the Internet Eyes site: http://interneteyes.co.uk/.
10. Terms and conditions: http://www.interneteyes.co.uk/terms-and-conditions.
11. Internet Eyes newsletter, November 2011.

References

Albrechtslund, A. (2008). Online social networking as participatory surveillance. *First Monday*, *13*(3). http://www.uic.edu/htbin/cgiwrap/bin/ojs/index.php/fm/article/view/2142/1949

Albrechtslund, A., & Dubbeld, L. (2005). The plays and arts of surveillance: Studying surveillance as entertainment. *Surveillance & Society*, *3*(2/3), 216–221.

Albrechtslund, A., & Nørgaard Glud, L. (2010). Empowering residents: A theoretical framework for negotiating surveillance technologies. *Surveillance & Society*, *8*(2), 235–250.

Andrejevic, M. (2007) *iSpy: Surveillance and power in the interactive era*. Lawrence: University Press of Kansas.

Andrejevic, M. (2005). The work of watching one another: Lateral surveillance, risk, and governance. *Surveillance & Society*, *2*(4), 479–497.

Andrejevic, A. (2004). *Reality TV: The work of being watched*. London: Rowman & Littlefield.

Ball, K., & Webster, F. (2003). The intensification of surveillance. In K. Ball & F. Webster (Eds.), *The intensification of surveillance: Crime, terrorism and warfare in the information age* (pp. 1–15). London: Pluto.

BBC News. (2010a, January 28). CCTV monitoring website launch delayed by review. *BBC News*. http://news.bbc.co.uk/2/hi/uk_news/8485056.stm

BBC News. (2010b, April 10). CCTV site Internet Eyes hopes to help catch criminals. *BBC News*. http://www.bbc.co.uk/news/uk-11460897

BBC News. (2009, July 10). Public to monitor CCTV from home. *BBC News*. http://news.bbc.co.uk/2/hi/uk_news/england/london/8293784.stm

Brown, W. (2006). American nightmare: Neoliberalism, neoconservatism, and de-democratization. *Political Theory*, *34*, 690–714.

Bruno, F. (2012). Surveillance and participation on Web 2.0. In K. Ball, K. Haggerty, & D. Lyon (Eds.), *Routledge handbook of surveillance studies* (pp. 343–351). London: Routledge.

Christensen, M., & Jansson, A. (2012). Fields, territories, and bridges: Networked communities and mediated surveillance in transnational social space. In C. Fuchs, K. Boersma, A. Albrechtslund, & M. Sandoval (Eds.), *Internet and surveillance: The challenges of Web 2.0 and social media* (pp. 220–238). New York: Routledge.

Doyle, A. (2006). An alternative current in surveillance and control: Broadcasting surveillance footage of crimes. In K. D. Haggerty & R. V. Ericson (Eds.), *The new politics of surveillance and visibility* (pp. 199–224). Toronto: University of Toronto Press.

Dubrofsky, R. E. (2009). Therapeutics of the self: Surveillance in the service of the therapeutic. In S. Magnet & K. Gates (Eds.), *The new media of surveillance* (pp. 127–148). New York: Routledge.

Ellerbrok, A. (2011). Playful biometrics: Controversial technology through the lens of play. *The Sociological Quarterly*, *52*, 528–547.

Ellerbrok, A. (2010). Empowerment: Analysing technologies of multiple variable visibility. *Surveillance & Society*, *8*(2), 200–220.

Farrier, C. (2010, October 7). Internet eyes citizen spy game—the new Stasi? *Disinformation.* http://disinfo.com/2010/10/internet-eyes-citizen-spy-game-the-new-stasi/#sthash.WX dUqIBC.dpbs

Fernandez, L. A., & Huey, L. (2009). Is resistance futile? Thoughts on resisting surveillance. *Surveillance & Society, 6*(3), 198–202.

Frohne, U. (2002). "Screen tests": Media narcissism, theatricality, and the internalized observer. In T. Y. Levin, U. Frohne, & P. Weibel (Eds.), *CTRL[SPACE]: Rhetorics of surveillance from Bentham to Big Brother* (pp. 253–277). Karlsruhe: ZKM Centre for Art and Media.

Fuchs, C., Boersma, K., Albrechtslund, A., & Sandoval, M. (2012). Introduction. Internet and surveillance. In C. Fuchs, K. Boersma, A. Albrechtslund, & M. Sandoval (Eds.), *Internet and surveillance. The challenges of Web 2.0 and social media* (pp. 1–28). New York: Routledge.

Garland, D. (2001). *The culture of control: Crime and social order in contemporary society.* Chicago: University of Chicago Press.

Gilliom, J. (2006). Struggling with surveillance: Resistance, consciousness and identity. In K. D. Haggerty & R. V. Ericson (Eds.), *The new politics of surveillance and visibility* (pp. 111–129). Toronto: University of Toronto Press.

Haggerty, K. (2006). Tear down the walls: On demolishing the panopticon. In D. Lyon (Ed.), *Theorizing surveillance: The panopticon and beyond* (pp. 23–45). Cullompton: Willan.

Hall, R. (2009). Of Ziploc bags and black holes: The aesthetics of transparency in the war on terror. In S. Magnet & K. Gates (Eds.), *The new media of surveillance* (pp. 41–68). New York: Routledge.

Hier, S. P. (2008). Thinking beyond moral panic: Risk, responsibility, and the politics of moralization. *Theoretical Criminology, 12*(2), 173–190.

Howe, J. (2006, June). The rise of crowdsourcing. *Wired.* http://www.wired.com/wired/archive/14. 06/crowds.html

Information Commissioner's Office. (2010). *Information Commissioner's report to Parliament on the state of surveillance.* http://www.ico.gov.uk/~/media/documents/library/Corporate/ Research_and_reports/surveillance_report_for_home_select_committee.ashx

Koskela, H. (2011). "Don't mess with Texas!": Texas Virtual Border Watch Program and the (botched) politics of responsibilization. *Crime, Media, Culture, 7*(1), 49–66.

Koskela, H. (2009). Hijacking surveillance? The new moral landscapes of amateur photographing. In K. F. Aas, H. O. Gundhus, & H. M. Lomell (Eds.), *Technologies of (in)security: The surveillance of everyday life* (pp. 147–167). London: Routledge/Cavendish.

Koskela, H. (2004). Webcams, TV shows and mobile phones: Empowering exhibitionism. *Surveillance & Society, 2*(2/3), 199–215.

Lyon, D. (2001). *Surveillance society: Monitoring everyday life.* Buckingham: Open University Press.

Marx, G. (2006). Soft surveillance: The growth of mandatory volunteerism in collecting personal information—"Hey buddy can you spare a DNA?" In T. Monahan (Ed.), *Surveillance and security: Technological politics and power in everyday life* (pp. 37–56). New York: Routledge.

Marx, G. (2002). What's new about the "new surveillance"? Classifying for change and continuity. *Surveillance & Society, 1*(1), 9–29.

Mathiesen, T. (2012). Preface. In C. Fuchs, K. Boersma, A. Albrechtslund, & M. Sandoval (Eds.), *Internet and surveillance: The challenges of Web 2.0 and social media* (pp. xv–xxi). New York: Routledge.

McGrath, J. (2012). Performing surveillance. In K. Ball, K. Haggerty, & D. Lyon (Eds.), *Routledge handbook of surveillance studies* (pp. 83–90). London: Routledge.

McGrath, J. (2004). *Loving Big Brother: Performance, privacy and surveillance space.* London: Routledge.

Monahan, T. (2011). Surveillance as cultural practice. *The Sociological Quarterly, 52,* 495–508.

Monahan, T. (2010). *Surveillance in the time of insecurity.* New Brunswick, NJ: Rutgers University Press.

Pinck, P. (2000). From sofa to the crime scene: Skycam, local news and the televisual city. In M. Balshaw & L. Kennedy (Eds.), *Urban space and representation* (pp. 55–68). London: Pluto.

Rose, N. (2000). Government and control. *British Journal of Criminology, 40,* 321–339.

Rose, N., & Miller, P. (1992). Political power beyond the state: Problematic of government. *British Journal of Sociology, 43,* 173–205.

Schienke, E. W., & IAA (2002). On the outside looking out: An interview with the Institute for Applied Autonomy (IAA). *Surveillance and Society, 1,* 102–119. http://www.surveillance-and-society.org/articles1/iaa.pdf

Shields, C. (1997). *Larry's party.* New York: Penguin.

Trottier, D., & Lyon, D. (2012). Key features of social media surveillance. In C. Fuchs, K. Boersma, A. Albrechtslund, & M. Sandoval (Eds.), *Internet and surveillance: The challenges of Web 2.0 and social media* (pp. 89–105). New York: Routledge.

Weibel, P. (2002). Pleasure and the panoptic principle. In T. Y. Levin, U. Frohne, & P. Weibel (Eds.), *CTRL[SPACE]: Rhetorics of surveillance from Bentham to Big Brother* (pp. 207–223). Karlsruhe: ZKM Centre for Art and Media.

Wilson, D., & Serisier, T. (2010). Video activism and the ambiguities of counter-surveillance. *Surveillance & Society, 8*(2), 166–180.

11

Sexual Bodies and Surveillance Excess on the Chinese Internet

Katrien Jacobs

Introduction

An explosion of sexually explicit media on the Chinese internet has caused a shift in awareness of surveillance culture, as unleashed expressivity and heightened censorship have become intermingled with the daily operations of netizen communities. The era of social media has also led to an internalization of surveillance as routines of gazing, acting out and abundantly sharing products. At the same time, since its establishment in 1949, the People's Republic of China has upheld a nationwide ban on sexually explicit media, imposing harsh punishments on those caught purchasing, producing or distributing materials deemed a violation of public morality. The mechanisms of censorship can be described as a panopticon-style reinforcement of upright morality, but one that is consistently undermined by underground circuits for erotic entertainment and a counterculture of activism and dissent. There have been attempts to disseminate pro-Communist ideology through government-hired netizen squads (also called the "50 cents party," *wǔmáo dǎng*) who infiltrate websites and social networks.[1] But despite these efforts, social norms and fashions are equally influenced by modern sex cultures and "peer-to-peer" types of intelligence about sensitive topics and taboo materials.

The People's Republic of China requires web users to gain government approval before opening any website or blog, and to submit contact information when accessing social networks on the internet. Governmental monitoring and censor-ship of the web primarily involves locating forbidden content, arranging visits between police officers and site administrators, shutting down host servers and mod-ifying pages that are linked to overseas servers. With the construction of a Golden Shield, later called the Great Fire Wall, a database-driven remote surveillance sys-tem was also created that offers immediate access to national and local records on every person in China. This system ultimately aims to integrate data from its vast surveillance networks of cameras, speech and face-recognition systems, smart cards and credit records. The Chinese government did not operate in a void while build-ing this Golden Shield as it collaborated with Western high-tech corporations who desired to expand their business into China. He Qinglian believes that the potential of a Chinese free-speech internet was further "hijacked" by these foreign corporations who aided the Chinese government in building an imposing system of surveillance and control (He, 2008:170).

In response to a widespread surveillance apparatus and the curtailing of civil rights, netizens employ subversive discourses and open displays of sexuality to crit-icize the prerogatives and ideologies of the nation-state. This chapter discusses a new ethos of sexual individualism and the employment of anonymous "mob" identities within sites for amateur or "D.I.Y." (do-it-yourself) pornography, internet activism and online vigilantes entitled "Human Flesh Search Engine" (*Renrou Sousuo*). These case studies were chosen to demonstrate that the social psychology of a "ruth-less gaze" has invaded the Chinese internet, that it has led to sexual liberation and movements towards democracy as well as a backlash of mob hatred and assault on people's freedom of expression and privacy.

The case studies were conducted by tracking and analyzing illegal porn collec-tions and sex scandals on the Chinese internet and by conducting interviews with young adults and porn consumers. At the same, the study followed the stirrings of a highly censored activist movement by looking at daily netizen postings on micro-blogs on Twitter and its Chinese equivalent, Weibo, as well as Facebook and its equivalent, Renren. Several accounts were created to follow the postings of activists, artists, sex radicals and media watchers between April 2009 and April 2011.[2]

Embodying and Sexualizing Surveillance Culture

In this analysis of sexually explicit media on the Chinese internet, surveillance cul-ture is presented alongside a global development towards peer-to-peer surveillance that has emerged alongside social networks. David Lyon writes that surveillance cul-ture has moved towards a dispersal of nation-state power and capitalism as modes of moral engineering and peer surveillance are practiced within micro-sites of work and play (Lyon, 2007:14). According to Siva Vaidhyanathan, the era of "panopticon" has morphed into a "cryptopticon," as disguised or less obtrusive types of surveillance by corporations and nation-states alike are affecting the social psychology of netizens. There has been a shift from a centrally controlled gaze of moral control towards decentralized mechanisms of tracking, classifying and supporting citizen communities, services and behaviors. As Vaidhyanathan writes:

> The forces at work in Europe, North America, and much of the rest of the world are the opposite of a Panopticon: They involve not the subjection of the individual to the gaze of a single, centralized authority, but the surveillance of the individual by all, always by many. We have a cryptopticon (for lack of a better word). Unlike Bentham's prisoners, we don't know the ways in which we are being watched or profiled—we simple know that we are. (Vaidhyanathan, 2011:112)

In the era of "big-data" surveillance, citizens are caught in webs of data and leave behind trails that can be easily used by government bureaucracies and private companies. The cryptopticon provides information architectures for people to spy on each other and to foster "open" play modes and radical identities, while systematically collecting, compiling and analyzing group behaviors. To some extent, the cryptopticon relies on its netizen groups to be aware of the power of recording devices, to bandy together and develop counterintelligence and do-it-yourself media environments.

For example, media activists Alessandro Ludovico and Hans Bernhard have criticized the surveillance mechanisms of the company Google by revealing its advertising programs and by automatically buying back market shares. In their act of civil disobedience entitled "Google Will Eat Itself," they wanted to reveal corporate greed underneath the workings of a "happy dictatorship." As they describe this type of power ironically:

> How can a dictator be funny for the people? One chance is to know how to entertain people, while continuing to influence every decision they make, so invisibly maintaining the totalitarian power untouched. Google's management knows very well how to entertain surfers....On the Google planet everything works and is funny. Everything is light (as the interface) and tasty (as the images search), resource-rich (as Gmail) or fast and updated (as Google News). (Ludovico & Bernhard, 2007)

The cryptopticon supports netizen communities in seemingly benign and humanitarian ways, as improved information architectures try to soothe and please consumers and watch them in their most relaxed and uninhibited modes of socializing (Vaidhyanathan, 2012). Massive social networks such as Facebook and Twitter, or their

Chinese equivalents, Weibo and Renren, have pushed netizens to keep up with varieties of networking and identity management, where hedonistic or social-radical identities can be developed and indulged. The ability to escape from restrictive moral attitudes and to question the immense pressures of a national surveillance culture constitutes a sense of freedom and vitality. These types of freedom provide entertainment and relief from blatant and antiquated forms of manipulation and censorship, but also entail a deeper embrace of the novel mechanisms of corporate surveillance.

The China–Google incident of 2010 showed that the coalescence of moral engineering and neo-liberalism reinforces a contradictory sense of empowerment within netizen communities. As Google was trying to extend its business operations in the People's Republic of China, the state illegally accessed some of their information to clamp down on dissidents and human rights. After a series of cyber attacks issued from within the People's Republic of China, Google stated that the Chinese Communist Party (CCP) had indeed used the company's services to spy on human rights activists. Google could not come to an agreement with the CCP government and closed its offices in China while moving to Hong Kong. Since Chinese netizens had been sharing information through Google services, there could be no guarantee that these data trails could be protected by the cryptopticon. Thus the era of cryptopticon poses extreme risks for netizens who participate in media activism and are still ruled by the laws of a totalitarian state.

It became apparent during this incident that the vying "owners" of the internet—the superpower governments and internet corporations—were both spying on netizens to build their networks of power and control. Netizens acknowledge feeling crushed and helpless about the excesses of surveillance culture. As explained by Tricia Wang:

> Google and China have their own visions for the social life of information and for the role of information in society. We should be equally critical of a corporation with algorithms that create a consensual consumer culture based on advertising clicks as we are of a country with policies that create a consensual citizenry based on obedience through a paternalistic form of governance. (Wang, 2010)

Netizens are continually tested and modulated by archaic government rhetoric and an expansionist consumer culture. Nonetheless, as a result of social media outlets, people demand to express themselves and debate ideology, while revealing their niche affections and affiliations.

Through the working of a cryptopticon, people have also learned how to carve out and claim their "privacy standards" precisely by reflecting on them, by trying to reveal and analyze them, by playing with them and constantly fine-tuning them. Modes of privacy are tested out as different online memberships and in different settings as ways to define the individual and maintain friendships. As Vaidhyanathan (2011) explains, the cryptopticon does not promote an idealized state of well-being, but warrants us to consider modulating behaviors and life choices within different networks and cultural contexts. This means, for example, that people can openly explore and pursue "eccentric" lifestyles or alternative sex cultures while still being "private" persons. This process of embodying privacy allows for a public sexualization of identity that is perhaps more of a novelty in the Chinese context, where Confucian morality and the totalitarian state have demanded a certain "numbness" concerning one's sex drive and sexual affairs. But these sexual outbursts have contributed a great deal towards the vitality of the Chinese internet.

New Individualism and Mob Identities

The Chinese Communist Party is concurrently pushing modes of global social networking and a unique type of Chinese morality or censorship. To some extent the push towards social media and citizens' emancipation is a result of global fashions and debates, but it is also reinforced through uniquely Chinese government guidelines and policies. For instance, in April 2010, the Chinese State Council published a white paper on internet policy, which stated that Chinese netizen culture would increasingly be "expansive and strong." The paper stated that there were 220 million bloggers in China and that 66% of internet users actively partake in civic debate, hence the Chinese internet produced millions of opinions on a daily basis. (Xinhua Agency, 2010). But these statistics were yet another example of government propaganda, and they were immediately refuted by the well-known blogger and activist Isaac Mao, who argued that censorship mechanisms were equally multiplying and shifting from the removal of specific content and sensitive keywords to entire websites and social networks (Nip, 2010). [3]

These discrepancies between government-issued reports and bloggers' counter-reports have opened up an era of identity management and online dissent, a way for people to step away from a long tradition of intimidation and self-censorship. As Isaac Mao explains:

China has a long tradition of people trying to fit into the group, moderating their behavior to avoid standing out conspicuously—a culture reinforced by the man-made collectivism of the past half-century. Blogs have leapfrogged this tradition, acting as a catalyst to encourage young people to become more individual. So this and other grassroots media are now emerging strongly to challenge China's social legacy. (Schokora, 2008)

Discussions amongst netizens also have helped create an atmosphere of reflexivity, intelligent feedback and tolerance. Even though there is still an urge to partake in a Communist-directed "upright" morality and public condemnation of dissidents, Chinese netizens have come to defend the values of non-standardized lifestyle choices and the diversification of thought. This also means that netizens more easily reveal their life choices and spy on each other's social whereabouts and mishaps.

For instance, mainstream social networks such as Facebook or its Chinese equivalent Renren (*renren wang*: literally, "everyone's network") tacitly encourage members to pry into each other's private lives as a collective routine that manifests social interest. While Facebook enjoys a huge popularity in Hong Kong, it was banned in the PRC (People's Republic of China) in July 2009 after a period of riots in Xinjiang province and the concomitant correspondences of Xinjiang independence activists. By January 2011, Renren had acquired a membership of 65 million active users even though it requires web users to register with their actual names and contact information. Its censorship rules are very strict, especially when it comes to tracking sensitive political keywords in its user-generated content. Following the Chinese law against sexually explicit images, Renren administrators will routinely remove all sexually explicit images that are occasionally uploaded and shared amongst friends. This ban on sexually explicit materials in social networks is also seen in other nation-states, but Chinese citizens have developed unique ways of commenting on the routines of uploading and deletion.

For instance, a gallery of D.I.Y. sex photos was uploaded on Renren on December 5, 2009, showing a naked girl playing with stuffed animals along with other toys. Renren members responded quickly by praising the photos: "Wow...how Brave!"..."This is crazy"..."My classmates and myself like these pictures, can you send some more?"..."Wow, but when will they be deleted again?"..."Are they still here? We are witnessing an important moment in history"..."Yes indeed, hope we can keep these as great memories!" Chinese surveillance culture has indeed come along with a new type of sexual camaraderie and a proliferation of sexually explicit materials.

Moreover, as has been pointed out by several media theorists, netizens invent vulgarities and sexual jokes to be able to talk back to the routines of government-issued surveillance and censorship. This new type of "sex talk" allows netizens to distinguish themselves stylistically from the language of government propaganda and the official bulletins of state-controlled news media (Qiang & Link, 2011). A counter-terminology of in jokes and swearwords circulates to resist or make fun of the pompous nature of government propaganda. These discourses aim at suggesting a distinctive social identity that is highly aware and critical of mechanisms of state control:

> Beginning from reflexive back-talk and sarcasm, this language is developing some new forms—new words, even new grammar—partly as a way to avoid Internet censorship, but partly also as a way for a generation who grew up with the Internet to assert its dis-

tinctive identity. Language is a way for Chinese netizens to create a new identity and to take distance from the monopoly of a cultural rhetoric of asexuality spread by the Communist Party. (Qiang & Link, 2011)

Qiang and Link also believe that these collectively invented discourses have a positive impact on netizens' self-education about identity and human rights. They coincide with discourses on "rights" of various kinds—the "right to know," the "right to express," the "right to monitor [officialdom]" and so on (Qiang & Link, 2011). This type of intelligence has created an opening in which netizens can hold and debate rights, while embodying the attitudes and aspirations of "a different type of people."

As will be shown, Chinese netizens are strategically rewriting individualism and collectivism to claim their sexual pleasures and rights, to foster a radical departure from a cultural rhetoric of asexuality and intimidation. Amongst this larger thrust towards sexual identity, the internet has spawned a generational wave of D.I.Y. pornography, as well as activists who criticize the PRC's war against pornography. Alongside the circulation of sexual novelties, netizens use strategies of humor and sarcasm to criticize the stringent morality lessons of Communism. Finally, netizens also embody an irate and revengeful mob mentality by assembling as a "Human Flesh Search Engine" to scrutinize individuals who are deemed to be suspect because of their involvement in cases of corruption, decadent lifestyles or sexual exploits.

D.I.Y. Pornography and the Sexualization of Surveillance

Even though the distribution of sexually explicit media can have serious legal consequences, people are sharing vulgarities and sexually explicit media within social networks. The Chinese internet has spawned waves of D.I.Y. pornography, in which individuals express the right to share their homemade sexually explicit materials. D.I.Y. porn sharing has developed historically within internet communities and goes back to peer-to-peer distribution within Usenet groups. As explained by porn researcher Sergio Messina, the Usenets groups are some of the most sophisticated networks to have influenced user-generated sexually explicit media. The Usenet groups fulfilled two of the original missions of the internet, which were to connect people through special-interest groups and to encourage do-it-yourself media making. One trend was a splintering and diversification of the established porn categories, a surfacing of micro-fetishes around a plethora of non-normative bodies and desires. These porn fetishes were sometimes co-opted again within commercial porn industries, but they were also able to resist such pressures as people were able to maintain friendship circles around D.I.Y. media-making (Jacobs, 2007:61–63).

In some cases, the D.I.Y. porn cultures have promoted an activist credo for radical or tolerant sex cultures. For instance, the European collective fuckforforest.com documents acts of naturism and public outdoor sexuality while raising money for activist purposes. As founders Tommy and Feona explain: "We live in a technological society. To document your sexuality can be an exciting experiment and you can learn a lot from watching yourselves. It is also great to test out your borders and limits. Documenting sex for us is not different than documenting any other experience. Many people like to film everything from weddings to funerals. We like to film sex." (personal communication, April 2009). The site further explains that erotic/pornographic consciousness is a positive value in reclaiming our identities as harmonious to the natural environment. Besides looking at snapshots of open-air sex, we can read blogs about their visits to political activist conferences interlaced with reports of sex encounters with locals or other activists.[4]

But unlike these pioneers of D.I.Y. porn in Euro-American cultures, who combine their sexual adventures with activist statements, the Chinese D.I.Y. collections are more concerned with acts of re-sexualizing China itself. For example, the Chinese internet is experiencing a new kind of D.I.Y. sex video shot by young adults in everyday locations such as classrooms, bath houses, computer labs and city parks. These videos have been archived and labeled as Doors or Gates (*men*, after the Watergate scandal in the U.S.) and carry the name of the exact location where the scene was shot, for example, East Building Kappa Female, Metro Gate, Shanghai Wash Gate, or Hunan Elevator Gate.

The popularity of these D.I.Y. videos is explained by an interviewee:

> These videos are now a novelty and are slightly in competition with commercial Japanese pornography. Of course it is important to make our own videos even if they look quite bad. Since everything is officially banned, then these videos fill the gap. (personal communication, June 2010)

These online collections create the impression that people are making D.I.Y. pornography all over China, in a wide variety of spaces and places. In some cases, it looks as if people were "caught in the act," as if their sex sessions were captured by a security camera or a government spy and/or uploaded by a peeping tom. In other cases, the camera is so close to the scene of action that the couple must be aware of its presence and insistent gaze, but they decide to ignore it in pursuit of their own sexual bliss.

The video "East Building Kappa Female" follows a group of schoolboys undressing a girl in a classroom. While the video at first portrays a scene of callous bullying, the boys then start caressing and kissing the girl at great length. She gets aroused and is then seen laughing and frolicking with her partners. One of the boys further manipulates the scenario by using his handheld camera to tease the Kappa female into responding to its very presence. The young woman is in fact very good at imitating a Japanese porn star who whimpers in combined pain and joy while being bullied into sexual action. In another longer D.I.Y. porn video, which was filmed in a computer lab, we can see a couple having sex on a chair in front of one of the computers. The image quality is grainy and very poor, indicating that the video may simply be shot by a security camera while the lab was deserted or closed. Indeed, the recording creates the illusion that the couple is having an illicit sex session. However, about 30 minutes into the movie, a third person appears in view who looks like a computer lab assistant. But rather than being shocked by the fornicating couple, she acts as if she does not notice anything or that indeed such sex sessions would be quite common in her lab. In actuality, the video must have been shot by a team of amateur video makers who carefully selected the location, the actors and participants, who all helped create an illusion of the average Chinese computer lab as a permissible sex space.

These D.I.Y. porn productions are circulating despite government warnings, but it is clear that the trend is a sensitive and potentially explosive topic when I attempt to solicit reactions from various interviewees. Still, some of them agree that D.I.Y. pornography can potentially act as a powerful and important incentive for sexual rights and social change. Yang explains it this way: "We have a common saying that if virtue rises one foot, vice will rise ten. The government will always have its policies against sex but we always know how to find it." (personal communication, June 2010). Yang is deeply attached to his strategy of "Jumping the Great Fire Wall" and searching for sexually explicit materials on illegal peer-to-peer downloading sites such as Emule and BitTorrent. Rather than hoping that the central government will legalize and organize his online pleasures through regulated e-commerce channels, he has devoted himself to the supplies he receives from these shadowy, black-market industries. He states that he even gains an educational benefit from these movies, as he learns, for instance, how to properly kiss and caress women. Thus, these D.I.Y. archives have become crucially important as they contribute to a new sexual identity, not only as a way of knowing something about pornography, but also as a way of belonging to and embodying the global internet age.

Sexual Rights and Pornography Activism

Chinese netizens are making use of various online identities to claim their civil rights, including the right to share D.I.Y. pornography or to engage in collective activism against heightened crackdowns and censorship. In some cases, these actions take place as individual outbursts or open artistic statements, but they also can appear as collective anonymous identities. For instance, a strategy of anonymity was taken up in the "2009 Declaration of Anonymous Netizens" that was posted on Global Voices

Online, a U.S.-based network for alternative news media, in response to the Chinese government's attempt to impose the Green Dam Youth Escort filtering software (Figure 11.1). As anonymous netizens addressed the Chinese Communist Party:

> We take no interest whatsoever in your archaic view of state power and your stale ideological teachings. You do not understand how your grand narrative dissipated in the face of Internetization. We are the sum of the world's entire online population. We are omnipresent….We are an army. We do not forgive. We do not forget. (Lam, 2009)

Figure 11.1. The image that accompanied the "2009 Declaration of Anonymous Netizens" action against internet porn filtering and censorship in China.

Matteo Pasquinelli has analyzed the activist uses of anonymous identity in his book *Animal Spirits: A Bestiary of the Commons*. Based on Virno's philosophy of the multitude, Pasquinelli introduces the concept of "immaterial civil war" where the "open animals of the world" combine creative talents to reveal internalized power structures. Pasquinelli makes reference to an old Jewish–Dutch proverb, "The greater the spirit, the greater the beast," to suggest a dialogic structure that would be present in innovative or radical web culture. As he writes: "At the level of base energies, aggressiveness, innovation and revolution all share the same wellspring—the same obscure source that feeds state power as well" (Pasquinelli, 2009:30). The traditional lines drawn between enemies, between the power bloc of a repressive nation-state and oppositional activists, becomes blurred. Each party makes use of a collective identity and popular emblems to adopt unique strategies of inspection and intimidation.

For instance, Chinese activists have collectively adopted an "animal spirit" to help in the fight against government censorship. The peculiar animal "Grass Mud Horse" (*cao ni ma*) became an internet meme in 2009 and was widely used as a defiant symbol that counteracted widespread internet censorship Figure 11.2). Ten mythical animals were created on the interactive encyclopedia Baidu Baike and people started using them as a mode of humorous, vulgar protest. Other symbolic animals were created, including the French-Croatian Squid, the Small Elegant Butterfly and the Chrysanthemum Silkworms. All of the animal names are homonyms in Chinese that can also vaguely refer to Chinese profanities; they utilize Chinese similar characters whose meaning changes when a different tone is applied.

The Grass Mud Horse is supposedly a species of the alpaca. The name is derived from *cao ni ma*, whose near-equivalent word translates as "f**k your mother." The greatest enemy of the Grass Mud Horse is the "river crab" whose name resembles *hexie*, meaning "harmony," referring to government censors who wish to create a "harmonious society" (*hexie shehui*). The Grass Mud Horse spurred people's imagination, as was evidenced in the thousands of image collages and mockumentaries that appeared online. The fad spread like a benign virus and was later popularized as a stuffed animal, an activist icon turned commodity. The popular theme song of the Grass Mud Horse was banned by the State Administration of Radio, Film, and Television in March 2009, together with the official blocking of the entire meme itself. The mythic figure survived and was later creatively conjoined with "Green Dam Girl," a satirical cartoon character who protects state interests. She compulsively preaches a rhetoric of "harmonizing the family," and behaves like a bossy government official who enjoys saddling people with moral directives. The surreal and humorous qualities of these figures tapped into a populist stream, or indeed pop culture itself, and helped to instigate and sustain a viral movement of protest.

Figure 11.2. The mythical animal "Grass Mud Horse" was invented in a fight against the government decision to have all PCs installed with the anti-pornography filtering software Green Dam Youth Escort.

The animal figure has meanwhile become a more widespread strategic icon of satire and dissent, as it became openly used by thousands of activists and by artists and scholars interested in joining pro-democracy movements. Artists and writers have contributed to the "grass mud horse movement" through creative acts of protest or by uploading their own representations of obscenities. For instance, Ai Weiwei, one of China's most influential artists and social commentators, ocassionally uses this icon in an expression of humor, strength and determination. In one of his most famous photographs, he jumps up naked while holding the "grass mud horse" in front of his genitals.

After his detainment in April 2010, one of the official government directives against Ai accused him of being an "inferior artist" who spreads "pornographic content."[5] The art work under investigation was Ai's photograph *One Tiger, Eight Breasts*, in which he appeared naked and surrounded by four other naked women. His most loyal supporters quickly responded with another campaign, "Listen Chinese Government, Nudity Is Not Pornography." They uploaded their own naked pictures, in some cases gathering in large orchestrated groups and using cut-outs of Ai's face to cover their genitals. In this way, netizens fought for the right to define and upload obscenities, acting out sexual humor and dissent in actions that are prohibited under the auspices of the harmonious society.

The Human Flesh Search Engine

There is also the phenomenon of revengeful mob activity on the Chinese internet that is called Human Flesh Search Engine (*Renrou Sousuo*), in which a group of anonymous netizens collaborate to make up a virtual people's court in order to condemn an individual who has been suspected of a moral or legal breach. They work as a group investigating people's personal details by stalking and spying on them, and sometimes harassing them in both the virtual and physical world. The sexual crusaders who have become targets of the Human Flesh Search Engine have included many types of "suspect individuals" from outspoken sex bloggers, to corrupt government officials who have extra-marital affairs with multiple mistresses, to individuals who are perceived to be immoral sex partners or sex radicals. For instance, in December 2008, a woman who had been blogging about her husband, Wang Fei and his alleged sex affair, committed suicide. Her death prompted an outpouring of hate mail and physical threats against Wang Fei that was instigated via the web.

Another example of this web mob mentality occurred in August 2009 when netizens launched a manhunt for the Shanghai-based "Chinabounder," a mysterious person of Caucasian origin who had infuriated netizens by boasting of his varied carnal encounters with Chinese women on his blog, "Sex and Shanghai" (Jones,

2007). A massive backlash occurred and 17,000 netizens formed a Human Flesh Search Engine that led to threats of murder and castration from those who claimed the Sex and Shanghai blogger had blackened China's good name. In March 2010 a much larger Human Flesh Search Engine invaded the internet in response to the sex diary by Han Feng, head of the Tobacco Department of Laibin City, Jiangxi Province. The diary was uploaded by netizen "han xian zi" on Tianya.cn, the most popular forum in China. The netizen later said that he was the husband of one of Han's lovers. Han Feng's diary was further disseminated online, which led to his dismissal from his official position and eventually to a jail sentence of 13 years.

Despite the fact that Han Feng was hounded and then condemned by the mobs, his diary reveals a fairly benign and reflective sexual crusader. His interweaving of personal sex statistics with the work duties of a Communist official gives a peculiar kind of surreal atmosphere to the confessional diary, as noted in the following entries:

November 6, Tuesday 11–25°C Sunny
I prepared for the "politeness and courtesy" lecture in the morning. At noon, I accompanied Li Dehui, who came from Xiamen, to have lunch and some wine. I stayed in the dormitory in the afternoon. At night, I had dinner with Huang Huiting and others and I drank quite some wine. Huang and his people are going to Chongqing and Chengdu tomorrow. I will send Su and Tan Shanfang to see them off. At 10ish, Tan Shanfang drove me over to her house. I made love for 3 times. We had one more session early in the morning. I did not ejaculate.

Han Feng admits that he is at once empowered and weakened by his extraordinary lifestyle, as he admits here:

December 4, Tuesday, 7–23°C Sunny
In the morning I stay in bed. At noon, Zhao Xin, who is from the Qinzhou Court came to deal with some business in the court here. He invited me to lunch and I asked Pan to come with me. We drank till 4ish. I was a little drunk and so was Pan. I asked to her to come to my room and I had sex with her. I remembered it was fierce. She's starting to guide me. There's a lot of love fluid. Pan and Mei invited me to midnight snack, and we invited Qin Gang and myself drank 2 bottles of western wine. I was drunk again.

May 5, Wed 13–22 °C Cloudy
The sex with Pan was too fierce. My whole body was sore and in pain. I stayed in the dormitory the whole day.

Of course, these diary entries shed light on the decadent lifestyles of Chinese Communist officials, but the collective impulse to single out and attack officials points to netizens' frustrations and the incapacity to pursue positive freedom.

Unlike the examples of the D.I.Y. pornography of porn activism, these types of peer surveillance do not reveal a true concern with identity or sexual rights as social change. Even if the Human Flesh Search Engine has the capacity to reveal aspects of social injustice within Chinese culture, the actions have drastic consequences and will rarely be motivated to operate outside the boundaries of blind revenge.

Conclusion

As surveillance methods are shifting from a panopticon-style gaze towards ubiquitous data mining by companies and government bureaucracies, netizens have developed novel ways of acting out countercultural identities and awareness of surveillance culture. Chinese netizens participate in surveillance excess by divulging new types of sexual humor and vulgarities, and by partaking in activism or underground circuits for porn sharing. Even though all sexually explicit materials are banned in China and the ban is reinforced through censorship, people fight back by defending sexualized individualism and by pursuing mob identities. These tendencies are reinforced by corporate social networks whose method of surveillance is one of encouragement of niche groups and user-generated contents. Vaidhyanathan shows that the method of cryptopticon seeks to smoothly infiltrate and track new fashions and lifestyles. It allows netizens to question and criticize corporations or the nation-state itself, but it finally offers no protection for illegal discourses, lifestyles or the communications of political dissidents.

The case studies in this chapter show that Chinese netizens fight for a sexualization of identity and the right to pornography. Homemade porn movies are a unique way for people to test out their own moral boundaries and to upload data on highly monitored sites of assembly and social networks. While the objective of Western-style D.I.Y. porn is to reveal identity and deviations from the sexual norm, Chinese D.I.Y. porn is concerned with acts of sexualizing China itself—individuals engage in ephemeral porn experiments in dispersed spaces and locations. Second, there is a movement of anonymous activists who have adopted alter egos to fabricate in-joke vulgarities and criticize the ongoing war on pornography. One phase of an incipient blossoming of porn activism was in 2009, when netizens contested stringent censorship of sexually explicit media through the collective use of the symbolic animal figure of the grass mud horse (*cao ni ma*).

The movement of the grass mud horse branched out into the various concepts of civil rights and artistic freedom. Perhaps the tactics of this movement can be compared to those of the international activist movement Anonymous, which revels in an anti-leader and anti-celebrity ethic and involves a criticism of the cult of individualism. As Gabriela Coleman explains:

> It purports to have no leaders, no hierarchical structure, nor any geographical epicenter. While there are forms of organization and cultural logics that undeniably shape its multiple expressions, it is a name that any individual or group can take on as their own. (Coleman, 2011)

But the playful use of animalistic alter egos has also paved the way for a different type of anonymous mob mentality, in which netizens band together in large groups to examine and attack suspect individuals. In this manner, the Chinese Human Flesh Search Engine wants to take revenge on individuals who are deemed to be symbols of corruption and sexual decadence. These activities also have a resemblance to the "trolling" activities of Anonymous, where web users collaborate to organize obnoxious campaigns such as phone pranks or online smear campaigns that can have damaging effects on a person's reputation. This is another way for netizens to claim their rights, to have an independent legal system that is protected from the infiltration of governmental officials. These tactics can be menacing power shields against the monopoly of Communist Party, but they easily revert back to an ideology of self-righteous morality and blind hatred.

These uniquely Chinese modes of online assembly are ways to respond to the excesses of the PRC's surveillance society, or the fact that citizens are subjected to centralized surveillance as well as multiple levels of data mining by the new corporate powers. The tendency for web users to sexualize modes of spying and acts of self-revelation has become engrained and accepted within social networks. Since the global era of cryptopticon, the pervasive technologies of surveillance and data mining have resulted in netizens testing out and playing with modes of privacy and identity (Vaidhyanathan, 2012). Chinese government officials have meanwhile responded to the era of cryptopticon by trying to issue "smart propaganda"—government directives and social guidelines that sound closer to street parlance and are more integrated into a language of the people. Qiang and Link have notes that official Communist rhetoric has made efforts to talk in the lingo of its critical people:

> It might be called "smart propaganda." The appearance of this new branch of the official language can be seen in considerable measure as a response to the rise of the Internet. The authorities have realized that if they want credibility with an international audience, they need to sound less rigid, and if they want to reach a Net-savvy younger generation in their own country, they had better adopt some of its lingo. (Qiang & Link, 2011)

The netizen culture resists infiltration attempts by their Communist government by constantly becoming a "new type of people" who share intelligence and aim at being radically different from the old. Netizens seek positive freedoms in identity revelation and sexuality, or the right to pursue eccentric lifestyles that differ from the norm. Hence the growing popularity of role models such as Ai Weiwei, who embodies the right to have a maverick personality and to gaze directly back at surveillance society. But on the dark side of confident activism lies the power of angry mobs, who may take on collective actions against sexual decadence within the Communist party and beyond. We can see that Chinese netizens have come to defend and berate radical sexuality, either in acts of courage to defy the "impotent" state, or angrily and chaotically as ways to judge the private lives of others. Either way, these highly emotional states permeate the networks and the goals of a more peaceful sexual liberation, which is to become tolerant of sexual others while being sexualized as individuals and sexually satisfied.

Notes

1. The 50 Cent Party (*wǔmáo dǎng*) are internet commentators hired by the Chinese government (both local and central) or the Communist Party to post comments favorable towards party policies in an attempt to shape and sway public opinion on various internet message boards. The commentators are said to be paid 50 cents for every post that either steers a discussion away from anti-party or sensitive content on domestic websites, bulletin board systems and chatrooms, or to conversely post commentary that advances the Communist party line.
2. Some of these online case studies have previously been mentioned in my book *People's Pornography: Sex and Surveillance on the Chinese Internet.* (U.K.: Intellect Books, 2011). For the present chapter, I have rethought them in terms of a theory of surveillance excess and its countercultures.
3. Isaac Mao showed that the self-congratulatory statistics issued in this report were actually wrong.
4. http://fuckforforest.com site is a pay porn site for people to learn about and support environmental activism and to access photos and videos of sex scenes in the outdoors. The collective solicits monthly membership fees, which are then redistributed to various environmental organizations. Paying members get access to the porn collection, or can get more actively involved.
5. On April 14, 2011, Beijing-backed Hong Kong newspaper *Wen Wei Po* reported Ai Weiwei as under investigation for tax evasion, bigamy and "spreading porn." His family denied the allegations. The case has not been resolved.

References

Coleman, E. G. (2011, April 6). Anonymous: From the Lulz to collective action. *The New Everyday.* http://mediacommons.futureofthebook.org/tne/pieces/anonymous-lulz-collective-action

He, Qinglian (2008). *The fog of censorship: Media control in China.* New York: Human Rights in China.

Jacobs, K. (2007). *Netporn: D.I.Y. web culture and sexual politics.* Lanham MD: Rowman & Littlefield.

Jones, G. (2007, February 12). The blogger who took on China. *The First Post.* http://www.the firstpost.co.uk/2231,news-comment,news-politics,the-blogger-who-took-on-china (Link no longer active)

Lam, O. (2009, June 24). China 2009 Declaration of anonymous netizens. *Global Voices Online.* http://advocacy.globalvoicesonline.org/2009/06/24/china-2009-declaration-of-the-anony-mous-netizens

Ludovico, A., & Bernhard, H. (2007). *Google will eat itself.* GWEI. http://gwei.org/index.php

Lyon, D. (2007). *Surveillance studies: An overview.* Malden MA: Polity.

Nip, A. (2010, June 20). Censors delete 95pc of blogs a day, forum told. *South China Morning Post.* http://www.scmp.com/article/717635/censors-delete-95pc-blogs-day-forum-told

Pasquinelli, M. (2009). *Animal spirits: A bestiary of the commons.* Rotterdam: Nai Publishers.

Qiang, X., & Link, P. (2011, November). *From grass-mud equestrians to right-conscious citizens: Language and thought on the Chinese internet.* Paper delivered at Restless China Publishing Conference, Chinese University of Hong Kong.

Schokora , A. (2008, August 6). *China's first blogger on the Chinese blogosphere.* Danwei.org. http://www.danwei.org/Internet/isaac_mao_and_the_chinese_blog.php (Link no longer active)

Vaidhyanathan, S. (2012, January). The cryptopticon: The new nature of surveillance. *The New School NYC.* http://soundcloud.com/thenewschoolnyc/the-cryptopticon-the-new

Vaidhyanathan, S. (2011). *The googlization of everything (and why we should worry).* Berkeley: University of California Press.

Wang, T. (2010, July 10). *Googlist realism: The Google–China saga posits free-information regimes as a new site of cultural imperialism and moral tensions.* CulturalBytes.com. http://culturalbyt.es/post/781876273/googoochinasaga

Xinhua Agency. (2010, June 8). *China issues white paper on internet policy.* http://www.china.org.cn/china/2010–06/08/content_20206978_3.htm

12

Post-Privacy and Ideology

Patrick Burkart & Jonas Anderson Schwarz

Introduction

Once the exclusive domain of policy wonks, certain counter-discourses about a "post-privacy" condition now circulate among some net activists, where none existed before the Anti-Counterfeiting Trade Agreement (ACTA) debates. The post-privacy position, articulated by Heller (2008, 2010, 2011) and Schramm (2012), is that digital privacy is both untenable and socially unrewarded, so privacy activism and even personal privacy hygiene is not worth the effort. The post-privacy debates reveal deep anxieties about the loss of control over domains previously associated with autonomy, especially self-presentation and personal visibility. The post-privacy thesis introduces a laissez-faire attitude towards surveillance at a time when, paradoxically, pirate politics has increased the salience of digital privacy as a social and legal norm in the information society (see Burkart, forthcoming). Pirate politics of the Swedish and German varieties tend to emphasize privacy absolutism as a key part of a government's obligation to protect digital rights. Post-privacy is hardly apolitical, but rather expresses a dominant ideology that acquiesces to status-quo privacy law and information policy.

Post-privacy challenges establishmentarian actors like the European Community (EC)—and also the more radical pirates—to articulate the specific means by which they would intend to realize greater privacy protections. In terms of social theory, post-privacy challenges critical media studies' assumptions about surveillance and social harm. Using identity to address authenticity, self-fashioning, queer pride and other individualistic factors, post-privacy arguments also challenge the tradition of political economy in critical media studies, which regards surveillance as a system-level promotion of conformity. The post-privacy thesis tends to avoid thematizing some of the disempowering and undemocratic consequences.

The threats to privacy emanating from corporate activities are well documented and summarized below. Less discussed, and more opaque, is the surveillance state currently under construction. A distinguishing feature of current EU-wide legal proposals such as ACTA and the Intellectual Property Rights Enforcement Directive (IPRED) has been the implementation of state surveillance by proxy—that is, its new reliance on internet service providers (ISPs) and private investigators to both detect and punish purported file-sharers through active, mass surveillance of internet connections, and through implementation of "graduated response" or "three-strikes" policies for cutting access to infringing users.[1] Under the new regime, ISPs' protected status as a neutral carrier would be reclassified; ISPs would share responsibilities for user infringements, and by order of the state, must actively police the network on behalf of private rights holders. Pirate parties in Sweden and Germany blossomed during the IPRED and ACTA debates, mobilizing opposition to these plans.

How can we make sense of cybernauts who are deeply knowledgeable about both kinds of surveillance but who are dismissive of any special privacy claims at all? We propose that it is possible to interpret the post-privacy ideology[2] through the ways actors position themselves regarding their praxis of maintaining personal online privacy under conditions of state and corporate surveillance—and that this praxis relates to the doxa and knowledge that would be relational to the ways this actor is socially embedded (Bourdieu, 1984; Calhoun, 2003). We argue that, while one might suspect that well-informed internet users tend to use preventive measures to protect their privacy online, post-privacy user attitudes exist that express high awareness of privacy risks but little or no willingness to compensate for lost privacy with protective measures. The ideology is understandable as an expression of hope that the market economy and consumer society will value and reward personal expression with new access to information. In considering the praxis, doxa and knowledge of online life under surveillance, we propose a hypothetical model of privacy awareness and behavior that can inform privacy policy debates while illuminating the confused psychology of post-privacy.

First, we discuss privacy as a concept amenable to ideological analysis. Gandy (1993) provides a sociological grounding for surveillance in systemic processes of special interest to critical media studies. We identify new, "panspectric" management strategies in which bio- and sociometric data play an organizing social role. We link the sociological importance of surveillance to the normative concept of privacy, and propose that, as a social value, privacy provides "contextual integrity" to individuals' everyday social interactions (Nissenbaum, 2004). In privacy pragmatics, privacy violations become recognizable as violations of foundational communication norms in everyday discourse, through objections to or grievances about surveillance and privacy risks. Context matters for both expectations of privacy and for formally observable behavior, and surveillance across mixed contexts can produce conflicts over privacy.

Next, we elaborate the European information policy context for intellectual property rights (IPR) harmonization under the IPRED and ACTA as a field of intense social conflict over surveillance policies and their legitimacy. With reference to findings by The Research Bay (a survey project on file-sharing sponsored by The Pirate Bay) and others, we consider how contextual integrity is a value in flux, as debates about post-privacy life compete today with proposals to create and enforce the "right to be forgotten"[3] and Pirate Party proposals to restrict data retention and online surveillance.

Finally, we present a model of personal privacy cognition and practice. The model considers a continuum of awareness (knowledge) of surveillance and justificatory belief in privacy, a continuum of belief (doxa) in investing time and effort into privacy, alongside a continuum of potential practices (praxis) for preserving and maintaining online privacy. While questions of privacy are attributed different meanings and views within different social fields—doxa could be said to act as investment or fidelity to a certain field—the resulting model begets a potentially complex analysis. Our descriptive model suggests a pirate field and a post-private field of study, with pirates exhibiting high-knowledge/high-doxa/high-praxis on the continua, and post-privacy users exhibiting high-knowledge/high-doxa/low-praxis. We conclude with reflections on the nature of the model. Since individual identities are multilayered and thus not tied to the logics of a given social field, a future elaboration of our model should be to further identify these fields, especially how they are constituted and demarcated.

Surveillance, Panspectric Management and Privacy in Critical Media Studies

Law and policy are ideological systems that depend upon underlying, local social structures for their growth, if not for their legitimacy. The policies and legal bases for surveillance have been suspect in Europe for a long time; its privacy policies mark these suspicions. A hermeneutic of suspicion also pervades the critical legal scholarship on privacy rights. The European experiences of the Second World War, in which genocide, discrimination and persecution was systematized using surveillance, informed the establishment and protection of legal personal privacy protections in the European Community. Notwithstanding these safeguards, the effectiveness of data privacy laws is generally weak, and continually threatened by reason of state and new business models.

Sweden's 1973 privacy law was an early forerunner. Comprehensive data-protection legislation now extends to 40 countries. In Germany, a right to "informational self-determination" and a "fundamental right to digital privacy" have been established by the Federal Constitutional Court, and the United Kingdom's 1998 Data Protection Act imposes considerable restrictions on data collection, storage and use by collectors of data on living persons (Raab, 2005:49). In the U.S., explicit legal proposals for safeguarding personal privacy have been rare.[4] The European Union adopted the European Directive of Data Protection[5] in 1998, but it is becoming increasingly clear that since then, there has been a shortage of jurisprudence and laws designated to safeguard personal data—especially when compared with the rapid expansion of IPR law to benefit corporate rights holders. The vagaries of cloud computing (Fleischer, 2012), a copyright system run amok and vastly expanded means for state and commercial surveillance and for interpersonal surveillance ("interveillance"; Jansson, 2012) all severely circumscribe public debates over privacy, such that a certain resignation about surveillance prevails as a permanent and inevitable state of affairs.

The digital economy's dependency on surveillance, the growth of the risk society and the informational state, and the blossoming of cyberspace has attracted persistent and critical scholarly attention. Following the dissemination throughout the social sciences of Foucault's work on state uses of the panopticon to enhance governmentality (1977), and Beck's work on the risk society (1982), Gandy's theory of surveillance (1989, 1993) trained critical attention in the social sciences on the use of the growing use of the "panoptic sort" in the private sector for discrimination through marketing and advertising. Through the years, he has focused on the social consequences of the spread of data mining and information retrieval throughout government services, particularly policing (2002) and finance (2009).

Continuing Gandy's analysis of surveillance for critical media studies, Andrejevic elaborates a Gandyian perspective on data centres, "big data," predictive modeling and internet enclosures on everyday life (2007, 2012). A dystopian vision of global Digital Rights Management (DRM), in which every digital device must request permission of rights holders to access any piece of digital media (Zittrain, 2008) considers how persistent surveillance is required increasingly for access control in media, finance and credit, and such public services as education and welfare. Burkart and McCourt (2006) explore the interaction of Customer Relationship Management (CRM) or personalization services and DRM in the operation of the "Celestial Jukebox," which together forms an underlying business model for new media that has come to engulf practically all interactive media experiences. CRM-DRM remains the underlying logic of the Celestial Jukebox, embodying surveillance in its core system architectures, and animating the emergent "Hollyweb."

DeLanda's (1991) notion of the "panspectron," a mode of military signals analysis developed since WWII, differs from the notion of panopticon (Foucault, 1977) in the nature of its gaze. "The Panspectron does not merely select certain bodies and certain (visual) data about them. Rather, it compiles information about all at the same time, using computers to select the segments of data relevant to its surveillance tasks" (DeLanda, 1991:206). Contemporary business management has begun increasingly to incorporate panspectron-type technologies (Palmås, 2011). Post-privacy reflects an acknowledgement of the Celestial Jukebox and panspectropy and also a suspension of the hermeneutic of suspicion about it.

Turning now from critical media studies and sociology to critical legal studies, Lessig (2006) sees information policy as layered, where the architectural layer of the network serves as a primary determination of the nature of regulation, with an economic system made possible by this architecture above it, followed by a third layer of social norms and hierarchies and a positive law as a fourth layer on top. Privacy is a practice that is enacted within nested routines that are often based in contractual agreements resting on these layers, but Lessig does not offer democratic criteria for evaluating it, as he does for instance with access policies.

Nissenbaum (2004) offers a rights-based approach to surveillance and privacy policy based on intersubjective judgments of private contexts. She theorizes privacy as being a social practice of maintaining "contextual integrity" by following both explicit and tacit rules of conduct. Private life is experience that can be distinguished by context from other kinds of experience that are commonly expected to be subjected to greater visibility. One's privacy contributes substantively to one's identity, or sense of self, through knowable and controllable contexts. Contextual integrity is maintained when two norms—norms of appropriateness and norms of flow or distribution—are upheld (2004:120). Bourdieu (see below) allows us to situate post-privacy and pirate politics as different vernacular politics of contextual integrity. They express fidelity to different norms of appropriateness and norms of distribution. In social action, they can both become laden with personal status that can be converted to cultural capital and competitive advantage.

In the U.S., the public interest orientation in information policy was finally abandoned with the Digital Millennium Copyright Act of 1998 (Elkin-Koren,

2000). Cyberliberties activism emerged in the breach (Burkart, 2010). The EU information policy environment, similarly, discloses a gradual de-linking of personal digital privacy and public interest regulation, such that it could be said that post-privacy is the system state of information policy. This is the case despite ongoing, pro-privacy campaigns such as the "right to be forgotten" (launched by EU Digital Agenda Commissioner Neelie Kroes) and despite the ascendancy of activist privacy absolutists in pirate politics in the European breach since the IPRED.

The struggle over privacy plays out in policy analysis covering three phases of data processing: collection, analysis and implementation. "While it is indeed difficult to control digital information once it has been created or gathered, it is possible to prevent data from being created" (Stalder, 1999). Stalder expresses concern that collection of personal data can take place without the user's full knowledge, or even without her explicit consent. Eleven years later, Best (2010) encounters a strong post-privacy attitude that habitually consents to all phases of data processing and surveillance. Best's subjects describe online surveillance as a worthwhile tradeoff between care and control, as a system of more immediate rewards and punishments and as an automatic process over which people have no control (p. 18). Corroborating these findings, Christensen (2011) also detects gratifying "sousveillance" and "interveillance" among users of social networking services (SNSs) in the Turkish diaspora in Sweden. Privacy law has not disrupted, or attempted to disrupt, social networking.

Current privacy law and policy does not aspire to reinforce contextual integrity, but instead, formalizes the public interest in privacy as a set of post-privacy assumptions about personal networking that materially benefits the social media owner-operators. Pro-privacy scholarship advocates for new privacy regulations—often on a purist, pirate model. Work by Zarsky shows how privacy regulations claim to strike a balance between data collectors' business initiatives and rights with protections for individuals, but acquiesce to data collection in the first instance (2004: 46). For future policymaking, Poe (2007:184–185) advocates a two-step regulation of private and public collectors and disclosers to prevent unwanted analysis, while Schneier (2008, 2009) and Fleischer (2012:122) argue that privacy regulations should extend to all forms of data processing with personally identifying information.

We propose, with Nissenbaum, that individuals' own, reflexive experiences of privacy overreach, transgression or even abuse can be sense-making exercises that help determine meaningful contexts for making privacy claims—or not making claims. They are most likely to be formed in the data implementation stage (Zarsky, 2004; see Jansson, 2012). Individual privacy claims will vary depending upon an individual's knowledge, doxa and praxis. Privacy "purists" (Zarsky, 2004) such as political pirates will exhibit high-doxa and high-praxis, while pragmatists will acknowledge the post-privacy condition by negotiating privacy praxis, and post-privacy purists will be highly cognizant of surveillance but abandon privacy praxis altogether. The next section addresses state surveillance by proxy as another variety of surveillance that may influence cybernauts' online attitudes and practices related to privacy.

Beyond the Net and the Self: Divergent Responses to Panspectropy

Corporate services and applications that trade usability and access for quanta of personal privacy include Google Street View, OkCupid.com, and PatientsLikeMe.com. They do so using business analytics software and sticky surveillance techniques targeted at clients from tracking sites. However, government surveillance is potentially moving to the transport layer of internet access in response to pressures to step up the social response to file sharing. In terms of network topography, surveillance is moving from the three-tier server architectures that enforce CRM and DRM regimes and enable persistent identity services to the ISPs themselves. ISPs are increasingly being treated as gatekeepers with greater responsibility for digital rights management. The old legal tradition that treated ISPs as neutral conduits for customer communications extended the legal indemnification of carriers for infringing content passing through the network (DeBeer & Clemmer, 2009). The requirements of the Celestial Jukebox for leak-proof IPR regimes have incrementally changed this legal tradition. The new situation stands to turn ISPs into privatized spy agencies required by public information law and policy. An early mover in this direction, France entrusted the national surveillance function to Trident Media Guard, a private firm charged with collecting data for graduated response warnings under HADOPI law (Creation and Internet law).

The end of ISP neutrality has been accompanied by impressive efforts to propagandize and reeducate citizens of their responsibilities to abide by maximalist copyright laws, and by regular news reporting on litigation campaigns waged against suspected file sharers and their hacktivist enablers like The Pirate Bay and Megaupload. The campaigns to inculcate fear, suspicion, uncertainty and doubts about infringing activities online are deliberate and documented strategies of the content industries and their trade associations. The response of many net-savvy internet users to the marketing of the IPRED, Data Retention Directive and ACTA was to initiate new privacy protection routines using cloaking and encryption (Larsson & Svensson, 2012).

Explaining Pirate Attitudes Towards Privacy and Surveillance

Pirate politics is centered on information policy and state action in the digital domain. In survey work, Bjereld and Oscarsson (2009) detected public awareness of, and opposition to, a Swedish surveillance program for internet and telephone traffic that is now operated by the military. In 2011, the Cybernorms research group at Sweden's Lund University conducted a global file-sharing survey known as the Research Bay Study, generating more than 75,000 responses in collaboration with The Pirate Bay, where the survey was posted on the front page for 72 hours. Of the 67,473 respondents who answered the survey question on anonymous practices, 17.8% acknowledged using VPNs (Virtual Private Network) or similar services for hiding their IP addresses. Another 51.4% said they did not use anonymization services, but showed an interest in them. A correlation between frequent uploading and anonymization was found: within the minority of users who upload files nearly every day, 30.9% used an anonymization service, while only 14% of those who said they never upload files at all did so. In the file-sharing community, at least, online anonymity can be seen as an active countermeasure against legal action that is perceived as illegitimate (Larsson, Svensson, de Kaminski, Rőnkkő, & Olsson, 2012:273). The small minority of more active file sharers (active uploaders) express more determination and privacy praxis, as shown by Andersson and Larsson (forthcoming). It is also not surprising that exclusive, closed communities sharing BitTorrent trackers require high degrees of security and anonymity; users of such networks are even vetted in order to gain membership (Balázs, forthcoming).

In a separate survey, a majority of Swedes expressed awareness of online privacy risks (Jansson, 2010:263). Those respondents were questioned about three privacy areas: electronic transactions, governmental surveillance and social media. A correlation emerges between high usage of social media and a reduced perception of risk with regards to it (Jansson, 2010:273). Familiarity with electronic transactions also reveals a similar correlation. Respondents interested in technology were considerably less concerned about privacy risks within social media and electronic transactions than those who were not interested in technology. However, technology-savvy users were more skeptical of "government supervision." This skepticism can be explained partly by gender differences, but perhaps also by correlations between interests in technology and pragmatism on the one hand, and between commitments to culture/politics and "privacy" as a perceived priority on the other (Jansson, 2010:272). While the Swedish survey data provide a useful glimpse into popular perceptions of privacy and surveillance risk, and divulge a post-privacy ideology among cybernauts, Sweden's internet history and cyberculture has unique characteristics that make generalizations to other populations difficult (Burkart, forthcoming). At the same time, Sweden could be read as a distinctive exponent of wider tendencies towards increasing individualization (management of the self, post-materialist values) in highly industrialized societies (Andersson, 2011).

Varieties of Post-Privacy

Purist post-privacy thinking emphasizes the "optimism towards a future where there is 'nothing to hide'" (Heller, 2008). Privacy maintenance, in this view, is the practice of hiding one's identity, rather than selecting contexts for sharing personal information. Privacy protections are not only pointless both legally and technically, but also counterproductive to people who socialize online. Heller's contentions are that the "new economy" rewards disclosure with even more information, and that individuals risk being left out of the "hive mind" if they are too reluctant to share. Moreover, self-disclosure fights social conformity, leads to better personalized services and presents one's authenticity to the world in a day and age when the absence of a unique and rich digital profile can create new suspicions.

Heller compares personal privacy hygiene to the experience of living a gay life in the closet, as compared to participating in a gay pride parade. Personal identities can be multiple and shared, and the notion of a static core identity is superannuated by postmodernism, the realities of adopting multiple personalities online and identity theft. Heller advances a manifesto: "Be what's fun to be, not what you supposedly 'are'" and do so guiltlessly, without letting identity be a "prison." Freedom comes through "total transparency," performing for multiple surveillance feeds, surveying the surveyors, and recognizing that there is no room for secrets of any kind. What is disclosed is not the "authentic" self anyway. A critical question to ask here, however, is whether all people have the ability, skill and tenacity to manage the disclosure or nondisclosure of the myriad features of everyday life online.

The mere assumption of a post-privacy condition is a very different symbolic stance than post-privacy practice. The post-privacy stance was described by science-fiction writer David Brin (1998), who—by outlining a future scenario of government and corporate monopolies on data monitoring—proposes the idea of "sousveillance" as a radical response to surveillance; abolishing the monopoly on surveillance information by giving everyone access to all information. This idea echoes appeals by Lyotard (1984:67) to open the closed databases amassing power-knowledge withheld from general access, and by Touraine, who rejects the "programmed society" altogether (1971). These diverse views open up a possibility of post-privacy as an alternative to the pirate path of liberal activism, and also as a rejection of the status quo and its Celestial Jukebox.

In another variant, post-privacy has a neoliberal valence. *The Economist* announced "the end of privacy" in 1999, after the implementation of the EU Data

Protection directive in October 1998—one of the few supranational legal initiatives in the field of digital IPR that buttress civic interests rather than trade interests. Privacy was seen as too costly to be commercially viable for industries dependent on the value of their information flows:

> Privacy is doomed for the same reason that it has been eroded so fast over the past two decades....Privacy is a residual value, hard to define or protect in the abstract. The cumulative effect of these bargains—each attractive on their own—will be the end of privacy....Policing the proliferating number of databases and the thriving trade in information would not only be costly in itself; it would also impose huge burdens on the economy. Moreover, such laws are based on a novel concept: that individuals have a property right in information about themselves. Broadly enforced, such a property right would be antithetical to an open society. It would pose a threat not only to commerce, but also to a free press and to much political activity, to say nothing of everyday conversation. (*The Economist*, 1999)

This position supports a claim that contextual integrity of all kinds would collapse if private property rights were extended to individuals for claims to their own personally identifying information. Stalder (1999) criticizes it as a prime example of neo-liberal ideology that considers private property rights over information as more natural or realistic than privacy rights.

The mutually antagonistic, purist-neoliberal moments of the post-privacy ideology are repeatedly revisited in an era of SNSs and personal data management, for example, as "datalove" purists confront hostile claims of IP ownership. The roll out of new search engines designed to harvest personal information—for example, Facebook's Social Graph Search—and the anticipation of the diffusion of Google Glass reveal these tensions widely.

The next section lays out the range of possible expectations about surveillance and privacy among internet users, and also the range of possible responses to privacy risks introduced by surveillance—reflecting high, medium and low states of awareness of actual surveillance practices, and similarly, a range of possible responses to surveillance and perceived privacy risks. High-knowledge, high-praxis internet users are characterized by politically active pirates, hacktivists and others who study and practice personal privacy protections in various online forums—private and public, commercial and noncommercial. The purist post-privacy advocate would disclose high-doxa/high-knowledge but low-praxis.[6]

Developing a Model of Contextual Integrity

Following Nissenbaum, we present a model of contextual integrity illustrated in different use-case scenarios that represent conditions of individuals' self-identification online. At a practical level, there are different degrees of identification, ranging from anonymity to pseudonymity to self-disclosure in online spheres of access. As a dynamic IP address is the only trace that users directly disclose when communicating online, it provides quasi-anonymity by default. It is quasi-anonymous because it is ultimately attributable to a user, but functionally, it identifies machines and not individual users. In virtual communities requesting or requiring user names, anonymity is sometimes preserved, but often pseudonymity is required for access, even if the user adopts the pseudonym "anonymous" or "anon." Lanier (2010) discusses recurring pseudonymity (where users have a recurring alias) and what he calls "drive-by anonymity" (where users make up a new alias each time). Figure 12.1 presents a model of the range of potential identifications.

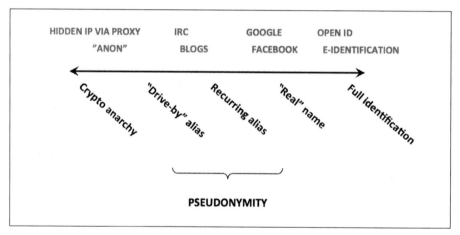

Figure 12.1. The Anonymity Spectrum (Constitutive to Praxis).

Anonymity, pseudonymity and full identification are communication practices that preserve different levels of privacy and vary by context. While adopting an anonymous or pseudonymous identity online may nominally preserve one's privacy at the beginning of a communication session, maintaining privacy depends upon controlling one's communication during the rest of the session.

Of course, this typology is not clear-cut. Privacy contexts can be mixed, and what has been called "the online disinhibition effect" (Suler, 2004) appears in different modes of, or opportunities for, anonymity. While a user thinks herself to be anonymous, she might in fact expose so much information (both textual and audiovisual) about herself that it would be possible to know her identity anyway, by means of triangulation.

Privacy and Doxa

We now turn to the subjective cognition of privacy and the awareness or lack of awareness of user privacy in the internet habitus. We adopt Bourdieu's notion of the habitus and its relation to fields of social action, and his notion of doxa as being the set of common assumptions and understandings underlying social practices in the absence of their becoming disputed or otherwise conflicted (Terdiman, 1987). Further discussion of Bourdieu's field theory and surveillance can be found in Christensen and Jansson (2012).

In addition to social stratification in terms of economic classes and ideologies, Bourdieu underscored the role of educational and cultural factors. A "field" can be seen as a social arena of struggle over the ways educational, social and cultural resources are distributed; the field could be said to arise when such resources are embodied as species of capital, and mutual acts of dedication to such capital are enacted. Capital only gains its value within the field; capital and field are mutually constitutive. Fields intersect vertically and horizontally, and different forms of capital are translatable into other forms of capital. Agency is determined by the extent to which participants are able to make an effective use of the resources they are endowed with; it is a function of the adaptation of their habitus in a specific field. The habitus is the subjective system of expectations and predispositions acquired through past experience and the mental structure through which one deals with the social world (Bourdieu, 1984, 1993).

The field is not merely a set of subjectively experienced ties among individuals; it thrives on collectively shared appreciations of value, and thus on objectivity. Nevertheless, in our schema we differentiate between field-bound beliefs and "objective" knowledge (which is, of course, never fully objective as the epistemic community where such claims are vetted is in itself a field; Rorty, 1991; Knorr-Cetina, 1999). We choose to separate the two—underscoring the difference between belief (doxa) and knowledge while admitting their fraught interrelation—as a heuristic: greater separation makes for a more fine-grained model.

The key feature of doxa is fidelity to the field, that is, investment into its norms, expectations and that which is taken for granted. This, in our interpretation, is essentially different than knowledge. Even for epistemological relativists, knowledge implies some kind of external benchmark, claims to validity, striving for objectivity (Harding, 1993/2004). Doxa can be thought of as "felt reality"; the taken-for-granted, preconscious understandings of the world and our place in it that shape our more conscious awarenesses (Calhoun, 2003:291). It precedes ideology (Calhoun, 2003:291). Knowledge could be attributed to what Östling (2012) calls the "rational" view on privacy, while doxa relates to what he calls the "human" view (fallible, limited by a situational horizon). Interestingly, in this latter view, privacy tends to be reified—for example, in terms of personal dignity, it is thought to have value in itself. But it is also tactical and context dependent—for example, in terms of the inherent value of privacy when divulging one's pregnancy to one's employer, family or (respectively) one's insurance company.

Actors gain status by displaying fidelity to certain aspects of a field, but perhaps more so by pursuing "distinction," seeking differentiation from the rest. Thus, there can be no such thing as disinterested actors within a field. The field is reconstituted every time a newcomer tries to enter the field of relations, or challenge the status quo, as heterodox behaviors act to expose that which is orthodox. At the same time, in order to challenge the existing doxic beliefs within the field, any newcomer is forced to take the field seriously, and to learn its rules (Bourdieu, 1991:127–128). In this sense, doxa has more to do with investment, interest and belief than with objective knowledge.

We hold that fields are never to be assumed a priori, but are always in flux, enacted through aggregated social action. Among those who hold that implementing personal privacy hygiene is sensible, a field arises. Likewise, among those who share the experience of sharing and downloading copyrighted content in ways that are not formally legal, a "pirate" field could be said to arise. As researchers specialized in these respective fields, our interest was sparked when noting that actors who would be expected to disclose a privacy field began confessing their assumptions of a post-privacy condition.

Specifically, we adapt a model of actor attributes developed by a "pro-IP" trade group in a study of "websites considered to be infringing copyright" and their users (PRS [Performing Right Society] for Music and Google, 2012:49–50). When approaching a new site or other communicative context where users have some control over their level of privacy protection, users in general (not only those intending to infringe copyright) consider privacy alongside other factors including content quality, community, cost of access, risk of prosecution, ease of use and content range (PRS for Music and Google, 2012: 49–50). Users who approach a new site offering context integrity may respond differently to privacy threats depending on their knowledge about it. Figure 12.2 represents the range of privacy praxis that users may exhibit.

If privacy is relational and socially constituted, the effective implementation of privacy-enhancing or privacy-eroding actions must be grounded in doxic belief; to believe in certain ways of enacting of privacy is to support certain views of what privacy is and how it can be enhanced or eroded. In a way, belief in privacy hinges on a particular form of mis-recognition, in that certain means and ends are highlighted by social actors, and taken to be objective facts. Based on these considerations, Figure 12.3 presents a spectrum of positions of belief in privacy, while Figure 12.4 presents a range of privacy practices informed by doxa.

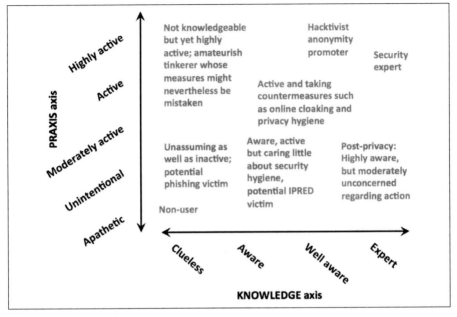

Figure 12.2. The Privacy PRAXIS-KNOWLEDGE Spectrum.

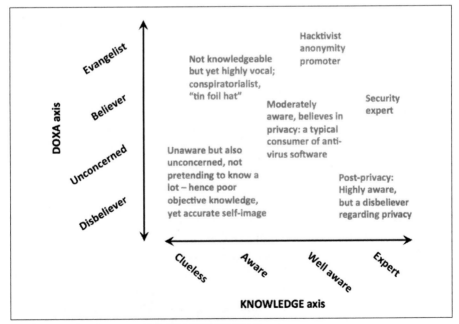

Figure 12.3. The Privacy DOXA-KNOWLEDGE Spectrum.

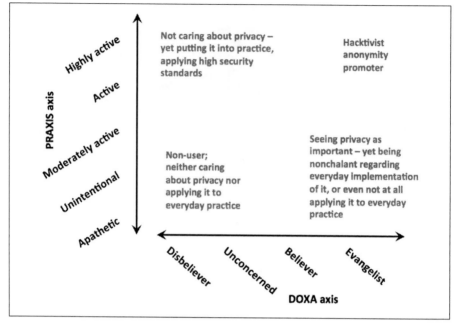

Figure 12.4. The Privacy PRAXIS-DOXA Spectrum.

One example of high-doxa/low-praxis would be the case of the technology journalist Honan (2012), who admits to having used passwords and security routines that were too weak, leading to hacked accounts. Another example would be academics who specialize in internet politics, yet implement conference websites that lack security, exposing participants' email addresses to spammers.

The low-doxa/high-praxis position seems like a theoretical artifact that is too contradictory to be tenable. What would be more tenable is low-knowledge/high-praxis, simply implying a subject whose objective knowledge about privacy would be low, yet nevertheless employing high privacy standards. In such cases, the high level of privacy might be a felicitous byproduct accruing to users who employ high technical standards in general, or a result of using equipment set up by someone else to be private and secure, or merely a coincidence.

In order to avoid the potential reductionism for which Bourdieu's approach has been criticized (cf. Calhoun, 2003), any analysis of this kind has to itself be reflexive, and allow for the possibility that actions are more than mere functions of the habitus (Sayer, 1999). Enumerating the disparities between doxa and praxis is a tool for revealing the analyst's own priorities as well as those of the subjects under scrutiny.

Larsson and Svensson (2012) propose that an awareness of being followed is matched by active privacy measures, and that both privacy doxa and praxis track the increasing governmentality of surveillance. This hypothesis is partially undermined, however, by the existence of post-privacy, in which high-knowledge/high-doxa is matched by low-praxis. Were we to continue hypothesis testing, we would conduct an empirical study of users searching for all possible combinations of privacy doxa and praxis. As it stands, however, we have merely outlined a theory of doxa, knowledge and praxis as these relate to online privacy and surveillance, set within a historical context of diminishing privacy protections through law and policy, and expectations about those protections. Whether or not diminishing expectations of privacy follow or precede the diminishing legal field for privacy is another interesting consideration.

Conclusion

Privacy law and policy are scaffolding built atop a normative foundation—which is, in turn, determined by the underlying material, economic and communicative infrastructures. The corporate world went the first round in testing the limits of privacy rights online. Now, state-sponsored agents are following suit. Online panspectropy of ordinary citizens by the state or by its ISP proxies grows in extent with the roll out of EU measures for harmonizing IPRs and their liability measures, law enforcement and trade. The passing from living memory of government abuses of privacy in World War II (Black, 2012), the rise of the post–9/11 security state, and the gathering of a billion users or more into digital enclosures puts the post-privacy ideology on questionable footing from an historical standpoint. What explains its dominance in contemporary privacy law and much popular communication?

The field of post-privacy could be understood as a subset of the relational positioning that internet users would take towards perceived public opinion about privacy with attitudes flaunted and beliefs firmly held. As fields are constitutive of capital, the act of distinguishing oneself from the herd of privacy absolutists is itself laden with status; a new relational field of flaunting a "post-privacy" sensibility is thus generated. Although this chapter critiques post-privacy as ideology, it merely hypothesizes the actual negotiation of such a post-privacy field. Besides allowing researchers to differentiate between (a) the actions of privacy advocates, (b) the beliefs held by them and (c) verifiable knowledge, several empirical tasks would arise from our model: What would the field of post-privacy turn upon? What is its main currency? Is it more plausible to characterize the post-privacy debate, in retrospect, as an even wider set of overlapping or contrasting fields? Further research could also explore the ways in which assumptions of a post-privacy condition would be different from explicitly demanding post-privacy. Would the latter constitute a form of praxis that is altogether different from, or merely a variation of, post-privacy praxis?

Notes

1. At the time of this writing, internet users in the U.S. face a "six-strikes" policy adopted by voluntary agreement of major ISPs. Here, we consider primarily the European policy arena.
2. The notion of ideology informing this essay is provided by Ricoeur (1986).
3. The right of the citizen to be forgotten by the servers operated by private firms was proposed by the European commissioner for Justice, Fundamental Rights, and Citizenship, Viviane Reding, in 2012.
4. A Federal Trade Commission proposal promotes a framework by which "consumers can compare the data practices of different companies and exercise choices based on privacy concerns, thereby encouraging companies to compete on privacy" (Federal Trade Commission, 2012:61).
5. Council Directive 95/46/EC 1995.
6. We do not claim to account for the motivations behind any speech acts online. For example, we do not assume that political pirates intend to violate copyright laws, nor do we assume that post-privacy adherents intend to abide by them scrupulously.

References

Andersson, J. (2011). The origins and impacts of the Swedish file-sharing movement: A case study. *Critical Studies in Peer Production (CSPP)*, *1*(1).

Andersson, J., & Larsson, S. (Forthcoming). The justifications of piracy: Differences in conceptualization and argumentation between active uploaders and other file-sharers. In M. Fredriksson & J. Arvanitakis (Eds.), *Piracy: Leakages from modernity*. Los Angeles, CA: Litwin Books.

Andrejevic, M. (2012, May). *Social media: Surveillance and exploitation 2.0*. 4th ICTs and Society Conference, Uppsala University.

Andrejevic, M. (2007). Surveillance in the digital enclosure. *The Communication Review, 10*, 295–317.

Balázs, B. (Forthcoming). Set the fox to watch the geese: Voluntary, bottom-up IP regimes in piratical file-sharing communities. In M. Fredriksson & J. Arvanitakis (Eds.), *Piracy: Leakages from modernity*. Los Angeles, CA: Litwin Books.

Beck, U. (1982). *Risk society: Towards a new modernity*. Newbury Park, CA: Sage.

Best, K. (2010). Living in the control society: Surveillance, users and digital screen technologies. *International Journal of Cultural Studies, 13*(1), 5–24.

Bjereld, U., & Oscarsson, H. (2009). Folket och FRA. In S. Holmberg & L. Weibull (Eds.), *Svensk höst: Trettiofyra kapitel om politik, medier och samhälle* (SOM-rapport nr 46, 293–298). Göteborg: SOM-institutet, Göteborg University. http://www.som.gu.se/digitalAssets/1294/1294523_293–298.pdf

Black, E. (2012). *IBM and the Holocaust: The strategic alliance between Nazi Germany and America's most powerful corporation*. Washington, DC: Dialog.

Bourdieu, P. (1993). *The field of cultural production*. Cambridge, U.K.: Polity.

Bourdieu, P. (1991). Några egenskaper hos fälten. In *Kultur & Kritik: Anföranden av Pierre Bourdieu* (J. Stierna, Trans.). Göteborg: Daidalos. (Originally a lecture in November 1976 at École normale supérieure, rue d'Ulm, Paris, published as Quelques propriétés des champs. In *Questions de sociologie*, 1984, pp. 113–120.)

Bourdieu, P. (1984). *Distinction: A social critique of the judgment of taste* (R. Nice, Trans.). Cambridge, MA: Harvard University Press.

Brin, D. (1998). *The transparent society*. New York: Perseus Books.

Burkart, P. (Forthcoming). *Pirate politics*. Cambridge, MA: MIT Press.

Burkart, P. (2010). *Music and cyberliberties*. Middletown, CT: Wesleyan University Press.

Burkart, P., & McCourt, T. (2006). *Digital music wars: Ownership and control of the celestial jukebox*. Lanham, MD: Rowman & Littlefield.

Calhoun, C. (2003). Pierre Bourdieu. In G. Ritzer (Ed.), *The Blackwell companion to major contemporary social theorists* (pp. 274–309). Cambridge, MA: Blackwell.

Christensen, M. (2011). Online social media, communicative practice and complicit surveillance in transnational contexts. In M. Christensen, A. Jansson, & C. Christensen (Eds.), *Online territories: Globalization, mediated practice and social space*. New York: Peter Lang.

Christensen, M., & Jansson, A. (2012). Fields, territories and bridges: Networked communities and mediated surveillance in transnational social space. In C. Fuchs, K. Boersma, A. Albrechtslund, & M. Sandoval (Eds.), *Internet and surveillance: The challenges of Web 2.0 and social media* (pp. 220–238). London: Routledge.

DeBeer, J. F., & Clemmer, C. D. (2009, Summer). Global trends in online copyright enforcement: A non-neutral role for network intermediaries? *Jurimetrics, 49*, 393–396.

DeLanda, M. (1991). *War in the age of intelligent machines*. New York: Zone.

The Economist (1999, May 1). The end of privacy: The surveillance society. *The Economist*, 21–23.

Elkin-Koren, N. (2000). The privatization of information policy. *Ethics and Information Technology, 2*, 201–209.

Federal Trade Commission. (2012, March 26). *Protecting consumer privacy in an era of rapid change: Recommendations for businesses and policymakers*. Washington, DC: Federal Trade Commission Report.

Fleischer, R. (2012). Molniga tider: Om integritetsdebattens förlamande dialektik. In J. Dalunde (Ed.), *Integritet i en digital värld: Sju texter om individ och internet*. Stockholm: Fores + Ivrig.

Foucault, M. (1977). *Discipline and punish: The birth of the prison* (A. Sheridan, Trans.). New York: Pantheon Books. .

Gandy, O. H., Jr. (2009). *Coming to terms with chance: Engaging rational discrimination and cumulative disadvantage*. Burlington, VT: Ashgate.

Gandy, O. H., Jr. (2002, July). Data mining and surveillance in the post-9.11 environment. Paper presented at the Political Economy Section, IAMCR Barcelona. http://www.asc.upenn.edu/usr/ogandy/iamcrdatamining.pdf

Gandy, O. H., Jr. (1993). *The panoptic sort: A political economy of personal information*. New York: Westview.

Gandy, O. H., Jr. (1989). The surveillance society: Information technology and bureaucratic social control. *Journal of Communication, 39*(3): 61–76.

Harding, S. (1993/2004). Rethinking standpoint epistemology: What is "strong objectivity"? In S. Harding (Ed.), *The feminist standpoint theory reader*. London: Routledge.

Heller, C. (2011). *Post-privacy: Prima leben ohne Privatsphäre.* Munich: Verlag C. H. Beck.

Heller, C. (2010, March 17). Die Ideologie Datenschutz. *Carta.* http://carta.info/24397/die-ideologie-datenschutz/

Heller, C. (2008, December). *Embracing post-privacy: Optimism towards a future where there is "nothing to hide."* Presentation at 25th Chaos Communication Congress. Berlin, Germany. http://events.ccc.de/congress/2008/Fahrplan/attachments/1222_postprivacy.pdf

Honan, M. (2012, December). Kill the password: Why a string of characters can't protect us anymore. *Wired.* http://www.wired.com/gadgetlab/2012/11/ff-mat-honan-password-hacker/

Jansson, A. (2012). Perceptions of surveillance: Reflexivity and trust in a mediatized world (the case of Sweden). *European Journal of Communication, 27*(4), 410–427.

Jansson, A. (2010). Integritetsrisker och nya medier. In S. Holmberg & W. Lennart (Eds.), *Nordiskt ljus.* Göteborg: SOM-institutet, Göteborg University.

Knorr-Cetina, K. D. (1999). *Epistemic cultures: How the sciences make knowledge.* Cambridge, MA: Harvard University Press.

Lanier, J. (2010). *You are not a gadget: A manifesto.* London: Allen Lane.

Larsson, S., & Svensson, M. (2012). Compliance or obscurity? Online anonymity as a consequence of fighting unauthorized file-sharing. *Policy and Internet, 2*(4), 77–105.

Larsson, S., Svensson, M., de Kaminski, M., Rônkkô, K., & Olsson, J. A. (2012). Law, norms, piracy and online anonymity: Practices of de-identification in the global file sharing community. *Journal of Research in Interactive Marketing, 6*(4), 260–280.

Lessig, L. (2006). *Code: Version 2.0.* New York: Basic Books.

Lyotard, J.-F. (1984). *The postmodern condition: A report on knowledge* (G. Bennington & B. Massumi, Trans.). Manchester, England: Manchester University Press.

Nissenbaum, H. (2004). Privacy as contextual integrity. *Washington Law Review, 79*(1), 119–158.

Östling, R. (2012). Varför värna den personliga integriteten? In J. Dalunde (Ed.), *Integritet i en digital värld* (pp. 63–77). Stockholm: Fores.

Palmås, K. (2011). Predicting what you'll do tomorrow: Panspectric surveillance and the contemporary corporation. *Surveillance & Society, 8*(3), 338–354.

Poe, G. A. (2007). *Privacy in database designs: A role-based approach* (Unpublished doctoral dissertation). Department of Information Systems/Decision Sciences, University of South Florida.

PRS for Music and Google. (2012). The six business models for copyright infringement: A data-driven study of websites considered to be infringing copyright. (Privately commissioned report.) http://www.prsformusic.com/aboutus/policyandresearch/researchandeconomics/Documents/TheSixBusinessModelsofCopyrightInfringement.pdf

Raab, C. (2005). Regulatory provisions for privacy protection. In S. Lace (Ed.), *The glass consumer: Life in a surveillance society* (pp. 45–68). Bristol, U.K.: Policy.

Ricoeur, P. (1986). *Time and narrative.* Chicago, IL: University of Chicago Press.

Rorty, R. (1991). *Objectivity, relativism, and truth: Philosophical papers, Volume I.* Cambridge, MA: Cambridge University Press.

Sayer, A. (1999). Bourdieu, Smith and disinterested judgement. *The Sociological Review, 47*(3), 403–431.

Schneier, B. (2009, November 19). A taxonomy of social networking data. Schneier on Security blog. http://www.schneier.com/blog/archives/2009/11/a_taxonomy_of_s.html

Schneier, B. (2008, March 6). The myth of the "transparent society." *Wired*, Security Matters blog. http://www.wired.com/politics/security/commentary/securitymatters/2008/03/security matters_0306

Schramm, J. (2012). *Klick mich: Bekenntnisse einer Internet-Exhibitionistin*. Munich: Knaus.

Stalder, F. (1999, May 11). The end of privacy as triumph of neoliberalism. *Nettime*. http://www.nettime.org/Lists-Archives/nettime-l-9905/msg00091.html

Suler, J. (2004). The online disinhibition effect. *Cyberpsychology & Behavior, 7*(3), 321–326.

Terdiman, R. (1987). Translator's introduction to Pierre Bourdieu, the force of law: Toward a sociology of the juridical field. *The Hastings Law Journal, 38*, 805–853.

Touraine, A. (1971). *The post-industrial society: Tomorrow's social history: Classes, conflicts, and culture in the programmed society*. New York: Random House.

Zarsky, T. Z. (2004). Desperately seeking solutions: Using implementation-based solutions for the troubles of information privacy in the age of data mining and the Internet Society. *Maine Law Review, 56*, 1–59.

Zittrain, J. (2008). *The future of the internet—and how to stop it*. New Haven: Yale University Press.

Contributors

Thomas Allmer studied Media and Communications at the University of Salzburg (Austria) and the Victoria University of Melbourne (Australia). He is a PhD candidate at the University of Salzburg and research associate in the project "Social Networking Sites in the Surveillance Society," funded by the Austrian Science Fund (FWF). In addition, Thomas is a member of the Unified Theory of Information Research Group and serves on the editorial board of *tripleC: Communication, Capitalism & Critique. Open Access Journal for a Global Sustainable Information Society*. Recent publications include *Towards a Critical Theory of Surveillance in Informational Capitalism* (Peter Lang, 2012). For further information, visit http://allmer.uti.at.

Jonas Andersson Schwarz is a media sociologist and researcher affiliated with Södertörn University College. He is the author of *Online File Sharing: Innovations in Media Consumption* (Routledge, forthcoming) and co-edited the *Efter the Pirate Bay* anthology (with Pelle Snickars; Mediehistoriskt arkiv). His current post-doc position, funded by Swedish research foundation Riksbankens Jubileumsfond in collaboration with the advertising agency Forsman & Bodenfors, aims at investigating internet user motivations. His research activities remain independent from the work for the agency.

Mark Andrejevic is an ARC QE II post-doctoral research fellow and deputy director at the Centre for Critical and Cultural Studies, University of Queensland. He is the author of *Infoglut* (Routledge, 2013), *iSpy: Surveillance and Power in the*

Interactive Era (University Press of Kansas, 2007) and *Reality TV: The Work of Being Watched* (Rowman & Littlefield, 2004); as well as numerous articles and book chapters on surveillance, digital media and popular culture. He is the director of the Personal Information Project, which studies public attitudes toward the collection and use of personal information.

David Barnard-Wills is an associate partner at Trilateral Research and Consulting. He has previously been a research fellow at the University of Birmingham, Cranfield University and the Parliamentary Office of Science and Technology. He holds a PhD from the School of Politics and International Relations, University of Nottingham. His research interests include privacy, discourse and the politics of surveillance, identity and security technologies. He is the author of *Surveillance and Identity: Discourse, Subjectivity and the State* (Ashgate Press, 2013). His research blog can be found at www.surveillantidentity.com.

Patrick Burkart is associate professor of Communication at Texas A&M University. He is author of *Pirate Politics* (MIT Press, forthcoming), *Music and Cyberliberties* (Wesleyan University Press, 2010) and *Digital Music Wars: Ownership and Control of the Celestial Jukebox* (with Tom McCourt; Rowman & Littlefield, 2006). He is co-editor of *Popular Communication: International Journal of Media and Culture* with Miyase Christensen, Mehdi Semati and Nabeel Zuberi.

Miyase Christensen is professor of Media and Communication Studies at Stockholm University and guest professor at the Department of Philosophy and History of Technology, the Royal Institute of Technology, Sweden. She is an editor of *Popular Communication: International Journal of Media and Culture* and the chair of the Ethnicity and Race in Communication Division of the International Communication Association. Christensen's research focuses on globalization processes and social change from a social theory perspective; technology, culture and identity; and the politics of popular communication. Christensen's latest co-edited books include *Media and the Politics of Arctic Climate Change: When the Ice Breaks* (Palgrave Macmillan, in-press), *Understanding Media and Culture in Turkey: Structures, Spaces, Voices* (Routledge, in-press) and *Online Territories: Globalization, Mediated Practice and Social Space* (Peter Lang, 2011). She is the author of *Connecting Europe* (Istanbul Bilgi University Press, 2009), and is currently working on a co-authored monograph (with A. Jansson) entitled *Cosmopolitanism and the Media: The Cartographies of Change* (Palgrave Macmillan, forthcoming).

Christian Fuchs is professor of social media at the University of Westminster. He is editor of *tripleC: Communication, Capitalism & Critique. Open Access Journal for a Global Sustainable Information Society*, co-founder of the ICT's and Society Network and chair of the European Sociological Association's Research Network 18: Sociology of Communications and Media Research. He has published many contributions in the realms of critical theory, social media/internet and society and critical information society studies.

Lee Humphreys is an assistant professor in Communication at Cornell University. She studies historical media practices, privacy, and everyday uses of mobile and social media. Her research has appeared in the *Journal of Communication, New Media & Society* and the *Journal of Computer-Mediated Communication*. With Paul Messaris, she co-edited the book *Digital Media: Transformations in Human Communication* (Peter Lang, 2006). She received her PhD from the Annenberg School for Communication at the University of Pennsylvania in 2007.

Katrien Jacobs is a scholar and artist who is an associate professor in cultural studies at the Chinese University of Hong Kong. Her work investigates the role of digital networks in people's experiences with the body, art and sexuality. She has lectured and published widely on pornography, censorship and media activism. Her recent book *People's Pornography: Sex and Surveillance on the Chinese Internet* has been widely commented on in the mass media. Her work can be found at www.libidot.org/blog.

André Jansson is a professor of Media and Communication Studies at Karlstad University, Sweden. His research mainly concerns media, identity and globalization processes, bridging the disciplinary divides between media studies, human geography and cultural sociology. Jansson's most recent work has been published in journals such as *Space and Culture, International Journal of Cultural Studies* and *Communication Theory*. His most recent book in English is the co-edited volume *Online Territories: Globalization, Mediated Practice and Social Space* (with M. Christensen and C. Christensen; Peter Lang, 2011).

Hille Koskela is a senior lecturer in the Department of Geosciences and Geography, University of Helsinki, Finland. Her research interests include video surveillance and the politics of control, the emotional experience of being watched and the responsibilization of the public in contributing to surveillance. She has published articles in journals such as *Surveillance and Society, Crime Media Culture* and *Theoretical Criminology*, and contributed to several international anthologies. Her current project deals with surveillance-related uses of online webcams.

Verena Kreilinger is a postgraduate student at the University of Salzburg, majoring in communication studies. She currently is a research associate in the project "Social Networking Sites in the Surveillance Society." Verena graduated from the University of Applied Sciences in Salzburg with a master's degree in Digital Media

Studies in 2007. Prior to joining the Unified Theory of Information Research Group, she worked in advertising and production. She is a member of the editorial team of *tripleC: Communication, Capitalism & Critique. Open Access Journal for a Global Sustainable Information Society* and a participant in the European Cooperation in Science and Technology Action "Living in Surveillance Societies."

David Lyon is director of the Surveillance Studies Centre at Queen's University, Kingston, Ontario, Canada. He has researched and written about surveillance since the mid-1980s, in sole-authored and collaborative projects. His books include *The Electronic Eye* (University of Minnesota Press, 1994), *Surveillance Society* (Open University Press, 2001), *Surveillance Studies* (Polity, 2007) and *Identifying Citizens* (Polity, 2009). With Zygmunt Bauman, he co-authored *Liquid Surveillance* (Polity, 2013). He leads a team making a report on surveillance in Canada and also exploring cultural, historical and ethical issues in surveillance. See sscqueens.org/davidlyon/.

Liisa A. Mäkinen is a social and public policy PhD student at University of Helsinki, Finland. Her research interests include participatory and responsibilized surveillance and gamification of surveillance. Her dissertation research examines new ways of conducting surveillance, especially the surveillant usage of webcams/surveillance cameras linked online and the participatory and playful visual surveillance they permit.

Jennie Germann Molz is an assistant professor of Sociology at the College of the Holy Cross in Massachusetts, USA. She is author of *Travel Connections: Tourism, Technology and Togetherness in a Mobile World* (Routledge, 2012) and a co-editor of the journal *Hospitality & Society*. She has published extensively on the topics of tourism, mobility, hospitality, globalization, cosmopolitanism and new technologies.

Sebastian Sevignani studied media and communication, philosophy and theology. After receiving his master's degree, he worked as research associate at University of Salzburgs's Department of Communication Studies and in the Austrian Science Fund (FWF)–financed project "Social Networking Sites in the Surveillance Society." His doctoral thesis focuses on the political economy of privacy in informational capitalism. Sebastian's further research interests encompass critical social theory, ideology, (digital) labour, social media and alternative modes of (media) production. He is a member of the Unified Theory of Information Research Group and a member of the editorial board of the journal *tripleC: Communication, Capitalism & Critique. Open Access Journal for a Global Sustainable Information Society*. For further information, visit http://sevignani.uti.at.

Nils Zurawski studied sociology, ethnology and geography in Münster, Germany, earning a master's in 1994 (Ethnicity and Migration); a PhD in 1999, with a thesis on *Virtual Ethnicity: Studies on Identity, Culture and Internet*; and a Habilitation in

2013 (TU Darmstadt) on *Space, Control, World view*. In 2000–2001 he conducted fieldwork in Northern Ireland. His research interests include surveillance (CCTV, consumption, theory, anthropology of surveillance), identity, urban studies, space, political anthropology, violence, internet and media and qualitative methods. Currently he is working as a researcher and associate professor at the University of Hamburg. He is also the editor of *Surveillance & Society, Kommunikation@Gesellschaft*. Blog: www.surveillance-studies.org.

Index

General Editor: *Steve Jones*

Digital Formations is the best source for critical, well-written books about digital technologies and modern life. Books in the series break new ground by emphasizing multiple methodological and theoretical approaches to deeply probe the formation and reformation of lived experience as it is refracted through digital interaction. Each volume in **Digital Formations** pushes forward our understanding of the intersections, and corresponding implications, between digital technologies and everyday life. The series examines broad issues in realms such as digital culture, electronic commerce, law, politics and governance, gender, the Internet, race, art, health and medicine, and education. The series emphasizes critical studies in the context of emergent and existing digital technologies.

Other recent titles include:

To order other books in this series please contact our Customer Service Department:

(800) 770-LANG (within the US)
(212) 647-7706 (outside the US)
(212) 647-7707 FAX

To find out more about the series or browse a full list of titles, please visit our website:

WWW.PETERLANG.COM